Third Edition

A Laboratory Course *in*

C++

Nell Dale

University of Texas, Austin

JONES AND BARTLETT PUBLISHERS
Sudbury, Massachusetts
BOSTON   TORONTO   LONDON   SINGAPORE

World Headquarters
Jones and Bartlett Publishers
40 Tall Pine Drive
Sudbury, MA 01776
978-443-5000
info@jbpub.com
www.jbpub.com

Jones and Bartlett Publishers
Canada
2406 Nikanna Road
Mississauga, ON L5C 2W6
CANADA

Jones and Bartlett Publishers
International
Barb House, Barb Mews
London W6 7PA
UK

ISBN: 0-7637-0063-0

Editor-in-Chief: J. Michael Stranz
Development and Product Manager: Amy Rose
Production Assistant: Tara McCormick
Cover Design: Night & Day Design
Compositor: Northeast Compositors, Inc.
Cover Printing: Courier Stoughton
Printing and Binding: Courier Stoughton

Printed in the United States of America

05 04 03   10 9 8 7 6 5 4 3 2

Need for Support in Learning C++

For about 20 years, the introductory computer science course had been taught mostly in Pascal. Over the last eight to ten years there has been a move toward C++ in place of Pascal. Even the strongest advocates for the change realized that C++ was going to be more difficult than Pascal for most beginning students to learn.

C, and later, C++ were designed for systems programming. Systems programmers are assumed to know what they mean and mean what they say. Therefore, C++ has very little runtime error checking and compiles some very weird code. Beginning students, on the other hand, often do not know what they mean and even more often do not mean what they say. Hence, it is essential that students understand the syntax and semantics of each construct as they go along. Closed laboratory activities seem an ideal way to make this happen.

Closed Laboratories in Computer Science

The Denning Report[1] introduced the term *closed laboratories* without defining exactly what they were. At least four different definitions subsequently surfaced.

1. A scheduled time when students work on their programming assignments under supervision.
2. A scheduled drill-and-practice time when students work on mini-problems under supervision.
3. The use of specially prepared laboratory materials where students interact with the computer as they would a microscope or Bunsen burner. The labs should help the student discover principles and solutions under supervision. This definition is closest to the spirit of the Denning Report.
4. A combination of two or more of the above.

---

[1] Denning, P. J. (chair) "Computing as a Discipline" *Communications of the ACM*, Vol. 32, No. 1, pp. 9-23.

With the publication of the Curriculum '91[2] report, laboratory exercises were suggested for many of the knowledge units. However, a precise definition of what constituted a closed laboratory activity was not included. And, in fact, many of the activities suggested could be done equally well in a non-supervised (or open) setting.

Laboratory activities as defined in this manual are a combination of definitions 2 and 3.

Open versus Closed Laboratories

Although the Denning Report and Curriculum '91 imply that laboratory exercises should be done under supervision, we do not feel that this is essential. Our view is that closed laboratory exercises are valuable for two reasons: the exercises themselves and the extra contact time with a faculty member or a teaching assistant. If a closed laboratory environment is not an option, the students can still benefit from working the exercises on their own.

Organization of the Manual

Each chapter contains three types of activities: Prelab, Inlab, and Postlab. The Prelab activities include a reading review assignment and simple paper and pencil exercises. The Inlab activities are broken into lessons, each of which represents a concept covered in the chapter. Each lesson is broken into exercises that thoroughly demonstrate the concept. The Postlab exercises are a collection of outside programming assignments appropriate for each chapter. Each exercise requires that the students apply the concepts covered in the chapter.

When this manual is being used in a closed-laboratory setting, we suggest that the Prelab activities be done before the students come to lab. The students can spend the first few minutes of the laboratory checking their answers (Lesson 1 for each chapter). The Inlab activities are designed to take approximately two hours, the usual time for a closed laboratory. However, an instructor can tailor the chapter to the level of the class by only assigning a partial set of exercises or by shortening the time allowed.

The Postlab activities present a selection of programming projects. We do not suggest that all of them be assigned. In most cases, one should be sufficient, unless there are several related problems.

If the manual is not being used in a closed-laboratory setting, an instructor can assign all or a selection of the Inlab activities to be done independently (see the section "Flexibility" below). In either a closed or open setting, many of the Inlab and Postlab activities can be done in groups.

Theoretical Basis for the Activities

The decision to break each chapter into three types of activities is based on the work of Benjamin Bloom, who developed a taxonomy of six increasingly difficult levels of achievement in the cognitive domain.[3] In developing the activities for this manual, we

---

[2] Tucker, A. B. (Ed.) "Computing Curricula 1991: Report of the ACM/IEEE-CS Joint Curriculum Task Force." Final Draft, December 17. ACM Order Number 201910. IEEE Computer Society Press Order Number 2220.

[3] Bloom, Benjamin *Taxonomy of Educational Objectives: Handbook I: Cognitive Domain*. New York: David McKay, 1956.

combined Bloom's six categories into three. These categories are defined below in terms of the concrete example of learning an algorithm (or language-related construct).

Recognition   The student can trace the algorithm and determine what the output should be for a given data set (no transfer).

Generation   The student can generate a very similar algorithm (near transfer).

Projection   The student can modify the algorithm to accomplish a major change (far transfer), can apply the algorithm in a different context, can combine related algorithms, and can compare algorithms.

The Prelab activities are at the recognition level. Most of the Inlab activities are at the generation level with a few projection-level activities included where appropriate. The Postlab activities are projection-level activities.

The activities are also influenced by the work of Kolb and others on how students learn.[4] The more actively involved students are in the learning process, the more they learn. Reading and writing are forms of active involvement. Therefore, the Prelab activities begin with a reading review, and many of the exercises ask the students to write explanations of what happened. Just watching a program run and looking at the answer is a passive activity, but having to write the answer down transforms the exercise into an active one.

Flexibility

A Laboratory Course in C++ is designed to allow the instructor maximum flexibility. Each chapter has an assignment cover sheet that provides a checklist in tabular form. The first column of the table in the Assignment Cover Sheet lists the chapter activities, in the second column students can check which activities have been assigned, in the third column they record what output is to be turned in, and the fourth column is for the instructor to use for grading. The pages are perforated so students can easily tear out sheets to turn in.

Changes in the Third Edition

The major change in this edition is the addition of a new chapter covering Templates and Exceptions. Although this chapter has been inserted after Linked Structures, the exercises only depend on array-based lists.

Support Materials

The programs, program shells (partial programs), and data files are available for students to download onto their computers at

http://www.problemsolvingcpp.jbpub.com.

A copy of most of the programs or program shells is listed before the exercises that use the program or program shell. Programs used for debugging exercises are not shown, however. Because some of the exercises ask the student to go back to the original version of a previous program or program shell, we suggest that the student make two copies and work from a copy.

---

[4] Svinicki, Marilla D., and Dixon Nancy M. "The Kolb Model Modified for Classroom Activities" *College Teaching*, Vol. 35, No. 4, Fall, pp. 141-146.

Student support materials are divided into subdirectories, one for each chapter. The programs and program shells are stored in files under the program name with a `.cpp` extension. Header files are stored with a `.h` extension.

If students are using a pre-standard version of C++, see

http://www.problemsolvingcpp.jbpub.com

for a guide of how to convert the programs on the disk to run with their compiler.

Acknowledgments

No author writes in a vacuum. There is always formal and informal feedback from colleagues. Thanks to those of you in my department who patiently answered "by the way" questions about C++. Thanks also to the following colleagues who have reviewed over the lifetime of the manuscript: Mary D. Medley, Augusta College; Susan Wallace, University of North Florida; Paul Ross, Millersville University of Pennsylvania; Jeanine Ingber, University of New Mexico, Albuquerque; James C. Miller, Bradley University; Ed Korntved, Northwest Nazarene College; Charles Dierbach, Towson State University; Mansar Zand, University of Nebraska, Omaha; Porter Scobey, Saint Mary's University; Kenrick J. Mock, Portland State; and Lee D. Cornell, Minnesota State University, Mankato. Special thanks to Mark Headington, University of Wisconsin–La Crosse, for his prompt and detailed answers to my questions.

To Michael, Amy, Mike, Sigrid, Bobbie, Tara, and Theresa: as always Thanks.

N.D.

Preface   v

1 Overview of Programming and Problem Solving   1

Prelab Activities   5

Prelab Assignment   9

      Lesson 1-1:   Check Prelab Exercises   11

      Lesson 1-2:   Basic File Operations   12

      Lesson 1-3:   Compiling and Running a Program   13

      Lesson 1-4:   Editing, Running, and Printing a Program File   14

      Lesson 1-5:   Running a Program with an Error   15

      Lesson 1-6:   Entering, Compiling, and Running a New Program   16

Postlab Activities   17

2 C++ Syntax and Semantics, and the Program Development Process   19

Prelab Activities   23

Prelab Assignment   29

      Lesson 2-1:   Check Prelab Exercises   31

      Lesson 2-2:   Components of a Program   32

      Lesson 2-3:   Sending Information to the Output Stream   33

      Lesson 2-4:   Debugging   34

Postlab Activities   37

3   **Arithmetic Expressions, Function Calls, and Output   39**

Prelab Activities   43

Prelab Assignment   49

    Lesson 3-1:   Check Prelab Exercises   51

    Lesson 3-2:   Arithmetic Operations   52

    Lesson 3-3:   Formatting Output   54

    Lesson 3-4:   Value-Returning Functions   56

    Lesson 3-5:   String Functions   57

    Lesson 3-6:   Debugging   58

Postlab Activities   61

4   **Program Input and the Software Design Process   63**

Prelab Activities   67

Prelab Assignment   71

    Lesson 4-1:   Check Prelab Exercises   73

    Lesson 4-2:   Input Statement and Data Consistency   74

    Lesson 4-3:   Input and Output with Files   78

    Lesson 4-4:   Program Design   80

    Lesson 4-5:   Debugging   82

Postlab Activities   83

5   **Conditions, Logical Expressions, and Selection Control Structures   85**

Prelab Activities   89

Prelab Assignment   95

    Lesson 5-1:   Check Prelab Exercises   97

    Lesson 5-2:   Boolean Expressions   98

    Lesson 5-3:   If-Then Statements   99

    Lesson 5-4:   If-Then-Else Statements   100

    Lesson 5-5:   Nested Logic   102

    Lesson 5-6:   Test Plan   104

    Lesson 5-7:   Debugging   105

Postlab Activities   107

6   **Looping   109**

Prelab Activities   113

Prelab Assignment   117

    Lesson 6-1:   Check Prelab Exercises   119

    Lesson 6-2:   Count-Controlled Loops   120

    Lesson 6-3:   Event-Controlled Loops   122

    Lesson 6-4:   Nested Logic   123

Lesson 6-5:   Debugging   125
Postlab Activities   127

7   **Functions   129**
Prelab Activities   133
Prelab Assignment   139
Lesson 7-1:   Check Prelab Exercises   141
Lesson 7-2:   Functions without Parameters   142
Lesson 7-3:   Functions with Value Parameters   144
Lesson 7-4:   Functions with Reference Parameters   146
Lesson 7-5:   Debugging   149
Postlab Activities   151

8   **Scope, Lifetime, and More on Functions   155**
Prelab Activities   159
Prelab Assignment   163
Lesson 8-1:   Check Prelab Exercises   165
Lesson 8-2:   Static and Automatic Variables   167
Lesson 8-3:   Value-Returning and Void Functions   168
Lesson 8-4:   Test Plan   171
Lesson 8-5:   Debugging   172
Postlab Activities   173

9   **Additional Control Structures   175**
Prelab Activities   179
Prelab Assignment   183
Lesson 9-1:   Check Prelab Exercises   186
Lesson 9-2:   Multi-Way Branching   187
Lesson 9-3:   Additional Control Structures   188
Lesson 9-4:   Test Plan   192
Lesson 9-5:   Debugging   193
Postlab Activities   195

10   **Simple Data Types: Built-In and User-Defined   197**
Prelab Activities   201
Prelab Assignment   207
Lesson 10-1:   Check Prelab Exercises   209
Lesson 10-2:   Numeric Data Types   210
Lesson 10-3:   Char Data Types   214
Lesson 10-4:   Enumeration Data Types   216
Lesson 10-5:   Debugging   218
Postlab Activities   219

11 Structured Types, Data Abstraction, and Classes   221

Prelab Activities   225
Prelab Assignment   231

    Lesson 11-1:   Check Prelab Exercises   235
    Lesson 11-2:   Record Data Type   236
    Lesson 11-3:   Hierarchical Records   238
    Lesson 11-4:   Class Data Type   239
    Lesson 11-5:   Header and Implementation Files   242
    Lesson 11-6:   Class Constructors   245
    Lesson 11-7:   Debugging   246

Postlab Activities   247

12 Arrays   249

Prelab Activities   253
Prelab Assignment   259

    Lesson 12-1:   Check Prelab Exercises   261
    Lesson 12-2:   One-Dimensional Array Data Types with Integer Indexes   262
    Lesson 12-3:   One-Dimensional Array Data Types with Enumeration Indexes   264
    Lesson 12-4:   Two-Dimensional Arrays   266
    Lesson 12-5:   Multidimensional Arrays   269
    Lesson 12-6:   Debugging   270

Postlab Activities   271

13 Array–Based Lists   273

Prelab Activities   277
Prelab Assignment   283

    Lesson 13-1:   Check Prelab Exercises   285
    Lesson 13-2:   Linear (Unsorted) List Operations   286
    Lesson 13-3:   Sorted List Operations   288
    Lesson 13-4:   C Strings   290
    Lesson 13-5:   Debugging   292

Postlab Activities   293

14 Object–Oriented Software Development   295

Prelab Activities   299
Prelab Assignment   303

    Lesson 14-1:   Check Prelab Exercises   305
    Lesson 14-2:   Classes   306

Lesson 14-3: Classes with Inheritance 307

Lesson 14-4: Virtual Methods 308

Lesson 14-5: Debugging 310

Postlab Activities 311

15 Pointers, Dynamic Data, and Reference Types 313

Prelab Activities 317

Prelab Assignment 323

Lesson 15-1: Check Prelab Exercises 325

Lesson 15-2: Pointer Variables 326

Lesson 15-3: Dynamic Data 327

Lesson 15-4: Classes and Dynamic Data 329

Lesson 15-5: Debugging 331

Postlab Activities 333

16 Linked Structures 335

Prelab Activities 339

Prelab Assignment 341

Lesson 16-1: Check Prelab Exercises 343

Lesson 16-2: Unordered Linked Lists 344

Lesson 16-3: Linked Lists of Objects 347

Lesson 16-4: Sorted Lists of Objects 349

Lesson 16-5: Debugging 350

Postlab Activities 351

17 Templates and Exceptions 353

Prelab Activities 357

Prelab Assignment 361

Lesson 17-1: Check Prelab Exercises 363

Lesson 17-2: Generic Data Types 365

Lesson 17-3: Generic Functions 366

Lesson 17-4: Exceptions 368

Lesson 17-5: Test Plan 369

Postlab Activities 371

18 Recursion 373

Prelab Activities 377

Prelab Assignment 379

Lesson 18-1: Check Prelab Exercises 380

Lesson 18-2: Simple Variables 381

Lesson 18-3: Structured Variables   382

Lesson 18-4: Debugging   383

Postlab Activities   385

Appendices   387

Glossary   397

Overview of Programming and Problem Solving

- ■ To be able to log on to a computer.
- ■ To be able to do the following tasks on a computer:
  - ■ Change the active (work) directory.
  - ■ List the files in a directory.
- ■ To be able to do the following tasks using an editor and a C++ compiler:
  - ■ Load a file containing a program.
  - ■ Alter a file containing a program.
  - ■ Save a file.
  - ■ Compile a program.
  - ■ Run a program.
  - ■ Change a program and rerun it.
  - ■ Correct a program with errors.
  - ■ Enter and run a program.
  - ■ Exit the system.

Chapter 1: Assignment Cover Sheet

Name _____   Date _____

Section _____

Fill in the following table showing which exercises have been assigned for each lesson and check what you are to submit: (1) lab sheets, (2) listings of output files, and/or (3) listings of programs. Your instructor or teaching assistant (TA) can use the Completed column for grading purposes.

Activities	Assigned: Check or list exercise numbers	Submit (1) (2) (3)			Completed
Prelab					
Review					
Prelab Assignment					
Inlab					
Lesson 1–1: Check Prelab Exercises					
Lesson 1–2: Basic File Operations					
Lesson 1–3: Compiling and Running a Program					
Lesson 1–4: Editing, Running, and Printing a Program File					
Lesson 1–5: Running a Program with an Error					
Lesson 1–6: Entering, Compiling, and Running a New Program					
Postlab					

Prelab Activities

Review

A computer is a programmable electronic device that can store, retrieve, and process data. The verbs *store*, *retrieve*, and *process* relate to the five basic physical components of the computer: the memory unit, the arithmetic/logic unit, the control unit, input devices, and output devices. These physical components are called computer *hardware*. The programs that are available to run on a computer are called *software*. Writing the programs that make up the software is called *programming*.

Programming

A program is a sequence of instructions written to perform a specific task. Programming is the process of defining the sequence of instructions. There are two phases in this process: determining the task that needs doing and expressing the solution in a sequence of instructions.

The process of programming always begins with a problem. Programs are not written in isolation; they are written to solve problems. Determining what needs to be done means outlining the solution to the problem. This first phase, then, is the problem-solving phase.

The second phase, expressing the solution in a sequence of instructions, is the implementation phase. Here, the general solution outlined in the problem-solving phase is converted into a specific solution (a program in a specific language). Testing is part of both phases. The general solution must be shown to be correct before it is translated into a program.

Let's demonstrate the process with the following problem.

Problem: Calculate the average rainfall over a period of days.

Discussion: To do the job by hand, you would write down the number of inches of rain that had fallen each day. Then you would add the figures up and divide the total by the number of days. This is exactly the algorithm we use in the program.

Algorithm (on next page):

Average Rainfall

```
Get total inches of rain
if total is zero then
    There wasn't any rain
otherwise
    Average <- total / number of days
```

Selection construct.

One thing is done if
there is no rain;
another thing is done
if there is rain.

Function construct.

The task of getting the total number of inches is stated in the
main algorithm without saying how it is done. This task is
expanded separately as a subalgorithm.

▶ Get Total Inches of Rain

```
for number of days
    Get inches
    Add to total
```

Loop construct.

The task of getting the number
of inches and adding it to the
total is repeated for each day.

Sequence construct.

The task of getting inches is followed immediately
by the task of adding the inches to the total.

The C++ program that implements this algorithm is given below. Don't worry if
you don't understand it. At this stage, you're not expected to. Before long, you will be
able to understand all of it.

Incidentally, the information between the symbols /* and the symbols */ is meant
for the human reader of the program. This kind of information is called a *comment* and
is ignored by the C++ compiler. Information from // to the end of a line is also a
comment.

```cpp
// Program Rain calculates the average rainfall over a period
// of days.  The number of days and the rain statistics are in
// file Rain.in.

#include <iostream>
#include <fstream>
#include <iomanip>
using namespace std;

void GetInches(ifstream&, int&, float&);
// Rain statistics are read from a file; the average is
// returned.

int main()
{
    float  average;          // average rainfall
    float totalRain;         // total accumulated rain
    int numberOfDays;        // number of days in calculation
    ifstream  rainFile;      // data file

    cout << fixed << showpoint;
    rainFile.open("Rain.In");
    GetInches(rainFile, numberOfDays, totalRain);
```

```
    if (totalRain == 0.0)
        cout  << "There was no rain during this period."
                << endl;
    else
    {
        average = totalRain / numberOfDays;
        cout  << "The average rain fall over "
                << numberOfDays;
        cout  << " days is " << setw(1)  << setprecision(3)
                << average  << endl;
    }

    return 0;
}

//************************************************************

void  GetInches(ifstream& rainFile, int& numberOfDays,
       float& totalRain)
// Pre:  rainFile has been opened.
//        numberOfDays is the first value on rainFile, followed
//        by numberOfDays real values representing inches of
//        rain.
// Post: numberOfDays is read from rainFile.
//        Number of inches of rain for numberOfDays are read
//        and their sum is returned in totalRain.

{
    float  inches;          // Day's worth of rain
    int  counter;           // loop control variable

    rainFile >> numberOfDays;
    totalRain = 0.0;
    counter = 1;
    while (counter <= numberOfDays)
    {
        rainFile >> inches;
        totalRain = totalRain + inches;
        counter++;
    }
}
```

Getting Started

Certain C++ systems provide an integrated environment for the creation and execution of C++ programs. For example, Turbo C++ and CodeWarrior, which run on PCs and Macs, provide such an environment. The compiler, the editor, and the runtime system are all bundled together into one system. Other C++ compilers come separately so that you must use a general-purpose editor to enter your program. You compile the program and then run it. There are far too many systems for us to describe any of them in detail. Therefore, we use an analogy to describe the process of entering and running your program.

When you first get on a machine (*log in*), the *operating system* is the software that is running. You can think of the operating system as a hallway that connects all the other pieces of software. You enter the name of the software you want to use, and the operating system provides it. When you finish using the software, you must come back to the operating system (the hallway) before you can use another piece of software.

Each piece of software is like a doorway. The operating system opens the door and ushers you into the room where the software you want to use is kept. In the *editor*, you create a file of written information. This file may contain a program or data for a program.

To those of you who have not worked with an editor before, think of it as a program that allows you to use your keyboard and screen like a very smart electronic typewriter. A *file* is the information that you type in through the keyboard. You see what you type on the screen. Commands to the editor do what you would do manually with a typewriter. These allow you to change and rearrange letters, words, and sentences. A file resides in an area in secondary storage, which has a name, and is used to hold a collection of data. The data itself is also referred to as a file.

When you are satisfied with what you've typed, you give your file a name and tell the editor to save it for you. Giving a file a name is like putting information into a folder with a label on it. You can pick up the file and carry it with you from one room to another.

When you leave the editor, the operating system comes back with a prompt that says it's ready for you to tell it where you want to go next. If you've created a C++ program, you say that you want to *compile* (translate) your file (go to the C++ room). The operating system opens the door, and you hand your file folder to the C++ compiler.

The C++ compiler attempts to translate your program. If the program contains grammatical errors (errors in syntax), the compiler tells you so. You then have to go back to the editing room to correct the mistakes. When your C++ program finally compiles correctly, the C++ compiler leaves the object program (the translated code) in a file.

You tell the operating system that you are ready to run the object program. The file containing the translated program is taken into the execute room, where it is run. It's here, in the execute room, that the problem your program was written to solve actually is solved.

When you're finished and ready to quit (*log out*), you tell the operating system. It opens the door marked exit, and you can leave.

Some systems bundle the editing room, the compiling room, and the executing room into one luxurious suite. For example, in Turbo C++ you enter this suite by saying "TC" to the operating system; in CodeWarrior, you say "CodeWarrior IDE." You are then handed a menu of the things that you can do: Create a new file, modify an old file, compile a program, or run a program. You even have the option of asking for help. You make a choice either by using a mouse (a pointing device) or by pressing a function key on the keyboard. Several of these choices then provide you with a second menu from which to choose. Integrated systems are *user-friendly* systems: You are never left stranded; you are always guided through the input (edit), compile, and run cycle by the use of these menus that appear at the top of your screen.

Chapter 1: Prelab Assignment

Name _____ Date _____

Section _____

Your instructor should provide a handout describing the system that you are using.

Exercise 1: What computer are you using?

Exercise 2: What operating system are you using?

Exercise 3: What C++ system are you using?

Exercise 4: Is your C++ system an integrated system, or is the editor separate from the compiler?

Exercise 5: If your editor is separate, which editor are you using?

Exercise 6: If you are not using an integrated system, what are the compile, run, and edit commands you are using?

Lesson 1–1: Check Prelab Exercises

Name _____ Date _____

Section _____

Exercise 1: What computer are you using? IBM-compatible PCs, Macintosh computers, and UNIX workstations are common in this course. You also might be using a terminal to a computer network.

Exercise 2: What operating system are you using? Windows ('95, '98, or 2000), DOS, Macintosh, and UNIX are common operating systems.

Exercise 3: What C++ system are you using? There are lots of choices, but it must be compatible with the operating system that you are using.

Exercise 4: Is your C++ system an integrated system, or is the editor separate from the compiler? You only have two choices here: either it is integrated or it is not.

Exercise 5: If your editor is separate, which editor are you using? Word and WordPerfect are two common editors on PCs. Emacs and vi are two editors for UNIX machines.

Exercise 6: If you are not using an integrated system, what are the compile, run, and edit commands you are using? You have to check with your instructor for this one.

Lesson 1–2: Basic File Operations

Name _____   Date _____

Section _____

Exercise 1: Follow your instructor's instructions on how to log on to the system.

Exercise 2: Regardless of the system you are using, the memory should be divided up into hierarchical subsections called directories. At any one time, you are in a directory. List all the contents of the directory you are in when you log on to the system.

Exercise 3: Enter the editor. Type your name on the screen and save the file.

Exercise 4: Bring file `rain.cpp` into your editor. Look through it carefully; it contains the C++ program shown in the review. Save the file.

Exercise 5: Bring file `rain2.cpp` into your editor. Examine it carefully. It is the same as file `rain.cpp` with the formatting changed. (Which is easier for the human to read?) Save the file.

Lesson 1–3: Compiling and Running a Program

Name _____   Date _____

Section _____

Exercise 1: Compile and run program `Rain` in file `rain.cpp`. How many inches of rain were there?

Exercise 2: Compile and run program `Rain` in file `rain2.cpp`. How many inches of rain were there?

Exercise 3: Are you surprised that the results were the same in Exercises 1 and 2? What does that tell you about the differences between how the compiler views the text of a program and how the user views the text of a program?

Exercise 4: Compile and run program `FirstOne` in file `firstone.cpp`. What is printed on the screen?

Lesson 1–4: Editing, Running, and Printing a Program File

Name _____   Date _____

Section _____

Exercise 1: Bring file `firstone.cpp` to the screen. Replace the name Nell Dale with your own name. Compile and run the program. What is printed on the screen?

Exercise 2: Did you notice that there is no period after the name and that the line of asterisks is not even? Go back and edit this program so that a period follows the name and the two lines contain the same number of asterisks. Compile and run your program. What is printed on the screen?

Exercise 3: Save your changed file.

Exercise 4: You now need to print out a copy of your changed file from Exercise 3 to turn in to your instructor. Follow your instructor's instructions on how to print a file.

Lesson 1–5: Running a Program with an Error

Name _____   Date _____

Section _____

Exercise 1: Compile program `Error` in file `error.cpp`. The error message you get and what happens when this occurs, depends on the C++ compiler you are using. Describe the error message, and tell what happened.

Exercise 2: Go back into the editor and correct the error. (There is a semicolon missing.) Compile and run your program. What is the output?

Lesson 1–6: Entering, Compiling, and Running a New Program

Name _____ Date _____

Section _____

Exercise 1: Enter the editor and key in the following program. You are not expected to understand what it does; just copy it exactly as shown.

```
// Program Area calculates the area of a square.
// The user is prompted to enter the number of inches on each
// side. Note that "endl" in line 7 ends in the letter "l" not
// the number one.

#include <iostream>
using namespace std;
int main ()
{
    int  inches;

    cout  << "Enter the number of inches on a side "
          << endl;
    cout  << "Press the return key."
          << endl;
    cin  >> inches;
    cout  << endl
          << "The area is "  << inches * inches  <<"."
          << endl;
    return 0;
}
```

Exercise 2: When you have finished keying in this program, try to compile it. If you have made any typing errors, correct them and try to compile the program again.

Exercise 3: When the program compiles without any errors, you are ready to run it. When the program is running, you are asked to input a number. Enter a number between 1 and 150. What number did you input? What was written on the screen?

Exercise 4: Exit the system.

Postlab Activities

Exercise 1: Key in the following program, compile it, and run it.

```cpp
// Program Stars prints three rows of asterisks.

#include <iostream>
using namespace std;

int main ()
{
    cout << "***********"  << endl;
    cout << " ********* "  << endl;
    cout << "  *******  "  << endl;
    return 0;
}
```

Exercise 2: Edit program Stars so that it prints five asterisks centered on the fourth line, three asterisks centered on the fifth line, and one asterisk centered on the sixth line. Compile and run your program.

Exercise 3: Using program Stars as a model, write a program that prints the same pattern on the screen but with a dollar sign symbol rather than an asterisk.

C++ Syntax and Semantics, and the Program Development Process

- To be able to compile and run a C++ program from disk.

- To be able to modify the various parts of a program and observe what these changes do to the program's output.

- To be able to construct output statements that send information to the output stream.

- To be able to construct an expression made up of characters, strings, and the concatenation operator.

- To be able to construct assignment statements to accomplish a stated task.

- To be able to debug a program with syntax errors.

- To be able to debug a program with logic errors.

Chapter 2: Assignment Cover Sheet

Name _____ Date _____

Section _____

Fill in the following table showing which exercises have been assigned for each lesson and check what you are to submit: (1) lab sheets, (2) listings of output files, and/or (3) listings of programs. Your instructor or teaching assistant (TA) can use the Completed column for grading purposes.

Activities	Assigned: Check or list exercise numbers	Submit (1) (2) (3)			Completed
Prelab					
Review					
Prelab Assignment					
Inlab					
Lesson 2–1: Check Prelab Exercises					
Lesson 2–2: Components of a Program					
Lesson 2–3: Sending Information to the Output Stream					
Lesson 2–4: Debugging					
Postlab					

Prelab Activities

Review

There are two basic parts to a C++ program: (1) instructions to the C++ preprocessor and compiler and (2) instructions that describe the processing to be done. However, before we can describe these instructions, we must have a way of naming things so that we can tell the compiler about them and describe what we want to have done to them. We name things (data types, data objects, and actions) by giving them an *identifier*. An identifier is made up of letters, numbers, and underscores, but must begin with a letter or an underscore. We use the words *identifier* and *name* interchangeably.

Beware: C++ is case sensitive. This means that Value, VALUE, value, and vaLue are four separate identifiers. In fact, we can construct 32 distinct identifiers from these five letters by varying the capitalization.

Program Structure

Let's examine the following C++ program. We have numbered the lines so that we can discuss them.

```
1.  // Program Rhyme prints out a nursery rhyme.

2.  #include <iostream>
3.  #include <string>
4.  using namespace std;

5.  const char SEMI_COLON = ';';
6.  const string VERB1 = "went up ";
7.  const string VERB2 = "down came ";
8   const string VERB3 = "washed ";
9.  const string VERB4 = "out came ";
10. const string VERB5 = "dried up ";

11. int main()
12. {
13.     string firstLine;
14.     string secondLine;
15.     string thirdLine;
16.     string fourthLine;

17.     firstLine = "The itsy bitsy spider " + VERB1 +
            "the water spout";
18.     secondLine = VERB2 + "the rain and " + VERB3 +
            "the spider out";
19.     thirdLine = VERB4 + "the sun and " + VERB5 +
            "all the rain";
20.     fourthLine = "and the itsy bitsy spider " + VERB1 +
            "the spout again";

21.     cout << firstLine  << SEMI_COLON  << endl;
22.     cout << secondLine << SEMI_COLON  << endl;
23.     cout << thirdLine  << SEMI_COLON;
```

```
24.    cout  << endl;
25.    cout  << fourthLine  << '.'  << endl;

26.    return 0;
27. }
```

Line 1 begins with a double slash (//) and is ignored by the translation system. Such lines are called comments and are meant for the reader of the program. They tell the user what the program is going to do. Comments begin with // and extend to the end of the line. Another way of entering comments into the program is to insert them between /* and */. Comments between /* and */ can extend across any number of lines.

Lines 2 and 3 are *include* directives to the C++ preprocessor. The preprocessor scans the program for lines beginning with a hash mark (#). The words "include <iostream>" tell the preprocessor to insert the contents of the file iostream in place of the directive. The angle brackets around the file name indicate that the file is in the standard *include directory*. This file includes constant, variable, and function declarations needed by the program. The words "include <string>" tell the preprocessor to insert the contents of the file string in place of the directive. This file contains the data type identifier string.

Line 4 is a *using* directive. This directive tells the compiler that all the identifiers in the std namespace are accessible to the program. This directive is explained in more detail in Chapter 8.

Lines 5 through 10 instruct the compiler to assign the constant identifier on the left of the equal sign a place in memory and to store the value on the right of the equal sign in that place. A constant declaration is made up of the reserved word const followed by a data type identifier; in this case char or string. char says that the value to be stored in the constant is one alphanumeric character. string says that the value to be stored in the constant is a string of characters. The data type identifier is followed by the name to be given to the constant. The constant name is followed by an equal sign and the value to be stored there. In line 5, a semicolon is stored in constant SEMI_COLON. In line 6, the string made up of the characters 'w', 'e', 'n', 't', and ' ' (blank) is stored in VERB1. By convention, most C++ programmers use all uppercase for constant identifiers.

Line 11 contains the words that begin the executable part of the program—that is, the part that contains statements that describe what you want to have done. A function performs an action and returns a result. The data type identifier int says that the value returned by function main is an integer. The compiler knows that main is a function because it is followed by a pair of parentheses. All C++ programs must have an int function main. Line 12 contains only one character: the left brace ({). This character begins a block that is the body of the function. The right brace (}) on line 27 is the closing brace of the block; it ends the body of the function. The body of the function contains the statements that are translated by the compiler and executed when the program is run.

Lines 13 through 16 contain the declarations of string variables. In line 13, firstLine is declared to be a string variable. The compiler assigns a memory location to firstLine. Nothing is stored in firstLine yet, but when values are stored there, they must be values of type string. In lines 14 through 16, string variables secondLine, thirdLine, and fourthLine are assigned memory locations.

Lines 17 through 20 are assignment statements. In an assignment statement, the expression on the right side of the equal sign is evaluated, and the result is stored in the variable whose identifier is on the left of the equal sign. In line 17, the expression is made up of a literal string constant, a named string constant, and another literal string constant. The operator that combines them is the *concatenation operator* (+). This binary operator takes two arguments. It appends the string on the right to the end of the string on the left. The result in line 17 is the string "The itsy bitsy spider went up the water spout". Lines 18 through 20 are evaluated the same way.

Lines 21 through 25 cause information to be written on the screen. cout, which is defined in file <iostream>, is a predefined variable that denotes an *output stream*. An output stream is just what it sounds like: a stream of characters sent to some output device. The operator << (double less-than signs) is called the *insertion operator*. The stream of characters described on the right of the insertion operator is sent to the output stream named on the left of the first insertion operator. Let's look at line 21 (repeated below) in detail.

```
21.    cout  << firstLine  << SEMI_COLON  << endl;
```

The output stream (cout) stands for the standard output, the screen. The leftmost insertion operator sends the string firstLine to cout; that is, the characters that make up the string are printed on the screen. The next insertion operator sends the char constant SEMI_COLON to cout. The third insertion operator sends a special feature called a *manipulator* to the output stream. endl is a manipulator that tells the output stream to go to a new line by writing the end-of-line marker. Thus, anything written after this statement begins on the next line of output.

Line 22 is similar to line 21: A string, a character, and the end-of-line manipulator are sent to the screen. Line 23 sends a string and a character, but does not send endl. Line 24 sends the end-of-line manipulator. Line 25 sends a string and a literal char value (a period) followed by the end-of-line manipulator.

We said that the executable part of the program is int function main. Because main is an int function, it must return an integer value. Line 26 says to return the value zero. By convention, main returns zero when the program executes with no errors. Line 27 ends function main and thus the program. The output from this program is:

```
The itsy bitsy spider went up the water spout;
down came the rain and washed the spider out;
out came the sun and dried up all the rain;
and the itsy bitsy spider went up the spout again.
```

Data Types

A data type is a set of values and a set of operations on these values. In the preceding program, we used the data type identifiers int, char, and string.

We used data type int in two ways in the preceding program. int precedes main, the name of the main function in the program, to indicate that the function returns a value of type int. In line 26 an int literal (zero) is returned as the result of the function main. In C++ there are four integral types that can be used to refer to an integer value (whole numbers with no fractional parts). These types are char, short, int, and long and are intended to represent integers of different sizes. The set of values for each of these integral data types is the range of numbers from the smallest value that can be represented through the largest value that can be represented. The operations on these values are the standard arithmetic operations allowed on integer values. We have more to say about integral values in the next chapter.

Data type char, the smallest integral data type, has an additional use: to describe one alphanumeric character. Each machine has a character set made up of all the alphanumeric characters that can be represented. If we need to represent a character in a program, we enclose it in single quotes. The following are seven alphanumeric characters available in all character sets.

```
'A'   'a'   '0'   ' '   '*'   '$'   '9'
```

Although arithmetic operations are defined on alphanumeric characters because they are type `char` (an integral type), such operations would not make any sense to us at this point. However, there is a collating sequence defined on each character set, so we can ask if one character comes before another character. Fortunately, the uppercase letters, the lowercase letters, and the digits are in order in all character sets. The relationship between these groups varies, however. We discuss manipulating `char` data in Chapter 5.

In program `Rhyme`, we used a `char` constant (SEMI_COLON) and a `char` literal (period).

We used four constants of data type `string`, VERB1, VERB2, VERB3, VERB4, and **VERB5**. We also used four variables of data type `string`, `firstLine`, `secondLine`, `thirdLine`, and `fourthLine`. Constants and variables of type `char` hold one alphanumeric character. If we want to store a sequence of characters, we declare a constant or variable to be of type `string`. We specify the characters in the string by putting them within double quotation marks. Notice that a `char` value is written within single quotation marks; a `string` value is within double quotation marks. Here are a few examples.

```
"blue sky"   "sun shine"   "I"   'I'
```

Note that "I" and 'I' are two different data types. The first is a `string` literal with one character; the second is `char` literal.

Concatenation is an operation defined on characters and strings. This binary operator (+ in C++) takes the character or string on the right of the operator and appends it to the character or string on the left of the operator. The only constraint is that at least one of the operands must be a string variable or named constant. This means that you cannot concatenate two string literals. The result of a concatenation operation is always a string.

The integral types are built into the C++ language, but type `string` is provided for us in file `<string>`. We used an include directive to gain access to it.

Operator Symbols

Here is a table of the C++ operators defined in this chapter.

Operator	Meaning
+	Concatenation
=	Assignment; evaluate expression on right and store in the variable named on the left
<<	Insertion; insert the character(s) (if a character or string literal) or the value (if a variable or constant) into the output stream named on the left of the first insertion operator

Words and Symbols with Special Meanings

Certain words have predefined meanings within the C++ language; these are called *reserved words*. For example, the names of data types are reserved words. In program `Rhyme`, there are six reserved words: `const`, `char`, `int`, `namespace`, `using`, and `return`. `const` directs the compiler to set up a constant; `int` and `char` are data type identifiers for integral values; and `return` signals the end of the function and usually sends back a value.

A hash mark, followed by the word `include` and a file name, is an instruction to the C++ preprocessor. It directs the preprocessor to insert the contents of the file into the program at that point.

Two slashes (`//`) signal that the characters from that point to the end of the line are comments and are to be ignored by the compiler. Characters written between `/*` and `*/` are also comments and are ignored by the compiler.

The statements that define constants (lines 5 through 10) and variables (lines 13 through 16) are called *declarations*. A C++ program is made up of declarations and one or more function definitions. A function definition is made up of a heading and a block. Line 11 is the function heading. The block begins with the left brace on line 12 and ends with the right brace on line 27.

Semicolons terminate statements in the C++ language. There are 21 semicolons in program `Rhyme`, so there are 21 statements in the program: seven statements in the declaration section and fourteen statements in the block of function `main`.

Chapter 2: Prelab Assignment

Name _____ Date _____

Section _____

Examine the following program and answer Exercises 1 through 5.

```cpp
// Program Lunch writes out the contents of a sandwich.

#include <iostream>
#include <string>
using namespace std;

const string HAM = "ham";
const string CHEESE = "cheese";
const string LETTUCE = "lettuce";
const string BREAD = "bread";

int main()
{
    string filling;
    string sandwich;

    filling = HAM + " and " + CHEESE + " with " + LETTUCE;
    sandwich = filling + " on white " + BREAD + '.';
    cout  << "Filling : "  << filling  << endl;
    cout  << "Sandwich : " << sandwich  << endl;

    return 0;
}
```

Exercise 1: What is written by program Lunch?

Exercise 2: List the identifiers that are defined in program Lunch.

Exercise 3: Which of these identifiers are named constants?

Exercise 4: List the literal constants.

Exercise 5: List the identifiers that are defined in <iostream>.

Lesson 2–1: Check Prelab Exercises

Name _____ Date _____

Section _____

Exercise 1: Run program `Lunch` to check your answer to Prelab Exercise 1. Was your answer completely correct? If it was not, explain where you made your mistake.

Exercise 2: The identifiers are HAM, CHEESE, LETTUCE, BREAD, `filling`, and `sandwich`.

Exercise 3: The named constants are HAM, CHEESE, LETTUCE, and BREAD.

Exercise 4: The literal string constants are " and ", " with ", " on white ", "Filling : ", and "Sandwich : ". The literal character constant is ".".

Exercise 5: `cout` and `endl` are defined in `<iostream>`.

Lesson 2-2: Components of a Program

Name _____   Date _____

Section _____

This lesson uses program `Greeting`. Compile and rerun the program after each modification.

```
// Program Greet prints a greeting on the screen.

#_____
#_____
using namespace std;

_____ string FIRST_NAME = "Sarah";
_____ string LAST_NAME = "Sunshine";
_____ _____ ()
{
    _____ message;
    _____ name;

    name = FIRST_NAME + LAST_NAME;
    message = "Good morning "  + name + '.';
    cout  << message  _____ endl;
    _____ 0;
}
```

Exercise 1: Program `Greet` prints a greeting on the screen. However, it is missing certain identifiers, reserved words, and operators that are necessary for it to compile. Replace each blank with the appropriate identifier, reserved word, or operator and run the program. Record the output.

Exercise 2: Replace the named constants with your first and last names and rerun the program.

Exercise 3: Make the greeting a named constant rather than a literal constant and rerun the program.

Exercise 4: Change the action part of the program so that the greeting is written on one line and your name is on the next line.

Lesson 2–3: Sending Information to the Output Stream

Name _____ Date _____

Section _____

Lesson 2–3 focuses on constructing output statements. Program Shell is the outline of a program. Use this shell for Exercises 1 through 3.

```
// Program Shell

#include <iostream>
using namespace std;

int main ()
{

    return 0;
}
```

Exercise 1: Write a program to print the following information single spaced on the screen. Use literal constants in the output statements themselves for each of the data items to be written on the screen. Run your program to verify that the output is as specified.

a. your name (last name, comma, blank, first name)
b. today's date (month:day:year)

Exercise 2: Change your program so that there is a space between the two lines of output.

Exercise 3: Change your program so that your first name is printed followed by your last name with a blank in between.

Lesson 2–4: Debugging

Name _____ Date _____

Section _____

Exercise 1: Program `Dinner` (on file `Dinner`) writes a dinner menu. Compile and run this program. Be forewarned: Bugs are lurking in the code. The lines of the program are numbered on the right in comments. Fill in the following chart, showing the errors and what you did to correct them. (This time you do not get a printed copy; you must use the file only.) If the errors are caused by missing code, explain in the Corrections column.

#	OK	Error	Corrections (if error)
1			
2			
3			
4			
5			
6			
7			
8			
9			
10			
11			
12			
13			
14			
15			
16			
17			

Exercise 2: Program `Dinner2` contains a syntactically correct version of program `Dinner`, but the output is not correct. What must you do to correct this problem?

Exercise 3: Program `Greet2` is a variation of program `Greet` in Lesson 2–2, but it doesn't produce the correct output. What is the problem?

Exercise 4: Correct program `Greet2` and rerun it.

Postlab Activities

Exercise 1: Write a program to print out the following lines from Dr. Seuss's *Horton Hatches the Egg.*[1]

I meant what I said
and I said what I meant
An elephant's faithful
one hundred percent

Put a border of asterisks around the entire quotation (all four sides). Each line of the quotation should be sent to the output stream in the same statement.

Exercise 2: Write a program that produces a cover sheet for your laboratory assignments. It should have the chapter number, the lessons that have been assigned, your instructor's name, your name, the date, and any other information that your instructor has requested.

Exercise 3: Write a program that writes a birthday message to your mother. Surround the message with asterisks.

---

[1] Dr. Seuss, *Horton Hatches the Egg* (New York: Random House, 1940).

Arithmetic Expressions, Function Calls, and Output

- To be able to write simple arithmetic expressions to accomplish a specified task.

- To be able to convert a value from one numeric type to another numeric type.

- To be able to write output statements that format data in specified ways.

- To be able to use value-returning library functions.

- To be able to use string functions to manipulate string data.

- To be able to debug a program with syntax errors.

- To be able to debug a program with logic errors.

Chapter 3: Assignment Cover Sheet

Name _____ Date _____

Section _____

Fill in the following table showing which exercises have been assigned for each lesson and check what you are to submit: (1) lab sheets, (2) listings of output files, and/or (3) listings of programs. Your instructor or teaching assistant (TA) can use the Completed column for grading purposes.

Activities	Assigned: Check or list exercise numbers	Submit (1) (2) (3)			Completed
Prelab					
Review					
Prelab Assignment					
Inlab					
Lesson 3–1: Check Prelab Exercises					
Lesson 3–2: Arithmetic Operations					
Lesson 3–3: Formatting Output					
Lesson 3–4: Value-Returning Functions					
Lesson 3–5: String Functions					
Lesson 3–6: Debugging					
Postlab					

Prelab Activities

Review

In Chapter 2, we showed how identifiers are constructed and said they name data types, data objects, and actions. We used the following three statements in program Rhyme.

```
const  char SEMI_COLON = ';';
const string VERB1 = "went up "
string firstLine;
```

The first named a `char` constant, `SEMI_COLON`, and stored a semicolon into it. The second named a `string` constant and stored the string "went up" into it. The third named a `string` variable `firstLine`, into which a value of type `string` can be stored.

As we said in Chapter 2, there are four integral types that can be used to refer to an integer value: `char`, `short`, `int`, and `long`. Although these types represent integers of different sizes, `char`'s most important role is representing an alphanumeric character. The actual number of bits used to represent each of these types varies from one computer to another, but the number of digits that can be represented increases from `char` (the smallest) to `long` (the largest). `float`, `double`, and `long double` are data type identifiers that refer to floating point numbers; that is, numbers with a whole and a fractional part.

Variables and constants of integral and floating point types can be combined into expressions using arithmetic operators. The operations between constants or variables of these types are addition (+), subtraction (-), multiplication (*), and division (/). If the operands of the division operation are integral, the result is the integral quotient. If the operands are floating point types, the result is a floating point type with the division carried out to as many decimal places as the type allows. There is an additional operator for integral types, the modulus operator (%). This operator returns the remainder from integer division.

In addition to the standard arithmetic operators, C++ provides an *increment* operator and a *decrement* operator. The increment operator ++ adds one to its operand; the decrement operator subtracts one from its operand. The increment and decrement operators can be either postfix operators or prefix operators. We only use them as postfix operators in this text.

Precedence Rules

The precedence rules of arithmetic apply to arithmetic expressions in a program. That is, the order of execution of an expression that contains more than one operation is determined by the precedence rules of arithmetic. These rules state that parentheses have the highest precedence, multiplication, division, and modulus have the next highest precedence, and addition and subtraction have the lowest. Because parentheses have the highest precedence, they can be used to change the order in which operations are executed. The C++ postfix increment and decrement operators have the highest precedence of any of the arithmetic operators.

Converting Numeric Types

If an integral and a floating point variable or constant are mixed in an operation, the integral value is changed temporarily to its equivalent floating point representation before the operation is executed. This automatic conversion of an integral value to a floating point value is called *type coercion*. Type coercion also occurs when a floating point value is assigned to an integral variable. Coercion from an integer to a floating point is exact. Although the two values are represented differently in memory, both representations are exact. However, when a floating point value is coerced into an integral value, loss of information occurs unless the floating point value is a whole number. That is, 1.0 can be coerced into 1, but what about 1.5? Is it coerced into 1 or 2? In C++, when a floating point value is coerced into an integral value, the floating point value is truncated. Thus, the floating point value 1.5 is coerced into 1.

Type changes can be made explicit by placing the value to be changed in parentheses and placing the name of the new type before it. That is,

```
intValue = 10.66;
```

and

```
intValue = int(10.66);
```

produce the same results. The first is implicit; the second is explicit. Explicit type changing is called *type casting* or *type conversion*, as opposed to implicit type changing, which is called *type coercion*. Explicit type conversion is more self-documenting and is therefore better style.

Value-Returning Functions

Every C++ program must have an `int` function `main` that forms the main program. That is, `main` is the name of the function that calculates what we want to have done (the action). We can also use functions to do specific tasks within our function `main`. When we want the task to be executed, we use the function name in an expression.

C++ provides a wealth of preprogrammed functions to use. These functions are collected into files and made available through the #include directive. For example, the <cmath> file includes such useful functions as `cos` and `sin`, which calculate the cosine and sine of a variable in radians, `pow`, which raises a value to a power, and `sqrt`, which takes the square root of a floating point value. These functions are all value-returning functions and are executed by using their names in an expression. Here is an example.

```
#include <cmath>
#include <iostream>
using namespace std;

cout  << pow(3.0, 4.0)  << sqrt(81.0)  << endl;
```

`pow(3.0, 4.0)` returns the value `81.0`; this value is written on the screen. `sqrt(81.0)` returns the value `9.0`, which is written on the screen. The values in the parentheses to the right of the function names are called *parameters* to the function. Parameters are the values that the functions use as input. In the case of `pow`, the first value is the one to be taken to a power and the second is the power. The parameter to `sqrt` is the value for which the square root is calculated.

You can write your own value-returning functions as well. Look at the following program.

```
// Program Miles prints miles in kilometers.

#include <iostream>
using namespace std;

float  Kilometers(int);

int main ()
{
    cout  << fixed  << showpoint;  // for decimal output
    cout  << "One mile is " << kilometers(1)
          << " kilometers."  << endl;
    cout  << "Ten miles is " << kilometers(10)
          << " kilometers."  << endl;
    cout  << "One hundred miles is "  << kilometers(100)
          << " kilometers."  << endl;
    return 0;
}

float  Kilometers(int miles)
{
    const float KILO = 1.609;
    return KILO * float(miles);
}
```

Function `Kilometers` is a user-defined value-returning function. It takes one `int` parameter that represents miles and returns that value expressed in kilometers. Function `Kilometers` is invoked by using its name in an output statement. That is, the value returned from the function is sent to the output stream. We discuss how to write value-returning functions in depth in Chapter 8.

Void Functions

C++ provides another type of function called a *void function*. A void function is the name of an action that does not return a single value. Value-returning functions like `main` have the data type of the value being returned before the name of the function (`int main`, for example). Void functions have the word `void` before the name of the function to indicate that they are not returning a single value. Rather than being used in an expression, void functions are used as statements in the body of other functions. We discuss void functions at great length in Chapter 7.

Output Formatting

We can control the vertical spacing of lines on the screen (or page) by using the `endl` manipulator described in Chapter 2. `endl` inserts an end-of-line character and forces the next output to begin on the next line. We can use successive `endl`'s to create blank lines. For example, the first of the following two statements creates three blank lines and writes the message "Happy New Year" on the fourth line.

```
cout  << endl  << endl  << endl  << "Happy New Year";
cout  << "!"
```

Where does the exclamation point go? Immediately following the *r* in *Year*. Characters are streamed to cout without line breaks unless endl is inserted into the stream.

We can put blanks in a line by including them within the strings that we are writing. For example, we can put extra blanks before and after the message as follows:

```
cout  << endl  << endl  << endl  <<    "  Happy New Year  ";
```

Note that we also added extra blanks before the double quote. These extra blanks have no effect on the output whatsoever. Only blanks within the strings are sent to cout.

When outputting numbers, it is useful to be able to state how many column positions the number should occupy. We can do this with another manipulator called setw. This manipulator (available in file <iomanip>) states how many columns the following data value is to occupy. For example,

```
intValue = 5;
cout  << setw(4)  << intValue;
```

prints the contents of intValue right-justified in four columns. The parameter to setw is an integer expression called the *fieldwidth*. If the fieldwidth is not large enough to contain the digits in the number, it is automatically expanded to the appropriate size. You specify the fieldwidth for floating point numbers the same way (don't forget to include the decimal point in your fieldwidth count). You can set the number of decimal places to be shown by the manipulator setprecision (also in file <iomanip>). For example,

```
realValue = 3.14159;
cout << setprecision(3) << realValue;
```

prints 3.142. Note that the last digit printed has been rounded. setprecision(3) remains in effect until the next setprecision is used, but setw applies only to the value immediately following.

There are two additional manipulators available in <iostream> that are useful when working with floating point numbers: fixed and showpoint. fixed forces all subsequent floating point output to be in decimal format, and showpoint forces all subsequent floating point output to show a decimal point even though the values are whole numbers.

Additional String Operations

In Chapter 2, we introduced the binary operation concatenation, which we used to combine strings and characters. Data type string provides four additional operations that are very useful when working with character data. They are length, find, size, and substr. Let's examine their syntax and semantics in the context of the following program.

```
// Program StrDemo demonstrates string functions.
#include <iostream>
#include <string>
using namespace std;

const string TITLE = "How much was the doggie in the window?";
const string CAT = "cat";
```

```
int main()
{
    cout  << TITLE.length()  << endl;
    cout  << TITLE.find("the")  << endl;
    cout  << TITLE.find(CAT)  << endl;
    cout  << TITLE.substr(17, 6)  << endl;
    cout  << TITLE.substr(17, 23)  << endl;
    cout  << TITLE.substr(17, 23).length()  << endl;
    return 0;
}
```

Output:

```
38
13
4294967295
doggie
doggie in the window?
21
```

The first line of output is 38, the number of characters in the constant string TITLE. (Recall that we use all uppercase letters for the names of string constants.) length is a function that is applied to an object of type string using *dot notation*: the name of the string object, followed by a dot (period), followed by the name of the function. length is a value returning function, so it is used in an expression. Although it does not have any parameters, it still must have parentheses to the right of the name.

Function find looks for its argument in the string to which it is applied. The second line of output is 13. "the" is found in TITLE beginning at the 13th position. How can that be? The "t" in "the" is the 14th character. Yes, well most humans start counting with one, but C++ begins counting with zero. "H" is in the zeroth position, making "the" start in the 13th position. The next line of output shows what happens when the string (or character) being searched for does not occur in the string object. A named constant npos is returned; npos is the largest value within the return value type of the function.

The next line of output demonstrates what the substr function does. It returns a substring of the object to which it is applied, beginning at the position specified by the first parameter. The length of the substring is specified in the second parameter. The fifth and sixth lines of output show what happens if the specified length of the substring exceeds the number of characters in the object string. substr(17, 23) asks for a substring of length 23 beginning at position 17. There are only 38 characters in the string TITLE, so this request cannot be fulfilled. In this case, the rest of the object string is returned beginning at position 17. The sixth line of input prints the length of the string returned (21). What happens if the beginning position is outside the string? The program crashes.

We said that there were four useful operations defined for type string. We have only shown three. What about the size function? Because many people think of the size of a string rather than the length of the string, both names are provided. The size function is identical to the length function.

Operator Symbols

Here is a table showing the C++ equivalent of the standard arithmetic operators and the other operations defined in this chapter.

Operator	Meaning
+	Unary plus
-	Unary minus
+	Addition
-	Subtraction
*	Multiplication
/	Floating point operands: floating point result Integer operands: quotient Mixed operands: floating point result
%	Modulus (remainder from integer division, operands must be integral)
++	Increment by one; can be prefix or postfix; as postfix has highest precedence
- -	Decrement by one; can be prefix or postfix; as postfix has highest precedence
length size	Functions that return the lengths of the objects to which they are applied
find	A function that searches the string object to which it is applied looking for a character or string specified in its parameter and returns the beginning position if a match is found and constant npos otherwise
substr	A function that returns a substring of the object to which it is applied beginning at the position specified in the first parameter and continuing until the substring is the length specified in the second parameter or the end of the object string is reached. If the beginning position is outside the string, the program crashes

Chapter 3: Prelab Assignment

Name _____ Date _____

Section _____

Examine the following program carefully and answer the question in Exercise 1.

```cpp
// Program Pres demonstrates the precedence of operators.

#include <iostream>
using namespace std;

int main ()
{

    cout  << fixed  << showpoint;
    cout << 4 + 3 * 5  << endl;
    cout << (4 + 3) * 5  <<endl;
    cout << 4 * 5 % 3 + 2  << endl;
    cout << (4 * (5 / 3) + 2)  << endl;
    return 0;
}
```

Exercise 1: Show what is written by each of the output statements.

Examine the following program carefully and then answer the questions in Exercises 2 and 3.

```cpp
// Program Format demonstrates the use of fieldwidth
// specifications.

#include <iostream>
#include <iomanip>
using namespace std;

const int  INT_NUMBER = 1066;
const float  FLT_NUMBER = 3.14159;
```

```
main ()
{
    float   fltValue;
    int     intValue;

    cout  << fixed  << showpoint;

    intValue = INT_NUMBER + FLT_NUMBER;
    fltValue = float(INT_NUMBER) + FLT_NUMBER;
    cout << INT_NUMBER  << endl;
    cout << intValue  << endl;
    cout << setw(10)  << intValue;
    cout << setw(10)  << intValue  << intValue /10  << endl;
    cout << setw(10)  << fltValue  << endl;
    cout << setprecision(10)  << fltValue  << endl;
    cout << setw(10)  << setprecision(3)  << fltValue
         << endl;
    cout << fltValue << endl;
    cout << intValue  << setw(3)  << intValue  << setw(7)
         << intValue
         << endl;
    return 0;
}
```

Exercise 2: Show what is written by each of the output statements.

Exercise 3: Circle a statement that contains type conversion, and underline a statement that contains type coercion.

Lesson 3–1: Check Prelab Exercises

Name _____ Date _____

Section _____

Exercise 1: Run program `Pres` to check your answers. Were your answers completely correct? If they were not, explain what was wrong.

Exercise 2: Run program `Format` to check your answers Were your answers completely correct? If they were not, explain what was wrong.

Exercise 3:

```
 intValue = INT NUMBER + FLT NUMBER;

 fltValue = float(INT_NUMBER) + FLT_NUMBER;
```

Lesson 3-2: Arithmetic Operations

Name _____ Date _____

Section _____

Use program Convert for Exercises 1 through 5. Study this program carefully. It converts a temperature from Fahrenheit to Celsius and a temperature from Celsius to Fahrenheit.

```
// Program Convert converts a temperature in Fahrenheit to
// Celsius and a temperature in Celsius to Fahrenheit.

#include <iostream>
using namespace std;

const int TEMP_IN_F = 32;
const int TEMP_IN_C = 0;

int main ()
{
    int fToC; // Place to store Celsius answer
    int cToF; // Place to store the Fahrenheit answer

    cToF = (9 * TEMP_IN_C / 5) + 32;
    fToC = 5 * (TEMP_IN_F - 32) / 9;
    cout << TEMP_IN_F  << " in Fahrenheit is "  << fToC
         << " in Celsius. "  << endl;
    return 0;
}
```

Exercise 1: Compile and run program Convert. What value is written out for fToC?

Exercise 2: Notice that the program computes two values (cToF and fToC) but only one value is written on the screen. Insert a second output statement that prints the value of cToF immediately below the value of fToC. Compile and run the program. (If you have trouble compiling your program, check to be sure that you have a semicolon after the second output statement.)

What was the output from your additional statement?

Exercise 3: Change the values for constants TEMP_IN_F and TEMP_IN_C to the following values and compile and rerun the program after each change. Record the values for fToC and cToF for each set of values.

TEMP_IN_F	TEMP_IN_C	fToC	cToF
a. 212	100	_____	_____
b. 100	50	_____	_____
c. 122	37	_____	_____
d. _____	_____	_____	_____
(You choose.)			

Exercise 4: Examine the output from b and c. There seems to be an inconsistency. Describe the inconsistency and make a hypothesis to explain it.

Exercise 5: Change the integer constants and variables to type float and rerun the program with the same data you used in Parts b and c in Exercise 3. Do the results confirm your hypothesis? Explain.

Exercise 6: Remove the parentheses from both assignment statements and rerun the program using the values that you used in Part c in Exercise 3.

What values are printed? fToC _____ cToF _____

These values are not the same ones that were printed in Exercise 5. Why?

Lesson 3–3: Formatting Output

Name _____ · _____   Date _____

Section _____ , ·· _____

Use the following program shell for Exercises 1 through 4.

```
// Program Numbers sends numbers to the output stream in
// specified formats.

#include <iostream>
#include <iomanip>
using namespace std;

int main ()
{
    cout << fixed  << showpoint;

    return 0;
}
```

Exercise 1: Write a program to print the following numbers right-justified in a column on the screen. Make the values named constants.

1066   1492   512   1   -23

Exercise 2: Add two statements to your program. Calculate the floating point result from dividing the sum of the first two values by the sum of the last three values and store it in `answer`. The second statement should write the contents of `answer` on the screen to four decimal places. (Do not forget to declare `answer`.)

The answer is _____.

Exercise 3: Write the following numbers right-justified in a column on the screen. Each of the data values should be written in formatted floating point notation with two decimal places. Use fieldwidth specifications rather than listing the numbers in your program with the proper formatting. You may use either literal constants or named constants.

23.62   46.0   43.4443   100.1   98.98

Exercise 4: Add two statements to your program for Exercise 3. The first statement should calculate the sum of the numbers and store the result in variable `sum`. The second statement should write `sum` on the screen, properly labeled.

The sum of the numbers is _____.

Use the following program shell for Exercises 5 and 6.

```
// Program Center sends strings to the output stream in
// specified formats.

#include <iostream>
#include <iomanip>
using namespace std;

int main ()
{

    return 0;
}
```

Exercise 5: Add the statements necessary to print the following strings centered in fields of 20 characters all on one line: "Good Morning", "Sarah", and "Sunshine!". Do not use manipulators. Compile and run your program; show your output.

Exercise 6: Repeat Exercise 5 using manipulators to help center your strings. Compile and run your program. Your output should be the same.

Exercise 7: Change the program in Exercise 6 so that the three strings print on three separate lines with a blank line in between each string.

Lesson 3–4: Value-Returning Functions

Name _____   Date _____

Section _____

Use the following shell for Exercises 1 and 2.

```
// Program Function demonstrates the use of library and
// user-defined functions.

#include <iostream>
#include <cmath>
using namespace std;

float Answer(float, float, float);

int main ()
{
    cout  << fixed  << showpoint;

    cout  << Answer(_____, _____, _____);
    return 0;
}
// Do you recognize this formula?
float Answer(float one, float two, float three)
{
    return ((- two + sqrt(pow(two, _____)
        - (4.0 * one * three))) / (2.0 * one));
}
```

Exercise 1: Fill in the blanks in function answer such that the value stored in parameter two is taken to the second power. Fill in the blanks in function main so that function Answer is invoked with 10.0 as the first parameter, 20.0 as the second parameter, and 5.0 as the third parameter. What is printed?

Exercise 2: Change the program in Exercise 1 so that function Answer is invoked with 5.0 as the first parameter, 20.0 as the second parameter, and 10.0 as the third parameter. What is printed?

Exercise 3: Change the program in Exercise 1 so that function Answer is invoked with 5.0 as the first parameter, 10.0 as the second parameter, and 20.0 as the third parameter . What happens? Explain why.

Lesson 3–5: String Functions

Name _____ Date _____

Section _____

Use the following program shell for Exercises 1, 2, and 3.

```
// Program Strings applies string functions.

#include <iostream>
#include <string>
using namespace std;

int main ()
{

    return 0;
}
```

Exercise 1: Write a named `string` constant made up of your first and last name with a blank in between. Write the statements to print out the result of applying `length` and `size` to your named constant object. Compile and run your program.

Exercise 2: Write the statements necessary to print your name, last name first, followed by a comma and your first name. Use function `substr` to accomplish this task. Compile and run your program.

Exercise 3: Write the statements necessary to print your last name, followed by a comma and your first initial. Compile and run your program.

Lesson 3–6: Debugging

Name _____ Date _____

Section _____

Exercise 1: Program Typos contains syntax errors. Correct the program, describe the errors, and show what is printed. (This time you do not get a printed copy; you must use only the file.)

List the syntax errors.

Show what is printed.

Exercise 2: The output from program Typos looks strange! Clearly, there are logic bugs lurking in the code. Find and correct these errors.

List the logic errors.

Show what is printed.

Exercise 3: Program Ounces converts a value in ounces to cups, quarts, and gallons. Compile and run this program. Be forewarned: A few bugs are lurking in the code. The elements (definitions, statements, and symbols) of the program are numbered on the left in comments. Fill in the following chart, listing the syntax errors and showing what you did to correct them.

#	OK	Error	Corrections (if error)
1			
2			
3			
4			
5			
6			
7			
8			
9			
10			
11			
12			
13			
14			
15			
16			

Exercise 4: Now that program Ounces compiles and runs, you must check the output for logic errors. List the logic errors that you find and indicate what you did to correct them. Run your corrected program.

Exercise 5: Did you double check the answers to be sure they were reasonable? Compare your solution to program Ounces2. Did you find all the logic errors?

Postlab Activities

Exercise 1: Write a program that prints the hundreds digit in a series of integer constants. For example, if constants ONE and TWO are 1456 and 254 respectively, your program should print 4 and 2. You may choose the integers yourself. Your output should include the original number followed by the digit in the hundreds position. Label your output appropriately.

Exercise 2: Write a program that prints the number 1349.9431 with three decimal places, with two decimal places, and with one decimal place.

Exercise 3: Write a program that prints each of the following values in two columns: 1234, 45, 7, 87, 99999. The first column is left-justified and the second column is right-justified.

Exercise 4: Write a program that takes a string of thirty hash marks (#) and prints six hash marks on five lines with a blank line in between. The variable that originally contains the thirty hash marks should contain the empty string at the end of your program.

Program Input and the Software Design Process

Objectives

■ To be able to determine how data must be input in order for a program to run correctly.

■ To be able to examine the input data to a program and the results and deduce the form of the input statements.

■ To be able to create a data file.

■ To be able to take a program that extracts data from the keyboard and change it to extract data from a file.

■ To be able to construct input and output statements that take their input from a file and send their output to a file.

■ To be able to distinguish between object-oriented design and functional design.

■ To be able to debug a program that inputs data from the keyboard and a file.

Chapter 4: Assignment Cover Sheet

Name _____ Date _____

Section _____

Fill in the following table showing which exercises have been assigned for each lesson and check what you are to submit: (1) lab sheets, (2) listings of output files, and/or (3) listings of programs. Your instructor or teaching assistant (TA) can use the Completed column for grading purposes.

Activities	Assigned: Check or list exercise numbers	Submit (1) (2) (3)			Completed
Prelab					
Review					
Prelab Assignment					
Inlab					
Lesson 4–1: Check Prelab Exercises					
Lesson 4–2: Input Statement and Data Consistency					
Lesson 4–3: Input and Output with Files					
Lesson 4–4: Program design					
Lesson 4–5: Debugging					
Postlab					

Prelab Activities

Review

Chapter 4 contains a great deal of new material: reading data from the keyboard, reading data from a file, creating a file, and learning a methodology for writing solutions to problems. Mastering these concepts here, before you go on to the next chapter, will save you much grief later on. We promise!

Input Streams

There are four ways that a value can be stored in a place in memory. You have already seen two methods in Chapter 2: A value can be stored by the compiler as the result of a constant declaration, or it can be stored as the result of an assignment statement. Chapter 4 introduces a third way: A value can be read into the program while the program is being executed. (We show you the fourth way in Chapter 8.)

In Chapter 2, we said that `cout` was an output stream. Characters inserted into this stream appear on the screen. That is, the insertion operator (`<<`) inserts strings and values from within the program into the output stream that appears on the screen. In an analogous fashion, we can extract data values from an input stream prepared at the keyboard and store them in variables in our program. `cin` is the input stream from the keyboard, and `>>` is the extraction operator.

`cout` is of type `ostream`, and `cin` is of type `istream`. `istream`, `ostream`, `cin`, and `cout` are defined in file `<iostream>` and accessed by using the preprocessor directive `#include <iostream>`. Whereas statements using `cout` and the insertion operator (`<<`) place values in the output stream, statements using `cin` and the extraction operator (`>>`) take values from the input stream and place them in variables in the program.

The data type of the place in which a value is stored determines how the value is read. If you are reading numeric data, whitespace characters are skipped and reading continues until a non-numeric character is encountered. Whitespace characters are blanks and certain nonprintable characters like end-of-line. If you are reading data into a variable of type `char`, whitespace characters are skipped and one character is read. If you are reading data into a variable of type `string`, whitespace characters are skipped and characters are read and stored until the next whitespace character is encountered (but not read).

There are as many values read from the input stream as there are extraction operator/place name pairs to the right of `cin`. The values are extracted one at a time from the input stream and stored in the places named in order. The first value read goes into the first place listed, the second value read goes into the second place listed, etc. The values read must be of the same type as the places into which they are to be stored, with the exception that a floating point value can be keyed as an integral value without a decimal point. The decimal point is automatically inserted in this case.

Because there are times when you do not want to skip whitespace before inputting a character, the `istream` data type provides a function to input the next character in the stream regardless of what it is. The function is named `get` and is applied as shown.

```
cin.get(character);
```

The next character in the input stream is returned in `char` variable `character`. If the previous input was a numeric value, `character` contains whatever inappropriate character ended the inputting of the value.

There are also times when you want to skip the rest of the values on a line and go to the beginning of the next line. A function named `ignore` defined in file `<iostream>` allows you to do this. It has two parameters. The first is an `int` expression and the second is a character. This function skips the number of characters specified in the first parameter or all the characters up to and including the character specified in the second parameter, whichever comes first. For example,

```
cin.ignore(80, '\n');
```

skips 80 characters or skips to the beginning of the next line depending on whether a newline character is encountered before 80 characters are skipped (read and discarded).

We said that initial whitespace is skipped when reading data into a variable of type `string` and that the next whitespace character encountered stops the reading. How, then, can we get blanks or other whitespace characters into a string? We must use function `getline`, which takes two parameters. The first is the name of the input stream, and the second is the name of the `string` variable into which the string is to be read. For example,

```
getline(cin, newString);
```

begins immediately reading and collecting characters into `newString` and continues until a newline character is encountered. The newline character is read but not stored in `newString`.

Keyboard Input Prompts

If your input is coming from the keyboard, someone is sitting at the keyboard waiting to enter the values at the proper time. The program should prompt the person to enter the values when it is ready to read them. For example, if the program needs the number of gallons of paint purchased and the price of a gallon, the person at the keyboard should be prompted with a message string something like this:

"Enter the number of gallons of paint (whole number) followed by the cost of a gallon (dollars and cents). Press return."

The statement that reads in the values follows the statement that writes the prompting message to the screen.

Files

If you want to prepare input data ahead, you may store the data in a file and direct the program to read its input from a file. If you want to save output data in a file to use later, you may direct the program to write data to a file. To read and/or write to a file, do the following things:

1. Request the preprocessor to include file `<fstream>` as well as file `<iostream>`. The former contains the declarations for defining input and output streams other than `cin` and `cout`.
2. Declare an input stream to be of type `ifstream` or an output stream to be of type `ofstream` (or both).

3. Prepare the streams for use by using the function named open provided in file <fstream>. The parameter for function open is the external name of the file. The external name is the name under which the file is stored on the disk.
4. Put the internal file name to the left of the insertion or extraction operator.

Here is an example program that reads four floating point data values from a file and writes them to another file in reverse order.

```
// Program IODemo demonstrates how to use files.

#include <iostream>
#include <fstream>
using namespace std;

int main()
{
    float val1, val2, val3, val4;       // declares 4 variables
    ifstream inData;                    // declares input stream
    ofstream outData;                   // declares output stream

    outData << fixed  << showpoint;

    inData.open("Data.In");
    // binds program variable inData to file "Data.In"
    outData.open("Data.Out");
    // binds program variable outData to file "Data.Out"

    inData  >> val1 >> val2 >> val3
            >> val4;                    // inputs 4 values
    outData  << val4  << endl;
    outData  << val3  << endl;
    outData  << val2  << endl;
    outData  << val1  << endl;          // outputs 4 values
    return 0;
}
```

Each file in your program has both an internal name and an external name. The internal name is what you call it in your program; the external name is the name the operating system knows it by. Somehow these two names must be associated with one another. This association is called *binding* and is done in function open. Notice that inData and outData are identifiers declared in your program; "Data.In" and "Data.Out" are character strings. Data.In is the name that was used when the input data file was created; Data.Out is the name of the file where the answers are stored.

Input Failure

The key to reading data in correctly (from either the keyboard or a file) is to make sure that the order and the form in which the data are keyed are consistent with the order and type of the identifiers on the input stream extraction statement. If your data and your input statements are not consistent, your program does not crash or give an error message, but every subsequent stream operation is ignored. An error causes the stream to enter the fail state, and any further references to a stream in the fail state are ignored. If you misspell the name of the file that is the parameter to function open (In.dat instead of Data.In, for example), the stream enters the fail state. Your program continues to operate, but all references to inData are ignored.

Creating a Data File

If you are using an integrated environment, such as Turbo C++ or CodeWarrior, an editor is provided for you in which to write your program. You may use this same editor to create a data file. That is, instead of writing a C++ program, you key in the data you want the program to read.

If you are using a general-purpose word processor to create your programs, such as Word or WordPerfect, you may use this same editor to create your data files. However, you need to save both your programs and your data files in text mode. General-purpose word processors have formatting information at the beginning of the file that you cannot see on the screen. This information must be removed from the file before the compiler can compile the program or the program can read data correctly. If the program file has formatting information, the compiler cannot compile the program and alerts you that there is a problem. If the data file has formatting information, you simply get the wrong answer.

Program Design

Object-oriented design is a methodology developed for large-scale programming projects. The solution to a problem using this technique is expressed in terms of self-contained entities called *objects*, which are composed of both data and operations that manipulate the data. Object-oriented design focuses on the objects and their interactions within a problem. Inheritance is a property of object-oriented design in which objects can inherit data and behavior from other objects.

Functional design (also called top-down or structured design) is like writing an outline for a paper. The main subheadings are listed, and then each subhead is further divided until no more subheadings are needed. In a functional design, the main subheadings are the tasks that must be accomplished for the problem to be solved. Each task (subheading) is further divided into the subtasks that must be accomplished before it is complete. Each subtask is further divided into the tasks necessary to complete its job. A task (or subtask) needs no further division when it becomes a concrete step, that is, when the task (or subtask) can be directly coded into a statement in a programming language.

To summarize, functional design methods focus on the *process* of transforming the input into the output, resulting in a hierarchy of tasks. Object-oriented design focuses on the *data objects* that are to be transformed, resulting in a hierarchy of objects. Grady Booch puts it this way: "Read the specification of the software you want to build. Underline the verbs if you are after procedural code, the nouns if you aim for an object-oriented program."[1]

We propose that you circle the nouns and underline the verbs. The nouns become objects; the verbs become operations. In a functional design, the verbs are the primary focus; in an object-oriented design, the nouns are the primary focus.

---

[1] Grady Booch, "What Is and Isn't Object Oriented Design." *American Programmer*, special issue on object orientation, vol. 2, no. 7–8, Summer 1989.

Chapter 4: Prelab Assignment

Name _____ Date _____

Section _____

Exercise 1: If file `Data.In` contains the values shown below, what does program `IODemo` write on file `Data.Out`?

```
5.5
6.6
7.7
8.8
```

Program `Frame` is an interactive program that reads the dimensions of a print and calculates the amount of wood needed to make a frame for it. Examine it carefully and then complete Exercises 2 through 6.

```cpp
// Program Frame prompts the user to input values representing
// the dimensions of a print.  The amount of wood needed for
// the frame is calculated and printed on the screen.

#include <iostream>
using namespace std;

int main ()
{
    int   side;          // vertical dimension in inches
    int   top;           // horizontal dimension in inches
    int   inchesOfWood;  // inches of wood needed

    cout  << "Enter the vertical dimension of your print."
          << endl;
    cout  << "The dimension should be in whole inches. "
          << "Press return."  << endl;
    cin  >> side;

    cout  << "Enter the horizontal dimension of your print."
          << endl;
    cout  << "The dimension should be in whole inches. "
          << "Press return."  << endl;
    cin  >> top;

    inchesOfWood = top + top + side + side;
    cout << "You need "  << inchesOfWood
         <<" inches of wood."  << endl;
    return 0;
}
```

Exercise 2: Program `Frame` prompts for and reads the vertical dimension of the print and then prompts for and reads the horizontal dimension of the print. How many lines of input does program `Frame` expect? Explain.

What happens if you key both values at the same time with a blank between them?

Exercise 3: Hand-simulate program `Frame` with the following three sets of input values; record the value for `inchesOfWood`.

top	side	inchesOfWood	
10		20	_____
13		5	_____
12		12	_____

Exercise 4: If the program is reorganized so that the prompts are together before the first input statement, what happens under the following reads? (The prompts are unchanged and the user follows them.)

a. `cin >> side >> top;`

b. `cin >> side;`
   `cin >> top;`

Exercise 5: What happens if you forget to put a space between the values for `side` and `top` in the input stream?

Exercise 6: Program `Frame` is to be changed to read from file `frame.in`. Mark all the changes on program `Frame`.

Lesson 4–1: Check Prelab Exercises

Name _____ Date _____

Section _____

Exercise 1: Run program `IODemo` and check your answer. Did one of the answers surprise you? Can you explain it?

Exercises 2 and 3: Program `Frame` expects two lines of input. You can tell because there are two accesses to `cin` with an output statement in between. Now, run program `Frame` to check the rest of your answers to Exercises 2 and 3 and answer the following questions.

What happened when you keyed both numbers on the same line?

Were your hand simulations correct? If not, why not?

Exercise 4: Programs `Frame2` and `Frame3` input the data as described in Parts a and b of this exercise, respectively. Run programs `Frame2` and `Frame3` to check your answers. Were your answers completely correct? If not, explain where you made your mistake(s).

Exercise 5: The program would input the combined numbers as one and store it in the first place named on the input statement (`side`). The program would then wait for the next value to be input.

Exercise 6: Compare your answers with program `Frame4`, which has the changes requested. (You will use this program later.)

Lesson 4–2: Input Statement and Data Consistency

Name _____   Date _____

Section _____

Exercises 1 through 3 use program shell `ReadData`.

```
// Program ReadData is a test bed for you to try various
// combinations of input statements with different data
// configurations.
// It determines the cost of a sheet of glass given the
// dimensions and the price per square foot of glass.

#include <iostream>
#include <iomanip>
using namespace std;

const  int IN_SQ_FT = 144;

int main ()
{
    int   length;         // measured in inches
    int   width;          // measured in inches
    float  price;         // sold by square foot
    float  cost;

    cout  << fixed  << showpoint;

    /*  TO BE FILLED IN. */

    cout  << "Width: "  << setw(5)  << width
          << " Length: "  << setw(5)  << length
          << " Price: "  << setw(6)  << setprecision(2)
          << price  << endl;
    cost = ((width * length) / IN_SQ_FT) * price;
    cout  << "The cost of the glass is $"  << setw(6)
          << cost  << endl;
    return 0;
}
```

Exercise 1: Write the appropriate prompts and input statements. (The data values should be keyed on one line with blanks between them.) Run program `ReadData` with the following data values and show the result.

Length	Width	Price
36	24	25.25

Exercise 2: Key in the values for `length` and `width` in reverse order. What happens?

Exercise 3: Key in the values for `price` and `length` in reverse order. What happens? Is the situation in Exercise 3 different from the situation in Exercise 2?

Exercise 4: Program `InOut` reads values from the keyboard but does not give any prompts. Compile and execute this program. Enter the following values from the keyboard exactly as shown. *Do not look at the code.*

```
11   12   13   14
21   22
31   32
41
51
```

What values are printed?

a _____   b _____   c _____   d _____   e _____
f _____   g _____   h _____

This program contains five input-related statements. What must these statements be to give the results shown?

Exercise 5: The input values that have been read in the previous tasks have all been numeric. This exercise uses program `CharRead` to read character variables.

```
// Program CharRead prompts for and reads four characters
// from the keyboard and then prints them.

#include <iostream>
using namespace std;
```

```
int main ()
{
    char   char1;
    char   char2;
    char   char3;
    char   char4;
    cout  << "Input four characters.  Press Return."  << endl;
    cin  >> char1  >> char2  >> char3  >> char4;
    cout  << char1  << char2  << char3  << char4;
    return 0;
}
```

Compile and run this program four times using the four sets of data values listed below. Key these values exactly as shown, including blanks.

Input Data	What Is Printed
abcd	_____
a b c d	_____
1b2c	_____
31 45	_____

Examine the results carefully. Do any of the results surprise you? (Remember that the extraction operator skips whitespace.)

Exercise 6: This exercise also reads character data.

```
// Program Char2Rd prompts for and reads four characters
// from the keyboard and then prints them.

#include <iostream>
using namespace std;

int main ()
{
    char   char1;
    char   char2;
    char   char3;
    char   char4;

    cout  << "Input four characters.  Press Return."  << endl;
    cin.get(char1);
    cin.get(char2);
    cin.get(char3);
    cin.get(char4);
    cout  << char1  << char2  << char3  << char4;
    return 0;
}
```

Compile and run this program four times using the four sets of data values listed below. Key these values exactly as shown, including blanks.

Input Data	What Is Printed
abcd	_____
a b c d	_____
1b2c	_____
31 45	_____

Examine the results carefully. Do any of the results surprise you? (Remember that the function get does not skip whitespace.)

Lesson 4–3: Input and Output with Files

Name _____ Date _____

Section _____

Program `Frame4` gets its input from a file.

```
// Program Frame4 reads input values that represent the
// dimensions of a print from a file and calculates and
// prints the amount of wood needed for a frame.

#include <iostream>
#include <fstream>
using namespace std;

int main ()
{
    ifstream  din;        // input stream
    int  side;            // vertical dimension in inches
    int  top;             // horizontal dimension in inches
    int  inchesOfWood;    // inches of wood needed

    din.open("Frame.In");
    din >> side >> top;
    cout << "Dimensions are " << top << " and "
         << side << "." << endl;
    inchesOfWood = top + top + side + side;
    cout << "You need " << inchesOfWood
         <<" inches of wood." << endl;
    return 0;
}
```

Exercise 1: Create a data file on the same directory as program `Frame4`, and name it `Frame.In`. Make the values in the file consistent with the input statements. Run program `Frame4` and record the output below.

Exercise 2: Why are there no prompts in program `Frame4`?

Exercise 3: Change program `Frame4` so that the output goes to file `dout`; `dout`'s external name should be `Frame.Out`. You must do the following tasks:

- Declare `dout` to be of type `ofstream`.
- Invoke function `open` to associate the internal name and the external name.
- Send the output to stream `dout`.

Run your changed program. Show what was written on file `Frame.Out`.

Exercises 4 and 5 use the following program shell StrRead.

```
// Program StrRead reads and writes strings.

#include <iostream>
#include <fstream>
#include <string>
using namespace std;

int main ()
{
    ifstream inFile;
    ofstream outFile;
    string   inString1;
    string   inString2;

    inFile.open("strData.in");
    outFile.open("outData");

    /*  TO BE FILLED IN.  */

    outFile  <<  inString1  <<  endl;
    outFile  <<  inString2  <<  endl;
    return 0;
}
```

`strData.in` contains the following information:

```
    Object-Oriented languages include C++ and Java.
List processing languages include Lisp and Scheme.
```

Exercise 4: Fill in the missing code in program `StrRead` so that `inString1` contains the characters "Object-Oriented" and `inString2` contains the characters "languages". Compile and run your program.

Exercise 5: Fill in the missing code in program `StrRead` so that `inString1` contains the entire first line of data and `inString2` contains the entire second line of data. Compile and run your program.

Lesson 4–4: Program Design

Name _____ Date _____

Section _____

Exercise 1: You love to travel, and you love to take photographs. When you finish this course, you are going to write a program to keep track of your photograph collection. You plan to use an object-oriented design for your program. In preparation for this project, list a tentative set of objects for the program and describe how they might interact. Give a list of possible operations for each object.

Possible Objects	Possible Operations for Objects	Interaction with Other Objects

Exercise 2: Write a functional design for the following problem. Maggie, your Labrador puppy, has eaten a hole in the carpet in the dining room. How much does it cost to replace the carpet? The input to your program should be the dimensions of the room and the price of the carpet. The output should be the cost written to the screen. Be sure to include prompts and echo-print the input along with the answer appropriately labeled.

Functional Design

Main   **Level 0**

On a separate sheet of paper, fill in as many levels of detail as are needed to make each statement a concrete step.

Exercise 3: Translate your functional design into C++ code and run your program.

Show your input.

How much does it cost to recarpet the dining room?

Lesson 4–5: Debugging

Name _____ Date _____

Section _____

Exercise 1: Program `FourVals` reads four `int` values from a file and writes them out with exactly one blank between them. The program doesn't even compile! Correct the syntax errors and run the program. Show your output.

Exercise 2: Now the program runs, but the output does not meet its specifications. Describe this logic error, correct it, and rerun the program. Show your output.

Exercise 3: Run your program, using file `Four2Val.in`. Describe what happens.

Exercise 4: Program `FourVals` makes an assumption about the data that is not stated in the problem.

What is this assumption?

How would you have to change program `FourVals` in order for it to work properly on file `Four2Val.in`?

Postlab Activities

Exercise 1: The dining room looks so nice with the new carpet that you decide to repaint the room. Write a functional design for a program that takes as input the dimensions of the room, the price of a gallon of paint, and the number of square feet that a gallon of paint covers. The output is what it will cost to paint the dining room. Echo your input and the answer on the screen, all appropriately labeled.

Exercise 2: Translate your design into a C++ program and run it.

Exercise 3: Write a functional design for a program to calculate how many calories your lunch contained. The input is on three lines: a character, *M*(eat), *V*(eggie), *D*(essert), followed by the associated calories. Read and echo-print the input. Write out the total number of calories in your lunch.

Exercise 4: Translate your design into a C++ program and run it.

Conditions, Logical Expressions, and Selection Control Structures

- ■ To be able to construct Boolean expressions to evaluate a given condition.

- ■ To be able to construct *if-then* statements to perform a specified task.

- ■ To be able to construct *if-then-else* statements to perform a specified task.

- ■ To be able to construct nested *if* statements to perform a specified task.

- ■ To be able to design and implement a test plan.

- ■ To be able to debug a program with a selection control structure.

Chapter 5: Assignment Cover Sheet

Name _____ Date _____

Section _____

Fill in the following table showing which exercises have been assigned for each lesson and check what you are to submit: (1) lab sheets, (2) listings of output files, and/or (3) listings of programs. Your instructor or teaching assistant (TA) can use the Completed column for grading purposes.

Activities	Assigned: Check or list exercise numbers	Submit (1) (2) (3)			Completed
Prelab					
Review					
Prelab Assignment					
Inlab					
Lesson 5–1: Check Prelab Exercises					
Lesson 5–2: Boolean Expressions					
Lesson 5–3: *if-then* Statements					
Lesson 5–4: *if-then-else* Statements					
Lesson 5–5: Nested Logic					
Lesson 5–6: Test Plan					
Lesson 5–7: Debugging					
Postlab					

Prelab Activities

Review

The physical order of a program is the order in which the statements are *listed*. The logical order of a program is the order in which the statements are *executed*. In this chapter, you learn to ask questions in your program and change the order in which the statements are executed, depending on the answers to your questions.

Boolean Data Type

To ask a question in a program, you make a statement. If your statement is true, the answer to the question is yes. If your statement is not true, the answer to the question is no. You make these statements in the form of *Boolean expressions*. A Boolean expression asserts (states) that something is true. The assertion is evaluated and if it is true, the Boolean expression is true. If the assertion is not true, the Boolean expression is false.

In C++, data type `bool` is used to represent Boolean data. Each `bool` constant or variable can contain one of two values: `true` or `false`.

Boolean Expressions

A Boolean expression can be a simple Boolean variable or constant or a more complex expression involving one or more of the relational operators. Relational operators take two operands and test for a relationship between them. The following table shows the relational operators and the C++ symbols that stand for them.

C++ Symbol	Relationship
`==`	Equal to
`!=`	Not equal to
`>`	Greater than
`<`	Less than
`>=`	Greater than or equal to
`<=`	Less than or equal to

For example, the Boolean expression

```
number1 < number2
```

is evaluated to `true` if the value stored in `number1` is less than the value stored in `number2`, and evaluated to `false` otherwise.

When a relational operator is applied between variables of type `char`, the assertion is in terms of where the two operands fall in the collating sequence of a particular character set. For example,

```
character1 < character2
```

is evaluated to `true` if the character stored in `character1` comes before the character stored in `character2` in the collating sequence of the machine on which the expression is being evaluated. Although the collating sequence varies among machines, you can think of it as being in alphabetic order. That is, *A* always comes before *B* and *a* always before *b*, but the relationship of *A* to *a* may vary.

We must be careful when applying the relational operators to floating point operands, particularly equal (==) and not equal (!=). Integer values can be represented exactly; floating point values with fractional parts often are not exact in the low-order decimal places. Therefore, you should compare floating point values for near equality. We have more to say about the problem of representing floating point values in Chapter 10. For now, *do not compare floating point numbers for equality.*

A simple Boolean expression is either a Boolean variable or constant or an expression involving the relational operators that evaluates to either true or false. These simple Boolean expressions can be combined using the logical operations defined on Boolean values. There are three Boolean operators: AND, OR, and NOT. Here is a table showing the meaning of these operators and the symbols that are used to represent them in C++.

C++ Symbol	Meaning
&&	AND is a binary Boolean operator. If both operands are true, the result is true. Otherwise, the result is false.
||	OR is a binary Boolean operator. If at least one of the operands is true, the result is true. Otherwise, if both are false, the result is false.
!	NOT is a unary Boolean operator. NOT changes the value of its operand: If the operand is true, the result is false; if the operand is false, the result is true.

If relational operators and Boolean operators are combined in the same expression in C++, the Boolean operator NOT (!) has the highest precedence, the relational operators have next higher precedence, and the Boolean operators AND (&&) and OR (\|\|) come last (in that order). Expressions in parentheses are always evaluated first.

For example, given the following expression (`stop` is a `bool` variable)

```
count <= 10 && sum >= limit || !stop
```

`!stop` is evaluated first, the expressions involving the relational operators are evaluated next, the && is applied, and finally the || is applied. C++ uses *short-circuit evaluation.* The evaluation is done in left-to-right order and halts as soon as the result is known. For example, in the above expression, if both of the arithmetic expressions are true, the evaluation stops because the left operand to the OR operation (|| operator) is true. There is no reason to evaluate the rest of the expression: true OR anything is true.

The following table summarizes the precedence of all the C++ operators we have seen so far.

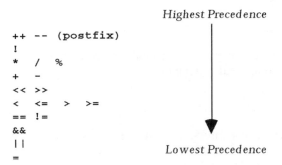

Highest Precedence

```
++ -- (postfix)
!
*  /  %
+  -
<< >>
<  <=  >  >=
== !=
&&
||
=
```

Lowest Precedence

if-then and *if-then-else* Statements

The *if* statement allows the programmer to change the logical order of a program; that is, make the order in which the statements are executed differ from the order in which they are listed in the program.

The *if-then* statement uses a Boolean expression to determine whether to execute a statement or to skip it.

```
if (number < 0)
    number = 0;
sum = sum + number;
```

The expression (number < 0) is evaluated. If the result is `true`, the statement `number = 0` is executed. If the result is `false`, the statement is skipped. In either case, the next statement to be executed is `sum = sum + number`. The statement that is either executed or skipped may be a *block*. A block is a group of statements in the action part of the program enclosed in braces.

The *if-then-else* statement uses a Boolean expression to determine which of two statements to execute.

```
cout << "Today is a ";
if (temperature <= 32)
    cout << "cold ";
else
    cout << "nice ";
cout << "day." << end
```

The characters "`Today is a `" are sent to the output stream. The expression (`temperature <= 32`) is evaluated. If the result is `true`, the characters "`cold `" are sent to the output stream. If the result is `false`, the characters "`nice `" are sent to the output stream. In either case, the next statement to be executed sends the characters "`day.`" to the output stream. Either of the statements may be a block (compound statement) as shown in the following example.

```
if (temperature <= 32)
{
    cout << "Today is a cold day." << endl;
    cout << "Sitting by the fire is appropriate." << endl;

}
```

```
else
{
    cout << "Today is a nice day." << endl;
    cout << "How about taking a walk?" << endl;
}
```

There is a point of C++ syntax that you should note: There is never a semicolon after the right brace of a block (compound statement).

Nested Logic

An *if-then* statement uses a Boolean expression to determine whether to execute a statement or skip it. An *if-then-else* statement uses a Boolean expression to determine which of two statements to execute. The statements to be executed or skipped can be simple statements or blocks (compound statements). There is no constraint on what the statements can be. This means that the statement to be skipped in an *if-then* statement can be another *if* statement. In the *if-then-else* statement, either or both of the choices can be another *if* statement. An *if* statement within another *if* statement is called a *nested if* statement.

The following is an example of a nested *if* statement.

```
cout << "Today is a ";
if (temperature <= 32)
    cout << "cold ";
else if (temperature <= 85)
    cout << "nice ";
else
    cout << "hot ";
cout << "day." << endl;
```

Notice that the nested *if* statement does not have to ask if the temperature is greater than 32 because we do not execute the else branch of the first *if* statement if the temperature is less than or equal to 32.

In nested *if* statements, there may be confusion as to which if an else belongs. In the absence of braces, the compiler pairs an else with the most recent if that doesn't have an else. You can override this pairing by enclosing the preceding if in braces to make the then clause of the outer *if* statement complete.

State of an I/O Stream

In Chapter 4, we said that all references to an input or output stream are ignored if the stream is in the fail state. The fail state is entered if the file that is the parameter to the open operation isn't found, if you try to input from a stream after all the values have been read, or if invalid data is encountered in the input stream. C++ provides a way to test the state of a stream: The stream name used in an expression returns true if the state if okay and false if the stream is in the fail state. Look at the following example.

```
// Program Area demonstrates stream testing.
#include <iostream>
#include <fstream>
using namespace std;
```

```
int main()
{
    int side1;              // one side of a rectangle
    int side2;              // the other side of a rectangle
    ifstream inData;        // file stream
    int area;               // area of rectangle

    inData.open("myData.dat");
    if (!inData)
    {
        cout  << "Input file not found." << endl;
        return 1;
    }
    inData >> side1 >> side2;
    if (!inData)
    {
        cout  << "Data format incorrect.";
        return 2;
    }
    area = side1 * side2;
    cout  << "Area is "  << area  << endl;
    return 0;
}
```

If the input file myData.dat cannot be found, 1 is returned to the operating system. If the data format on file inData is incorrect, 2 is returned to the operating system. If there are no input errors, 0 is returned to the operating system. Notice that the function main is exited as soon as a value is returned. Therefore, there are three ways that this function can be completed: two with an error (return 1 or 2) and one with no error (return 0). Returning 0 means normal completion of a program; returning any other value signals an error. When you are writing your program, you may choose the values to return to indicate different error conditions.

Test Plans

How do you test a specific program to determine its correctness? You design and implement a *test plan*. A test plan for a program is a document that specifies the test cases that should be run, the reason for each test case, and the expected output from each case. The test cases should be chosen carefully. The *code-coverage* approach designs test cases to ensure that each statement in the program is executed. The *data-coverage* approach designs test cases to ensure that the limits of the allowable data are covered. Often, testing is a combination of code and data coverage.

Implementing a test plan means that you run each of the test cases described in the test plan and record the results. If the results are not as expected, you must go back to your design and find and correct the error(s). The process stops when each of the test cases gives the expected results. Note that an implemented test plan gives you a measure of confidence that your program is correct; however, all you know for sure is that your program works correctly on your test cases. Therefore, the quality of your test cases is extremely important.

An example of a test plan for the code fragment that tests temperatures is shown on the next page. We assume that the fragment is embedded in a program that reads in a data value that represents a temperature.

Reason for Test Case	Input Values	Expected Output	Observed Output
Test first end point	32	Today is a cold day.	
Test second end point	85	Today is a nice day.	
Test value below first end point	31	Today is a cold day.	
Test value between end points	45	Today is a nice day.	
Test value above second end point	86	Today is a hot day.	
Test negative value	−10	Today is a cold day.	

To implement this test plan, the program is run six times, once for each test case. The results are written in the Observed Output column.

Warning

The assignment operator (=) and the equality test operator (==) can easily be miskeyed one for the other. What happens if this occurs? Unfortunately, the program does not crash; it continues to execute but probably gives incorrect results. Look at the following two statements.

```
aValue == aValue + 1;     // aValue = aValue + 1 is meant

if (value1 = value2)      // if (value1 == value2) is meant
```

The first statement returns `false`: `aValue` can never be equal to `aValue + 1`. The semicolon ends the statement, so nothing happens to the value returned (`aValue + 1`) and execution continues with the next statement. `aValue` has not been changed. In the second case, although we think of `value1 = value2` as being an assignment statement, it is technically just an expression that does two things: It returns the value of the expression on the right of the equal sign, and it stores this value in the place on the left. Here, the value returned is the content of `value2`. Because of the way C++ implements values of type `bool`, if `value2` does not contain zero, `true` is returned; if `value2` contains zero, `false` is returned. We have more to say about the assignment statement actually being an expression in Chapter 11.

The moral of this story is to be very careful when you key your program. A simple keying error can cause logic errors that the compiler does not catch and that are very difficult for the user to find. Great care and a good test plan are essential to C++ programming.

Chapter 5: Prelab Assignment

Name _____ Date _____

Section _____

Examine program `Convert` and answer the questions in Exercises 1 through 3.

```cpp
// Program Convert converts a temperature from Fahrenheit to
// Celsius or a temperature from Celsius to Fahrenheit
// depending on whether the user enters an F or a C.

#include <iostream>
using namespace std;

int main ()
{
    char letter;         // Place to store input letter
    int tempIn;          // Temperature to be converted
    int tempOut;         // Converted temperature

    cout  <<"Input Menu"  << endl  << endl;
    cout  <<"F: Convert from Fahrenheit to Celsius"  << endl;
    cout  <<"C: Convert from Celsius to Fahrenheit"  << endl;
    cout  <<"Type a C or an F, then press return."  << endl;
    cout  <<"Type an integer number, then press return."
          << endl;

    cin  >> letter;
    cin  >> tempIn;

    if (letter == 'C')
        tempOut = (9 * tempIn / 5) + 32;
    else
        tempOut = 5 * (tempIn - 32) / 9;
    cout  << "Temperature to convert: "  << tempIn  << endl;
    cout  << "Converted temperature: "  << tempOut << endl;

    return 0;
}
```

Exercise 1: If the letter *C* and the value 100 are input, what is the output?

Exercise 2: If the letter *F* and the value 32 are input, what is the output?

Exercise 3: If the letter *c* and the value 0 are input, what is the output?

Exercise 4: Examine the following pairs of expressions and determine if they are equivalent. Put a T in the Result column if they are the same and an F if they are not.

Expression 1	Expression 2	Result
! (A == B)	A != B	_____
! ((A == B) || (A == C))	(A != B) && (A != C)	_____
! ((A == B) && (C > D))	(A != B) || (C <= D)	_____

Exercise 5: Examine the following pairs of expressions and determine if they are equivalent. Put a T in the Result column if they are the same and an F if they are not.

Expression 1	Expression 2	Result
!A && B	B && !A	_____
!A || B	B || !A	_____
!(A && B)	A || B	_____
A && B || C	A && (B || C)	_____
(A && B || C)	!(A || B && C)	_____

Lesson 5–1: Check Prelab Exercises

Name _____ Date _____

Section _____

Run program `Convert` to check your answers to Prelab Exercises 1 through 3 and answer the following questions.

Exercise 1: Was your answer completely correct? If it was not, explain where you made your mistake.

Exercise 2: Was your answer completely correct? If it was not, explain where you made your mistake.

Exercise 3: Was your answer completely correct? If it was not, explain where you made your mistake.

Exercise 4: The answers are T, T, and T.

Exercise 5: The answers are T, T, F, F, and F.

Lesson 5-2: Boolean Expressions

Name _____   Date _____

Section _____

Use program Shell1 **for Exercises 1 and 2.**

```
// Program Shell1 prints appropriate messages based on a
// grade read from the keyboard.

#include <iostream>
using namespace std;

int main ()
{
    int grade;

    cout  << "Enter an integer grade between 50 and 100."
          << "  Press return. "  << endl;
    cin  >> grade;

    if  /* TO BE FILLED IN  */
        cout  << "Congratulations!"  << endl;
    return 0;
}
```

Exercise 1: When completed, program Shell1 reads an integer value and writes an appropriate message. Fill in the Boolean expression beside the if so that "Congratulations!" is written if the numeric grade is greater than or equal to 80. Run the program five times entering the following values for grade: 50, 100, 80, 81, and 79.

"Congratulations!" is printed _____ time(s) in the five runs.

Exercise 2: Change the Boolean expression in Exercise 1 so that "Try harder" is printed if the numeric grade is less than 70. Run the program with the same data listed for Exercise 1.

"Try harder" is printed _____ time(s) in the five runs.

Exercise 3: Change the Boolean expression so that "Average" is printed if the numeric grade is less than 80 but greater than 70. Run the program with the same data listed for Exercise 1.

"Average" is printed_____ time(s) in the five runs.

Lesson 5-3: if-then Statements

Name _____ Date _____

Section _____

Use program `Shell2` for the exercises in this lesson. This program prompts for and reads an integer value, and then prints a message based on this value.

```
// Program Shell2 prints appropriate messages based on a
// pressure reading input from the keyboard.

#include <iostream>
using namespace std;

main ()
{
    int  pressure;

    cout << "Enter an integer pressure reading. "
        << " Press Return."  << endl;
    cin >> pressure;
    /* FILL IN Code appropriate to exercise */
    return 0;
}
```

Exercise 1: Insert a statement that writes the following warning to the screen if the pressure reading is greater than 100.

"Warning!! Pressure reading above danger limit."

Run your program eight times using the following values as input: 5, 75, 80, 99, 0, 100, 110, 199

"Warning !! Pressure reading above danger limit." is printed _____ times.

If your answer is 2, your *if* statement is correct. If your answer is 3, the relational operator on your expression is incorrect. It should be greater than, not greater than or equal to. Rerun your corrected program.

Exercise 2: Insert a statement in program `Shell2` that writes the following message if the pressure reading is lower than 100 but greater than 5.

"Everything seems normal."

Run your program eight times using the same data that you used in Exercise 1.

"Everything seems normal" is printed _____ times.

Lesson 5–4: if-then-else Statements

Name _____ Date _____

Section _____

Exercise 1: Take program `Shell2` in Lesson 5–3 and change it so that it prints the message in both Lesson 5–3, Exercise 1, and Lesson 5–3, Exercise 2. Run the program with the data set for Lesson 5–3, Exercise 1.

"Warning !! Pressure reading above danger limit." is printed _____ times.

"Everything seems normal" is printed _____ times.

Use program `Shell3` for Exercises 2, 3, and 4.

```
// Program Shell3 calculates a person's percentage of
// calories from fat and prints an appropriate message.

#include <iostream>
#include <string>
using namespace std;

int main ()
{
    string foodItem;
    int    gramsOfFat;
    int    calories;
    float fatCalPercent;

    cout  << "Enter the name of a food item."
          << "  Press return."  << endl;
    getline(cin, foodItem);

    cout  << "Enter the grams of fat; press return."  << endl;
    cin   >> gramsOfFat;

    cout  << "Enter the number of calories; press return."
          << endl;
    cin   >> calories;

    /* TO BE FILLED IN */
    return 0;
}
```

Exercise 2: The American Heart Association recommends that no more than 30 percent of a person's daily calories come from fat. Each gram of fat is nine calories. Given the grams of fat and the number of calories in an item, we can calculate the percentage of calories that comes from fat.

Add statements to program She113 to print the item and the percentage of calories that come from fat (fatCalPercent). Run your program four times with the following data:

Item	Grams of Fat	Calories	Percent from Fat
Tuna	1	60	_____
Spaetzle	2	170	_____
V8 Juice	0	35	_____
Corned Beef	7	200	_____

Exercise 3: Add a statement to program She113 from Exercise 2 that prints one of the following two messages depending on the percentage of calories from fat (value of fatCalPercent).

"This item is Heart Healthy!"
"This item is NOT Heart Healthy!!"

Run your program using the data in Exercise 2.

Which of the items are heart healthy?

Exercise 4: Your test should look like one of the following where fatCalOK is a bool variable:

```
fatCalOK = fatCalPercent <= 0.30;
if (fatCalOK)

if (fatCalPercent <= 0.30)

fatCalOK = fatCalPercent <= 0.30;
if (fatCalOK == true)

if ((fatCalPercent <= 0.30) == true)
```

Circle the one that you used in your program. If you used the first or the second, you understand Boolean expressions and *if* statements. If you used one of the others, you are correct, but you have redundant code. A Boolean variable contains one of the constants true or false, and a Boolean expression returns true or false. You do not need to compare the Boolean variable or expression with the value true.

Lesson 5–5: Nested Logic

Name _____ Date _____

Section _____

Use the following shell for the exercises in this lesson.

```
// Program Shell4 reads in a temperature and prints an
// appropriate message.

#include <iostream>
using namespace std;

int main ()
{
    int  temperature;

    cout << "Enter the temperature in your room." << endl;
    cin >> temperature;

    /* TO BE FILLED IN */
    return 0;
}
```

Exercise 1: Add five *if-then* statements to program `Shell4` so that one of the following messages is printed based on the value of `temperature`.

Temperature	Message
> 90	"Visit a neighbor."
<= 90, > 80	"Turn on air conditioning."
<= 80, > 70	"Do nothing."
<= 70, >55	"Turn on heat."
<= 55	"Visit a neighbor."

Run your program as many times as it takes to write each message exactly once. What data values did you use?

Exercise 2: Rewrite the program in Exercise 1 using nested logic (i.e., *if-then-else* where the *else* branch is an *if* statement). Rerun the program with the same data. Did you get the same answers? Explain.

Exercise 3: Complete program `HiScore` so that it reads and prints three test scores, then labels and prints the largest of the three.

```
// Program HiScore reads and prints three test scores.
// The largest value of the three is printed with an
// appropriate message.
// Assumption: The scores are unique.

#include <iostream>
using namespace std;

int main ()
{
    int   test1Score;
    int   test2Score;
    int   test3Score;

    cout  << "Enter score for test 1; press return."  << endl;
    cin  >> test1Score;
    cout  << "Enter score for test 2; press return."  << endl;
    cin  >> test2Score;
    cout  << "Enter score for test 3; press return."  << endl;
    cin  >> test3Score;

    cout  << "The three test scores are: "  << endl;
    cout  << test1Score  << endl;
    cout  << test2Score  << endl;
    cout  << test3Score  << endl;

    /* TO BE FILLED IN */
    return 0;
}
```

Fill in the missing statement(s) in program `HiScore` so that the largest of the three input values (scores) is printed and labeled as the highest test score. You may use a nested *if* statement or a series of *if* statements. For example, if `test2Score` with a value of 98 is the largest, your output might look as follows:

```
The value for test 2 is the highest; it is 98.
```

Your message may be different, but it must include the largest value and which test had that value. Run your program three times using the three sets of input values listed below.

Input values			*What Is printed*
100	80	70	_____
70	80	100	_____
80	100	60	_____

Lesson 5–6: Test Plan

Name _____ Date _____

Section _____

Exercise 1: Design a test plan for program HiScore in Lesson 5–5. (Hint: There should be at least six test cases.)

Reason for Test Case	Input Values	Expected Output	Observed Output

Exercise 2: Implement the test plan designed in Exercise 1. You may show the results in the chart in Exercise 1.

Lesson 5–7 Debugging

Name _____ Date _____

Section _____

Exercise 1: Program AddSub is supposed to read in a letter and two integer values and print either the sum of the two values or the difference of the two values depending on the letter read. It is such a simple program, but it doesn't even compile! Correct the program and describe the errors.

Exercise 2: Now that the program compiles, run it with the following sets of values.

Input Values	Means	What Is printed
A 10 20	add 10 and 20	_____
A 20 10	add 20 and 10	_____
S 10 20	subtract 20 from 10	_____
S 20 10	subtract 10 from 20	_____

Exercise 3: Unless you corrected the logic errors in Exercise 1, your answers are incorrect. Locate the logic errors and rerun your program until you get the correct answers. Describe the errors.

Postlab Activities

Exercise 1: Your history instructor gives three tests worth 50 points each. You can drop one of the first two grades. The final grade is the sum of the best of the first two grades and the third grade. Given three test grades, write a program that calculates the final letter grade using the following cut-off points.

>= 90	A
< 90, >= 80	B
< 80, >= 70	C
< 70, >= 60	D
< 60	F

Exercise 2: Write a program to determine if the digits in a three-digit number are all odd, all even, or mixed odd and even. Your program should prompt the user to input a three-digit number and echo-print the number. If the digits in the number are all odd, write "This number contains all odd digits." If the digits are all even, write "This number contains all even digits." If the number contains both odd and even digits, write "This number contains both odd and even digits." Use integer division and modulus to access the digits in the number.

Exercise 3: The world outside of the United States has switched to Celsius. You are going to travel in England, where the temperature is given in Celsius. A friend said that a quick approximation of the Fahrenheit equivalent of a Celsius number is to take the number, double it, and add 32. Write a program that takes as input a temperature in Celsius and calculates both the approximated Fahrenheit equivalent and the actual Fahrenheit equivalent. Write out all three values. If the approximation and the actual value are within two degrees, write out "Close enough." If they are not within two degrees, write out "Will not do."

Exercise 4: High cholesterol is a problem for millions of people. Write a program that prompts for and inputs LDL (bad cholesterol) and HDL (good cholesterol) readings in milligrams per deciliter and prints the appropriate message based on the values shown below.

LDL:	< 100	"Great!"
	< 130	"Pretty good!"
	< 160	"Borderline"
	<190	"High!"
	>189	"Dangerously high!"
HDL:	< 4 0	"Too low!"
	< 60	"OK"
	> 59	"Great!"
LDL/HDL	< 3.22	"Good ratio"
	>3.21	"Bad ratio"

Looping

- To be able to modify a program containing a *while* statement.

- To be able to construct a count-controlled loop to implement a specified task.

- To be able to construct an event-controlled loop to implement a specified task.

- To be able to construct a loop nested within another loop.

- To be able to test the state of an I/O stream.

- To be able to answer questions about a loop that you have implemented.

Chapter 6: Assignment Cover Sheet

Name _____   Date _____

Section _____

Fill in the following table showing which exercises have been assigned for each lesson and check what you are to submit: (1) lab sheets, (2) listings of output files, and/or (3) listings of programs. Your instructor or teaching assistant (TA) can use the Completed column for grading purposes.

Activities	Assigned: Check or list exercise numbers	Submit (1) (2) (3)			Completed
Prelab					
Review					
Prelab Assignment					
Inlab					
Lesson 6–1: Check Prelab Exercises					
Lesson 6–2: Count-Controlled Loops					
Lesson 6–3: Event-Controlled Loops					
Lesson 6–4: Nested Logic					
Lesson 6–5: Debugging					
Postlab					

Prelab Activities

Review

In Chapter 5, we looked at Boolean expressions and how they can be used in the *if* statement to make a choice. In this chapter, we examine how Boolean expressions can be used in a *while* statement to make the program repeat a statement or group of statements. Such repetitions are called *loops*.

while Statement

The *if* statement allows the program to skip the execution of a statement or choose between one of two statements to be executed based on the value of a Boolean expression. In contrast, the *while* statement allows a program to continue executing a statement as long as the value of a Boolean expression is true. When the Boolean expression becomes false, execution of the program continues with the statement immediately following the *while* statement. Look at the following code fragment.

```
sum = 0;
count = 1;
while (count <= 10)
{
    cin >> value;
    sum = sum + value;
    count++;
}
cout << "The sum of the 10 numbers is " << sum;
```

The variables `sum` and `count` are assigned the values 0 and 1 respectively. The Boolean expression (`count <= 10`) is evaluated. The value in `count` is less than or equal to 10, so the expression is `true` and the block (compound statement) associated with the *while* is executed. A number is extracted from the standard input stream and added to `sum`. The value in `count` is incremented by 1.

At this point, the logical order of the program diverges from the physical order. The *while* expression is evaluated again. Because the value stored in `count` is still less than or equal to 10, the compound statement associated with the *while* is executed again. This process continues until `count` contains the value 11. At that time, the expression is no longer `true`, the body of the *while* statement is not executed again, and execution continues with the statement immediately following the *while* statement that sends the labeled answer to the output stream.

Types of Loops

There are two basic types of loops: count-controlled and event-controlled. A *count-controlled loop* is one that is executed a certain number of times. The expression that controls the loop becomes false when the loop has executed the prescribed number of times. An *event-controlled loop* is one whose execution is controlled by the occurrence of an event within the loop itself. The previous example is a count-controlled loop that executes 10 times. Let's look at an example of an event-controlled loop that reads and sums values from `cin` until a negative value is encountered.

```
sum = 0;

cin  >> value;

// Set moreData to true if the first data item is not
// negative; false otherwise.
moreData = value >= 0;

while (moreData)
{
    sum = sum + value;
    cin  >> value;
    moreData = value >= 0; // Reset moreData
}
cout  << "The sum of the values prior to a negative value is "
      << sum  << endl;
```

`sum` is set to zero and the first data item (`value`) is read outside of the loop. `value` is compared to zero and the result is stored in `moreData`. If the first data item is less than zero, `moreData` is `false`, and the body of the loop is not executed. If the first data item is greater than or equal to zero, `moreData` is `true`, and the body of the loop is entered. `value` is added to `sum`, and the next data item is read. This new data item is compared to zero, and `moreData` is reset. The expression is tested again. This process continues until a value of less than zero is read and `moreData` becomes `false`. When this happens, the body of the *while* is not executed again, and the sum of the nonnegative numbers is sent to the output stream.

Reading the first value outside of the body of the loop is called a *priming read*. When a priming read is used before a loop, the input values are processed at the beginning of the loop body and a subsequent read occurs at the end of the loop body.

Notice the difference between these two loops. The first reads ten values and sums them; the second reads and sums values until a negative number if read. The first is count-controlled; the second is event-controlled. The second loop is called a sentinel-controlled loop because reading a sentinel (a negative number) is the event that controls it.

EOF Loops

In Chapter 5, we stated that running out of data puts the input stream into the fail state. We also said that the stream name can be used to test to see if the stream is in the fail state. We can put these two facts together to construct a very useful event-controlled loop for reading data values. We can read and process data values until the stream goes into the fail state. When the last data value has been read, the stream is at the end of the file (called EOF). The stream is fine until another data value is requested. At that point, the stream goes into the fail state. This means that we must try to read one more value than exists on the stream in order to let the fail state control the reading. The following loop reads and sums values until there is no more data.

```
sum = 0;
cin >> value;
while (cin)
{
    sum = sum + value;
    cin >> value;
}
```

Because cin does not go into the fail state until we try to access a value when the stream is at EOF, we must use a priming read as we did in the previous example. If there is a value, (cin) returns true and the body of the loop is entered where the value is added to sum and a new value is read. After the last value has been processed, the attempt to read one more value causes cin to enter the fail state. When the *while* expression is tested the last time, (cin) returns false and the loop is not repeated.

Proper Loop Operation

For obvious reasons, the *while* statement is called a loop or looping statement. The statement that is being executed within the loop is called the *body* of the loop.

There are three basic steps that must be done for a loop to operate properly.

1. The variables in the expression (the counter or event) must be set (initialized) before the *while* statement is executed the first time.
2. The expression must test the status of the counter or event correctly so that the body of the loop executes when it is supposed to and terminates at the proper time.
3. The counter or the status of the event must be updated within the loop. If the counter or the status of the event is not updated, the loop never stops executing. This situation is called an *infinite loop*.

Nested Loops

The body of the loop can contain any type of statement including another *while* statement. The following program counts the number of characters on each line in a file. We know that the manipulator endl forces the next characters sent to the output stream to begin a new line. How can we recognize a new line on the input stream? A new line begins following the symbol '\n'. We must be sure to use function get defined in file <iostream>, not the extraction operator, to input each character.

```cpp
// Program LineCt counts the number of characters per line
// and the number of lines in a file.
// There is a '\n' before the EOF.

#include <iostream>
#include <fstream>
using namespace std;

int main()
{
    int  lineNo;
    char character;
    int  number;
    ifstream inData;

    inData.open("Data.In");
    lineNo = 0;
    inData.get(character);
    while (inData)
    {
        lineNo++;
        number = 0;
```

```
        while (character != '\n')
        {
            number++;
            inData.get(character);
        }
        cout  << "Line "  << lineNo  << " contains "
              << number  << " characters."  << endl;
        inData.get(character);
    }
    return 0;
}
```

Chapter 6: Prelab Assignment

Name _____ Date _____

Section _____

Read program Count **carefully.**

```cpp
// Program Count prompts for, reads, echo prints, and sums a
// fixed number of integer values.  The sum is printed.

#include <iostream>
using namespace std;

const int  LIMIT = 10;

int main ()
{
    int  counter;               // loop-control variable
    int  sum;                   // summing variable
    int  dataValue;             // input value
    counter = 1;
    sum = 0;

    // Input and sum integer data values.
    while (counter <= LIMIT)
    {
        cout  << "Enter an integer value.  Press return."
            << endl;
        cin  >> dataValue;
        sum = sum + dataValue;
        counter++;
    }
    cout  << "Sum is "  << sum  << endl;
    return 0;
}
```

Exercise 1: What is printed, if the following data values are entered as prompted?

8   5   3   -2   0   9   1   7   3   10

Exercise 2: Is the loop in program Count a count-controlled loop or an event-controlled loop? Explain.

Read program Count2 **carefully.**

```cpp
// Program Count2 prompts for, reads, and sums integer
// values until a negative number is read.  The input
// values and the sum are printed.

#include <iostream>
using namespace std;

int main ()
{
    int   sum;        // summing variable
    int   dataValue;  // input value
    sum = 0;
    cout  << "To stop processing, enter a negative"
          << " value."  << endl;
    cout  << " Enter an integer value; press return."
          << endl;
    // Read first data value to prepare for loop.
    cin  >> dataValue;

    // Input and sum integer data values
    while (dataValue > 0)
    {
        sum = sum + dataValue;
        cout  << "Enter an integer value; press return."
              << endl;
        cin  >> dataValue;
    }
    cout  << "Sum is "  << sum  << endl;
    return 0;
}
```

Exercise 3: What is printed, if the following data values are entered one per line?

8   5   3   -2   0   9   1   7   3   10

Exercise 4: Is the loop in program Count2 a count-controlled loop or an event-controlled loop? Explain.

Lesson 6-1: Check Prelab Exercises

Name _____   Date _____

Section _____

Exercise 1: Run program Count to check your answers. Were they correct? If not, why not?

Exercise 2: The loop in program Count is a count-controlled loop because the loop body is executed a specified number of times.

Exercise 3: Run program Count2 to check your answers. Were they correct? If not, why not?

Exercise 4: The loop in program Count2 is an event-controlled loop because input of a negative data value (the event) stops it.

Lesson 6–2: Count–Controlled Loops

Name _____ Date _____

Section _____

Exercise 1: Change program Count so that the number of values to be read (limit) is input from the keyboard rather than being set as a named constant. Run your program using a value of 10 and entering the data listed for Prelab Exercise 1. (Don't forget to prompt for limit.) Your answer should be the same. If it is not, you have an error.

Run your program again entering a value of your choice for limit, followed by limit integer values. List limit, your data, and the sum.

Exercise 2: Run program Count entering one fewer data value than called for. What happens? Explain.

Exercise 3: Run program Count entering one more data value than called for. What happens? Explain.

Exercise 4: Examine program Shell1. When completed, program Shell1 prompts for and reads a one-digit number, then adds the numbers from zero to the number, inclusive, and prints the sum.

```
// Program Shell1 prompts for and reads a one-digit number.
// Values between 0 and the digit (inclusive) are summed.

#include <iostream>
using namespace std;

int main ()
{
    int  counter;   // loop-control variable
    int  sum;       // running sum
    int  digit;

    cout  << "Enter a one-digit number; press return."
          << endl;
    cin  >> digit;
    counter =  /* TO BE FILLED IN */
    sum  =     /* TO BE FILLED IN */

    while /* TO BE FILLED IN  */
    {
      /*  TO BE FILLED IN */
    }
    cout  << "Sum of digits between 0 and "
          << digit  << " is "  << sum  << endl;
    return 0;
}
```

Fill in the appropriate initializations and the body of the *while* loop so that the sum of the digits from zero through `digit` (the input value) is computed. Run your program four times using 0, 3, 7, and 9 as the input values.

Answer for 0: _____   Answer for 3: _____

Answer for 7: _____   Answer for 9: _____

Exercise 5: Program `Shell3` in Lesson 5–4 read and printed a string representing a food item. You had to run the program four times, once for each item. What a waste of effort! Rewrite the program so that all the processing is done at one time. That is, enclose the entire program in a count-controlled loop that executes four times. Were your answers the same?

Item	Grams of Fat	Calories	Percent from Fat
Tuna	1	60	_____
Spaetzle	2	170	_____
V8 Juice	0	35	_____
CornedBeef	7	200	_____

Lesson 6–3: Event-Controlled Loops

Name _____ Date _____

Section _____

Use program Shell2 for Exercises 1 and 2.

```
// Program Shell2 counts the number of uppercase letters
// on a line.

#include <iostream>
using namespace std;

int main ()
{
    char letter;
    int  letterCt;

  /* TO BE FILLED IN */
    return 0;
}
```

Exercise 1: Fill in the body of program Shell2 so that the number of uppercase letters on a line of input is printed. Run your program with the following input and show the result. (Hint: Remember that relational operators can be applied between two variables of type char. The assertions being made relate to the variables' relative positions in the collating sequence. In Chapter 10, we show you a better way to work with character data.)

AbbaDabbaDoo

Exercise 2: Change program Shell2 from Exercise 1 so that the counting stops if the input line contains a digit. Run your program with the following data and show the results.

ABBA1DABBA2Doo

Exercise 3: Change program Shell2 from Exercise 1 so that it counts uppercase and lowercase letters. Run your program with the following data and show the result.

Abba#Dabba#2Doo

Lesson 6–4: Nested Logic

Name _____ Date _____

Section _____

Exercise 1: Rewrite your solution to Lesson 6–2, Exercise 4, so that the processing is repeated until a negative digit is read. That is, embed your solution within another loop that continues to prompt for a digit and calculates the sum of the digits from zero through `digit` as long as `digit` is positive. The process stops when `digit` is negative. Be sure to add this information to the prompt. Rewrite the program documentation at the beginning of the program to reflect this change. Run your program once using the same data you used in Lesson 6–2, Exercise 4.

What additional documentation did you include?

Is the outer loop a count-controlled loop or an event-controlled loop?

Exercise 2: Examine program `Shell3`. When completed, this program prompts for and reads an integer value and prints a warning message based on the input value.

Pressure	Message
< 0	"Error in input."
>= 0, < 50	"Pressure in the normal range."
>= 50, < 100	"Pressure on the high side."
> = 100	"Evacuate plant!!!!"

```
// Program Shell3 prints appropriate messages based
// on a pressure reading read from a file.  Processing
// continues until the plant is evacuated because of
// a pressure reading over 100.

#include <iostream>
#include <fstream>
using namespace std;

int main ()
{
    int  pressure;
    ifstream  data;
```

```
    data.open("Shell3.Dl");

/* LOOP TO BE FILLED IN */

    data  >> pressure;

    /* FILL IN Code to print the message */

    return 0;
}
```

What kind of a loop is being used?

How many times was each message printed?

"Error in input."   _____
"Pressure in the normal range." _____
"Pressure on the high side." _____
"Evacuate plant!!!!"   _____

Exercise 3: The program to check pressure readings (your solution to Exercise 2) continues to run as long as the pressure readings are within the safe range. The program only halts when an unsafe reading is read. Plant maintenance has decided that the process should also be halted after 60 safe readings. Rewrite your solution from Exercise 2 to end the program when a dangerous reading occurs or when 60 safe readings have been read. Run your program twice, using Shell3.D2 and Shell3.D3 as input.

What was the result using Shell3.D2?

What was the result using Shell3.D3?

Exercise 4: Program Shell3, as modified in Exercise 3, seems to be both an event-controlled loop and a count-controlled loop. However, we classify any loop that is not a pure count-controlled loop as an event-controlled loop. Explain why.

Exercise 5: Plant maintenance has decided to add one more modification. If all the pressure readings are safe but there are less than 60 of them, stream data goes into the fail state. Rewrite the program so that it prints the message "Insufficient data." if there are less than 60 safe readings. Also, print out how many pressure readings there were. Use the state of the input stream as the loop control. Run your program using Shell3.D4. How many pressure readings are there?

Lesson 6–5: Debugging

Name _____ Date _____

Section _____

Exercise 1: Program SumNums reads and counts nonnegative integers until there are no more data values. You run the program using file SumNums.D1, and the program says that there are no values on the file. You know that there are nine values on the file and that seven of them are nonnegative. Locate the bug and describe it.

Exercise 2: The program now runs, but it gives the wrong answer. Locate and describe this bug.

Exercise 3: The answer is different but still wrong! Keep looking. Describe the error.

Postlab Activities

Exercise 1: Write a program to print a triangle composed of a symbol. The number of lines in the triangle and the symbol should be entered as input from the keyboard. For example, if the input values are 7 and #, the output is as follows:

```
      #
     ###
    #####
   #######
  #########
 ###########
#############
```

In your program documentation, describe the loop(s) used as count-controlled or event-controlled.

Exercise 2: File `History.d1` contains a brief history of computing. There are no indentations in this file. Write a program to read this file, inserting five blank spaces at the beginning of each paragraph. You can recognize a paragraph because a blank line appears before the first line of each paragraph. Write the changed file on `History.d2`. In your program documentation, describe the loop(s) used as count-controlled or event-controlled.

Exercise 3: How many nonblank characters are there in file `History.d1`? Add a counter to your program from Exercise 2 that keeps track of the number of nonblank characters in the file. Print this number to the screen. Do not include '\n' in your nonblank count.

Exercise 4: As a child, did you ever play the game "One potato, two potato, . . . " to determine who would be "it"? The complete rhyme is given below:

One potato, two potato, three potato, four;
Five potato, six potato, seven potato, more.
O U T spells "out you go."

A child is pointed to during each phrase. There are four phrases each in lines 1 and 2 and seven phrases in line 3, so the last child pointed to is the 15th one. If there are fewer than 15 children, you go around the circle again. The child pointed to when the word *go* is said is "out." The game begins again with the remaining children, starting again with the first child. The last child remaining is "it."

Simulate this game in a computer program. The input is the number of children; the output is which child is "it."

Exercise 5: Modify the game in Exercise 4 so that rather than beginning again with child number 1, you start again with the child following the last one out.

Exercise 6: In Chapter 5, Postlab Exercise 3, you were asked to determine the accuracy of an approximation of a translation of a temperature from Celsius to Fahrenheit. The Fahrenheit approximation is the Celsius number doubled plus 32. Write a program that creates a table with three columns. The first column contains temperatures in Celsius, the second contains the Fahrenheit approximation, and the third contains the actual Fahrenheit equivalent. Run your program using at least 10 data values. Examine your table and write a paragraph discussing the accuracy of the approximation.

Exercise 7: There is a temperature for which Fahrenheit and Celsius are the same. This value can be determined both algebraically and experimentally. Solve the problem algebraically first and then write a program that determines if a solution exists by experimentation.

Functions

- To be able to write and invoke a parameterless void function to implement a specified task.

- To be able to write and invoke a void function with value parameters to execute a specified task.

- To be able to write and invoke a void function with reference parameters to execute a specified task.

- To be able to debug a program with a function.

Chapter 7: Assignment Cover Sheet

Name _____ Date _____

Section _____

Fill in the following table showing which exercises have been assigned for each lesson and check what you are to submit: (1) lab sheets, (2) listings of output files, and/or (3) listings of programs. Your instructor or teaching assistant (TA) can use the Completed column for grading purposes.

Activities	Assigned: Check or list exercise numbers	Submit (1)	(2)	(3)	Completed
Prelab					
Review					
Prelab Assignment					
Inlab					
Lesson 7–1: Check Prelab Exercises					
Lesson 7–2: Functions without Parameters					
Lesson 7–3: Functions with Value Parameters					
Lesson 7–4: Functions with Reference Parameters					
Lesson 7–5: Debugging					
Postlab					

Prelab Activities

Review

Identifiers can name actions as well as data objects. There are two types of named actions in C++: value-returning functions and void functions. The name of a value-returning function is used in an expression; the action is executed and the returned value is substituted in the expression. `sqrt` and `pow` are named actions that are value-returning functions. The name of a void function is used as a statement in the executable part of a program. The action is executed, and the program continues with the next statement. The `get` in `cin.get` and the `open` in `inData.open` are void-function identifiers that name actions or processes. Both value-returning and void functions can be used to implement modules in functional decomposition. In this chapter, we focus on how to write void functions.

Using the name of a function in an expression or as a statement is called *invoking* or *calling* the function.

Defining Void Functions

A void function has a heading that names the function followed by a pair of parentheses. (The function identifier is preceded by the word `void`.) A list of the identifiers that the function needs can be inserted within the parentheses. This list of identifiers is called a *parameter list*.

Each identifier on the parameter list must have its type listed. These identifiers are used in the statements in the executable part of the function. When the function is invoked, there is a list of identifiers in parentheses after the function name. This list of identifiers is called the *argument list*. The identifiers on the argument list name the places that the function actually uses during execution. The parameter list and the argument list must match up in number and type because each argument is substituted for its corresponding parameter when the function is executed. (You may see formal parameter list used for parameter list, and actual parameter list used for argument list.)

Let's examine the syntax in the context of an example. Before we look at a function with parameters, let's look at the case where the function does not need any information from the outside and therefore has no parameter list. The task is to write a box that looks as follows:

```
. . . . . . . . . . . . . . . . . . . .
.                                      .
.                                      .
. . . . . . . . . . . . . . . . . . . .
```

There are 20 periods on the first line, 2 periods on the second and third lines separated by 18 blanks each, and the fourth line is identical to the first line. Function `WriteBox` produces this output.

```
void WriteBox()                          // name of the action
// Post: A box (20 x 4) is printed using periods.
{                                        // begin action
  cout << "...................." << endl;
  cout << "." << setw(19)  << "."  << endl;
  cout << "." << setw(19)  << "."  << endl;
  cout << "...................." << endl;
}                                           // end action
```

The reserved word void precedes the name of the action. There is no parameter list, but the parentheses that enclose the parameter list must be present. The braces enclose the function body, the action part of the function. The four output statements write the box described above.

How does WriteBox get executed? The name of the action, WriteBox, is used as a statement in your program.

```
WriteBox();    // function invocation or 'call'
```

How does all this fit together? *Where* in the program? What *is* the program? A complete program containing function WriteBox is shown below. Notice that the function definition is set off with a row of asterisks before it. This design makes the parts of the program easier to distinguish for the human reader—the compiler doesn't care.

```
// Program Box writes a box using periods.

#include <iostream>
#include <iomanip>
using namespace std;

void WriteBox();                      // function prototype
// Post: A (20 x 4) box of dots is written on the screen.

int main()
{
    cout << "A box: "  << endl;
    WriteBox();
    cout << "Box has been drawn."  << endl;
    return 0;
}

//*********************************************

void WriteBox()              // name of the action
// Post: A box (20 x 4) is printed using periods.

{                                        // begin action
  cout << "...................." << endl;
  cout << "." << setw(19)  << "."  << endl;
  cout << "." << setw(19)  << "."  << endl;
  cout << "...................." << endl;
}                                        // end action
```

Physical Order and Logical Order

The text of the function definitions can be in any physical order. The logical order of executing the compiled program begins with the first statement in function main, which sends the characters "A box: " to the output stream. Function WriteBox is then executed. When function WriteBox is finished, control passes to the statement immediately following the call to WriteBox, and "**Box has been drawn.**" is sent to the output stream.

Most C++ programmers put function main first in the physical order of the program with the other function definitions following. Each function is separated by a row of some delimiter symbol. We use a row of asterisks. Because most C++ programs have function main listed first and each identifier must be declared before it is used, we have a problem. The functions invoked in function main are not known to the compiler because they have not been defined yet. We solve this dilemma by using a *function prototype.* A function prototype is the function heading without the body of the function. Look back at program Box; the comments identify the prototype for function WriteBox. Note that the function prototype ends with a semicolon, but the heading in the function definition does not.

Exiting a Function

We have seen with value-returning functions that the function is exited when a return statement is executed. That is, control is passed back to the place in the expression where the call occurred when a value is returned. How do you exit a void function? Control passes back to the statement immediately following the function call when the last statement in the function is executed or when a return that doesn't include an expression is executed. A return with no expression can occur only in a void function.

Functions with Parameters

Now, let's look at an example of a program with a function that has a parameter list.

```
// Program Demo prompts for and reads two integer
// values that represent the sides of a rectangle.
// The area of the rectangle is calculated and printed.

#include <iostream>
using namespace std;

void GetData(int&, int&);                // function prototype
// GetData gets two integer values.

int main()
{
    int   height;
    int   width;
    int   area;

    GetData(height, width);
    area = height * width;

    cout << "The area of the "  << height  << " by "
         << width  << " rectangle is "  << area  << endl;
    return 0;
}
```

```
//***********************************************************

void GetData(int& firstValue, int& secondValue)
// Post: The user has been prompted to input two values
//       representing the length and width of a rectangle.
//       These values have been read and returned in
//       firstValue and secondValue.
{
    cout  << "Enter two integer values representing "
          << "a rectangle.  Press return."  << endl;
    cin  >> firstValue  >> secondValue;
}
```

The identifiers on the parameter list of function `GetData` are `firstValue` and `secondValue`, which are both of type `int`. The identifiers on the argument list are `height` and `width`. When function `GetData` is executed, `height` (the argument) is substituted for `firstValue` (the parameter) and `width` (the argument) is substituted for `secondValue` (the parameter). The names used on the parameter list and the argument lists are immaterial; the individual items are matched solely by position.

The function prototype can have the names of the parameters listed, but the compiler only needs to know the number of parameters and their data types. Therefore, the function prototype for `GetData` has just the data types listed. (We explain the ampersands in the next section.)

Value and Reference Parameters

In C++, there are two types of parameters: *value parameters* and *reference parameters*. If the parameter is a value parameter, a *copy* of the value of the argument is passed to the function. If the parameter is a reference parameter, the *address* of the argument is passed to the function. This means that if a value parameter is changed within a function, only the copy is changed. However, if a reference parameter is changed within a function, the argument is changed. How can you tell which parameters are value and which are reference? Reference parameters have the ampersand (&) following their type identifier in the function prototype and function heading. Value parameters are the default parameter type, so they have nothing following their type identifiers.

The parameters for function `GetData` are reference parameters because the ampersand follows their type identifiers.

Parameters that send back values to the calling function are called output parameters (or outgoing). Parameters that only give information to the function are called input parameters (incoming). Parameters that both give information to the function and transmit information back are called in/out parameters (or incoming/outgoing). Output parameters and in/out parameters *must be reference parameters*. Input parameters should be value parameters so that the function cannot inadvertently change the actual parameter. C++ requires that all files must be passed as reference parameters.

The task of function `GetData` is to prompt for and read two integer values from the standard input stream. Because these values are needed by the calling function, they are reference parameters. If we change program `Demo` so that the last output statement is put into a function, `PrintData`, with three parameters (`height`, `width`, and `area`), should the parameters be value parameters or reference parameters? Because these values are not changed, they should be value parameters.

If a function needs no information and returns no values to the calling routine, then the function doesn't need parameters. Function `main` is a function with no parameters. Notice, however, that function prototypes, function headings, and function calls must always have the parentheses even if there are no parameters.

Local Variables

Any user-defined function has a heading and a body, and the body is a block. Therefore, any function can include variable declarations. Declarations declared within a block are called *local variables*. Local variables are created when the function is called and disappear when the function finishes executing. Local variables are accessible only from within the block in which they are defined.

Documentation of Functions

There is a need-to-know principle in programming that says that the user of a function needs to know only *what* the function does, not *how* it does it. One way to implement this principle is to have the documentation on each function prototype state what the function does—just enough information for the program reader to understand the function's purpose. On the other hand, the documentation in the function heading and the body is for the person reading the details, usually the one responsible for maintaining the code. Therefore, the documentation in the function definition can state how the function is implemented.

As long as our programs are small enough to include all of the function definitions in the same file with function `main`, we use an informal style of documenting the function prototypes and definitions. In later chapters, when we separate the function prototypes and function definitions into different files, we use a more formal style in which preconditions describe the state of the parameters on input to the function and postconditions describe the state of the parameters on output from the function. Preconditions state what the function assumes is true on entry; postconditions state what the function guarantees to be true on exit from the function, provided the preconditions are true. Preconditions and postconditions can be written in many different ways, ranging from simple English sentences to statements in formal logic.

In this formal documentation style, the function prototype becomes the *interface* to the function. It includes the formal description of the purpose of the function and a description of the parameters at the logical level. The implementation details are hidden within the definition of the function. The hiding of the implementation details within a separate block with a formally specified interface is called *encapsulation*. When our programs are large enough to warrant it, we use this style of documentation to emphasize encapsulation.

Data flow refers to information going into and out of a function. The direction of data flow can be documented by using one of the following statements as a comment beside each parameter in the prototype: 'in', 'out', 'in/out'. Note that 'out' and 'in/out' parameters must be designated as reference parameters.

Chapter 7: Prelab Assignment

Name _____ Date _____

Section _____

Examine program Stars carefully.

```cpp
// Program Stars prints NUM_STARS on the screen.

#include <iostream>
using namespace std;

const int   NUM_STARS = 10;

void PrintStars();
// Prints NUM_STARS stars on the screen.

int main ()
{
    cout  << "The next line contains "  << NUM_STARS
          << " stars. "  << endl;
    PrintStars();
    PrintStars();
    return 0;
}
//**************************************************
void PrintStars ()
// Post: NUM_STARS asterisks are sent to cout.

{
    cout << "**********"  << endl;
    return;
}
```

Exercise 1: Show below exactly what program Stars writes on the screen.

Exercise 2: Trace the execution of program Demo on page 135. The data is keyed as follows:

10   23

What is printed?

Exercise 3: If the values in the data line are entered in reverse order, what is printed?

Lesson 7–1: Check Prelab Exercises

Name _____ Date _____

Section _____

Exercise 1: Run program `Stars` to check your answer to Exercise 1. Were you correct? If not, explain your error. (Did the output statement mislead you? What should the output statement say?)

Exercise 2: Run program `Demo` to check your answers to Exercise 2. Discuss your results.

Exercise 3: Run program `Demo` to check your answers to Exercise 3. Discuss your results.

Lesson 7–2: Functions without Parameters

Name _____ Date _____

Section _____

Lesson 1 uses program `Shell1`.

```cpp
// Program Shell1 is a program shell with a function.

#include <iostream>
using namespace std;

void  Print();
// FILL IN the documentation.

main ()
{
    Print();
    return 0;
}

//**************************************

void  Print()
// FILL IN the documentation.
{
    /* TO BE FILLED IN */
}
```

Exercise 1: Fill in the code for function `Print` so that it prints your name and address (on two separate lines) enclosed or boxed in dollar signs on the screen. Don't forget to fill in the appropriate documentation for function `Print`. Run your program and show your documentation and your output.

Exercise 2: Change function `Print` so that it reads the name and address from file `data.in`. Make your input file a reference parameter to function `Print`. Use '\n' to control your loops. You may assume that the name is on one line and the address is on the next line. Run your program and show your documentation and your output. (Did you remember to change the documentation for function `Print`?)

Lesson 7–3: Functions with Value Parameters

Name _____ Date _____

Section _____

Use program Shell2 for Exercises 1 through 3.

Writing boxes on the screen is fun. Program Shell2 is the shell of a program that prompts the user to enter an integer number. When completed, this number is read and passed to function Print as parameter numSigns. The function prints a box of dollar signs on the screen that is numSigns by (numSigns / 2). For example, if numSigns is 10, the following box is printed on the screen.

```
$$$$$$$$$$
$        $
$        $
$        $
$$$$$$$$$$
```

Note the interior dimensions are (numSigns–2) x (numSigns / 2–2).

```cpp
// Program Shell2 prompts for the number of dollar signs for
// the top of the box.  That number / 2 - 2  lines are
// printed with dollar signs on the sides.

#include <iostream>
using namespace std;

void  Print(int numSigns);
// FILL IN documentation.

int main ()
{
    int  number;

    cout  << "Enter the number of dollar signs for the top: "
          << "press return."
    cout  << "Enter end-of-file character to quit."  << endl;
    cin >> number;
    while (cin)
    {
        /* FILL IN call to Print */
        cout  << "Enter the number of dollar signs for "
              << "the top: press return."
        cout  << "Enter end-of-file character to quit."
              << endl;
        cin >> number;
    }
    return 0;
}
```

```
//*****************************************

void  Print(int numSigns)
// FILL IN documentation.
{
    /* FILL IN code to print numSigns $'s */

    /* FILL IN code to print (numSigns / 2)-2 lines with    */
    /* $'s lining up under the left-most and right-most      */
    /* $ ones on the top line.                               */

    /* FILL IN code to print numSigns $'s                    */

}
```

Exercise 1: Fill in the missing code in function `Print` and the invoking statement in function `main`. Compile and run your program using 4, 10, and 7.

Exercise 2: Change your program so that when the number of dollar signs is odd, it uses

```
(numSigns + 1) / 2 - 2
```

as the inside height dimension.

Exercise 3: Rewrite your solution to Exercise 2 so that the symbol used as the border is also read as data and passed to function `Print` as a parameter.

To make the symbol a parameter requires the following changes:

- Prompt for and read the symbol.
- Add the symbol and its type (or just the type) to the parameter list of the function prototype.
- Add the symbol and its type to the parameter list of the function prototype.
- Add the symbol to argument list.

Run the program three times using &, %, and *A* as symbols and 4, 10, and 7 as the number of symbols to use.

Lesson 7–4: Functions with Reference Parameters

Name _____ Date _____

Section _____

Exercise 1: To do this exercise look at program Shell3. This program reads two real numbers, miles and hours, and prints milesPerHour on the screen. Function GetData prompts the user for the appropriate values, reads them, and returns them to function main.

```cpp
// Program Shell3 reads miles and hours and prints miles
// per hour.

#include <iostream>
#include <iomanip>
using namespace std;

/* FILL IN the function prototype for GetData */

int main ()
{
    float  miles;
    float  hours;
    float  milesPerHour;

    cout  << fixed  << showpoint;

    /* FILL IN code to invoke function GetData */

    milesPerHour = miles / hours;
    cout  << setw(10)  << miles
          << setw(10)  << hours
          << setw(10)  << milesPerHour  << endl;
    return 0;
}

//*******************************************************

/* FILL IN the function heading for GetData */
{
    /* FILL IN Code to prompt for miles and hours */
    /* FILL IN Code to read miles and hours */
}
```

Fill in the missing code, and compile and run your program three times using the values shown on the next page.

Miles	Hours	Miles per Hour
120.1	2.2	_____
332.0	5.5	_____
1250.0	20.0	_____

Exercise 2: Run program Shell3 three more times, entering the hours first and the miles second. Fill in the answers below.

Miles	Hours	Miles per Hour
2.2	120.1	_____
5.5	332.0	_____
20.0	1250.0	_____

Exercise 3: Explain why the answers are different in Exercises 1 and 2.

Exercise 4: Complete program Shell4. When completed, the program reads, counts, and averages the numbers stored in a file.

```cpp
// Program Shell4 averages the values on file dataFile.

#include <iostream>
#include <fstream>
using namespace std;

void  ReadAndSum(ifstream&, int&, float&);
// Reads, counts, and averages values on a file.

int main ()
{
    ifstream  dataFile;
    int  numberOfValues;
    float  average;

    cout  << fixed  << showpoint;

    dataFile.open("Shell4.dat");

    /* FILL IN the invoking statement for ReadAndSum */

    cout  << "The average of "  << numberOfValues
          << " values is "  << average  << endl;
    return 0;
}
```

```
//*****************************************

void  ReadAndSum /* TO BE FILLED IN */
// FILL IN documentation.
{
  /* TO BE FILLED IN */
}
```
_____

Fill in function ReadAndSum to read, count, and average all the numbers in dataFile.
Run the program using the data on Shell4.dat.

List the Parameters	Reference or Value?
_____	_____
_____	_____
_____	_____

The average of _____ values is   _____.

_____

Exercise 5: Lesson 6–4, Exercise 1, contains a loop nested within a loop. The outer loop prompts for and inputs a digit. The inner loop sums the integers from zero through the digit. Rewrite your solution to this task so that the summing of the digits from zero through the input digit is done in void function SumDigits. The digit should be an input parameter and the sum of the digits should be an output parameter. Rerun your changed version with the same data: 0, 3, 7, and 9. The results should be the same.

Exercise 6: Write a void function, Count, that takes a file name as input and returns the number of characters on the current line of the file. The function main should call the function within a loop that runs until the file stream fails (end of file) and prints the answers on the screen. Test your program using CharCt.dl.

How many lines are there?

How many characters are there on each line?

Exercise 7: Write a void function, FindMinimum, that takes as input a file of integers and returns as output the minimum value on the file. (Remember that all file parameters must be passed by reference.) Write a main function that calls FindMinimum and prints out the minimum value. Use file Numbers.dat. What is printed?

Lesson 7–5: Debugging

Name _____ Date _____

Section _____

Exercise 1: Program Triangle inputs three values representing the lengths of the three sides of a triangle. If the three sides represent an equilateral triangle, "Equilateral" is printed. If the three sides represent an isosceles triangle, "Isosceles" is printed. If the three sides are all different, "Scalene" is printed. There is one problem: The program doesn't work. Debug it.

What errors did you find?

Show the last three lines of output.

Exercise 2: Look carefully at the last three answers. Did you notice that they are wrong? Yes, they have two equal sides—but they are not triangles at all! For the values to represent a triangle, the sum of any two must be greater than or equal to the third. Add this error checking to the program and print out a message stating that the sides do not represent a triangle. Show the last three lines of output.

Exercise 3: Program Triangle has no documentation and non-problem-specific identifiers. Add appropriate documentation and make the identifiers more meaningful. How did the lack of documentation and the poor choice of identifiers make debugging more difficult?

Postlab Activities

Exercise 1: The American Heart Association publishes brochures describing what it means to be "Heart Healthy." We should watch our cholesterol and make sure that no more than 30 percent of our caloric intake comes from fat. Write a program that reads all the food items eaten in a day along with the fat (in grams) and the calorie content. (Assume that each food item appears on a line by itself, with the fat and calories on the following line with a blank in between.) Echo-print your input on file `Diet.out`, followed by a statement that describes the day's food intake as heart healthy or not heart healthy. Your program should be interactive. Each module in your functional design should be implemented as a function.

Exercise 2: The following test plan is designed to test the program from Exercise 1. Execute this test plan. Because of the amount of input required to test this program, we have used a different format for the test plan.

```
General Cases
  Input¹
      food      : Egg McMuffin with orange juice and coffee.
      fat grams: 11
      calories : 360
      food      : Chunky chicken salad with iced tea.
      fat grams: 6
      calories : 198
      food      : Regular hamburger with small fries and diet
                    coke.
      fat grams: 21
      calories : 476
  Expected Output
    input echo printed
    'Warning!  You had too many fat calories today.'
  Actual Output
```

```
  Input
    food        : Whole-grain cereal with low-fat milk and orange
                    juice.
    fat grams: 3
```

---

[1] The nutritional information shown here came from a McDonald's placemat. Egg McMuffin, McLean Deluxe, and McDonald's are registered trademarks.

```
calories : 280
food     : Chunky chicken salad with iced tea.
fat grams: 6
calories : 198
food     : McLean deluxe, side salad, and diet coke.
fat grams: 12
calories : 375
```

Expected Output
  input echo printed
  'Congratulations! You had a Heart Healthy day.'
Actual Output

```




```

End Cases
  Input
    food   : <eoln>
    fat grams: 0
    calories : 0
  Expected Output
    input echo printed with food taking up no characters
    'Congratulations! You had a Heart Healthy day.'
  Actual Output

```




```

  Input
    food   : 47 A's
    fat grams: 0
    calories : 0
  Expected Output
    input echo printed with food taking up 46 characters
    'Congratulations! You had a Heart Healthy day.'

Actual Output

Exercise 3: You are going on a round-the-world trip and wonder how many miles you must cover to go from one time zone to another. Write a program that writes out a table showing how many statute miles you must cover to go from one time zone to another when you are at the equator, 30° N and S, 60° N and S, and 180° N and S. You may ignore any local time differences. You must use at least one void function.

Exercise 4: Alter the program you wrote in Exercise 3 so that it prints out both statute miles and nautical miles for the latitudes requested.

Scope, Lifetime, and More on Functions

- To be able to determine which variables are global, which variables are local, and which variables are nonlocal.

- To be able to differentiate between declarations and definitions.

- To be able to differentiate between static and automatic variables.

- To be able to define and invoke a numeric value-returning function to implement a specified task.

- To be able to define and invoke a Boolean value-returning function to implement a specified task.

Chapter 8: Assignment Cover Sheet

Name _____ Date _____

Section _____

Fill in the following table showing which exercises have been assigned for each lesson and check what you are to submit: (1) lab sheets, (2) listings of output files, and/or (3) listings of programs. Your instructor or teaching assistant (TA) can use the Completed column for grading purposes.

Activities	Assigned: Check or list exercise numbers	Submit (1) (2) (3)			Completed
Prelab					
Review					
Prelab Assignment					
Inlab					
Lesson 8–1: Check Prelab Exercises					
Lesson 8–2: Static and Automatic Variables					
Lesson 8–3: Value-Returning and Void Functions					
Lesson 8–4: Test Plan					
Lesson 8–5: Debugging					
Postlab					

Prelab Activities

Review

In Chapter 7, we said that local variables are those declared within a block. The block does not have to be the body of a function—local identifiers can be declared within *any* block. In a large program, there may be several variables with the same identifier—*name*, for example. How do we know which variable is meant and where each variable is accessible? The answers to these questions are provided by scope rules.

Scope of an Identifier

There are four categories of scope for an identifier in C++: class scope, local scope, namespace scope, and global scope. Class scope is defined in Chapter 11. Local scope is the scope of an identifier defined within a block and extending from the point where the identifier is declared to the end of the block. Global scope is the scope of an identifier declared outside all functions and extending to the end of the file containing the program.

Function names in C++ have global scope. Once a function name has been declared, any subsequent function can call it. In C++ you cannot nest a function definition within another function. When a function defines a local identifier with the same name as a global identifier, the local identifier takes precedence. That is, the local identifier hides the existence of the global identifier. For obvious reasons this principle is called *name precedence* or *name hiding.*

The rules of C++ that govern who knows what, where, and when are called *scope rules.*

- A function name has global scope.
- The scope of a global identifier extends from its declaration to the end of the file in which it is defined.
- The scope of a parameter is the same as the scope of a local variable declared in the outermost block of the function body.
- The scope of a local identifier includes all statements following the declaration of the identifier to the end of the block in which it is declared and includes any nested blocks, unless a local identifier of the same name is declared in a nested block.
- The scope of an identifier begins with its most recent declaration.

The last three rules mean that if a local identifier in a block is the same as a global or nonlocal identifier to the block, the local identifier blocks access to the other identifier. That is, the block's reference is to its own local identifier.

To summarize, any variable or constant declared outside all functions is a *global identifier.* Any global identifier is known (and can be accessed directly) by any function that does not declare a variable or constant with the same name. Local identifiers of a function are *nonlocal* (but accessible) to any block nested within it.

If global identifiers are accessible to all functions, why don't we just make all identifiers global and do away with parameter lists? Good programming practice dictates that communication between the modules of our program should be explicitly stated. This practice limits the possibility of one module accidentally interfering with another. In other words, each function is given only what it needs to know. This is how we write "good" programs.

The avoidance of global variables is especially critical in a team environment, where one person should not have to check with everyone else before using or changing a variable because it might be global.

Namespaces

As a concept, namespace is the same as scope. In C++, namespace is a language feature that allows a programmer to create a named scope. The authors of `<iostream>`, for example, enclosed the definitions and declarations within a namespace called `std`. To access streams `cin` and `cout` and the manipulator `endl`, we used the statement

```
using namespace std;
```

near the front of our programs. This statement told the compiler that all identifiers defined in namespace `std` (defined in file `iostream`) are assessable to the parts of the program that are within the scope of the using directive.

Declarations and Definitions

In Chapter 7, we used a function prototype to tell the compiler that a function with certain parameters would be defined later. The function prototype is a declaration that is not also a definition. The function definition includes a heading and a body.

One need for a function prototype comes about because most C++ programmers put function `main` physically first in the file. `main` invokes other functions, so the names of the other functions and their parameter types must be known before function `main` is compiled. In our example, if we had put the function definition physically before `main`, the prototype would not have been necessary, and the function definition would have been both a declaration and a definition. However, function prototypes cannot be eliminated simply by moving `main`, because we might have a function that calls a second function, and that second function also calls the first function.

The distinction between a declaration and a definition is that memory space is reserved in a definition. In a function definition, the space for the compiled code of the function body is reserved. There are times when we want to declare a variable but not define it. That is, we want to let the compiler know about a global variable defined in another file. Look at the following two statements.

```
int   myValue;
extern int   anotherValue;
```

The first statement is both a declaration and a definition. Space is reserved for the variable `myValue` of data type `int`. The second statement is a declaration only. Your program can reference `anotherValue`, but the compiler does not reserve space for it. The reserved word `extern` tells the compiler that `anotherValue` is a global variable located in another file.

More about Variables

The *lifetime* of a variable is the time during program execution when the variable has storage assigned to it. The lifetime of a global variable is the entire execution of the program. The lifetime of a local variable is the execution of the block in which it is declared. There are times when we want to have the value of a local variable remain between calls to the same function. For example, to know how many times a function is called during the execution of a program, we would like to use a local function variable as a counter and increment it each time the function is called. However, if space is allocated each time the function is called and deallocated when the function finishes executing, we can't guarantee that the space for the local variable is the same for each function invocation. In fact, it most likely would not be.

Therefore, C++ lets the user determine the lifetime of each local variable by assigning it a storage class: static or automatic. If you want the lifetime of a local variable to extend to the entire run of the program, you preface the data type identifier with the reserved word `static` when the variable is defined. The default storage class is automatic in which storage is allocated on entry and deallocated on exit from a block.

Any variable may be initialized when it is defined. This is the fourth way to assign a value to a place in memory. To initialize a variable, follow the variable identifier with an equal sign and an expression. The expression is called an *initializer*. The initializing process differs depending on whether the variable being initialized is static or automatic. For a static variable, the initializer must be a constant expression, and its value is stored only once. For an automatic variable, the initializer can be any expression, and its value is stored each time the variable is assigned storage.

User-Defined Value-Returning Functions

With void functions, we use the function name as a statement in our program to represent the action that the function performs. Value-returning functions are used when the action returns a single value and that value is used in an expression. For example, let's write a function that returns the smallest of its three input values.

```
// Program PrintMin prints the smallest of three input values.

#include <iostream>
using namespace std;

int  Minimum(int, int, int);     // function prototype
// Returns the minimum of three distinct values.

int main()
{
    int   one;
    int   two;
    int   three;

    cout  << "Input three integer values; press return." << endl;
    cin  >> one  >> two  >> three;
    cout  << "The minimum value of "  << one  << ", "  << two
          << ", and "  << three  << " is "
          << Minimum(one, two, three)  << "."  << endl;
    return 0;
}
```

```
//****************************************************

int  Minimum(int first, int second, int third)
// Pre:  Input values are distinct; that is, no duplicates.
// Post: Return minimum of three distinct int values.

{
    if (first < second && first < third)
        return first;
    else if (second < first && second < third)
        return second;
    else if (third < first && third < second)
        return third;
}
```

The function prototype declares a function of data type `int`. This means that the type of the value returned to the calling function is `int`. Because a value-returning function always sends back one value, we designate the type of the value before the function name. We call this data type the *function type*. However, *function value type*, *function return type*, or *function result type* is more accurate.

In this example, the function invocation occurs in the output statement in function `main`. Function `Minimum` is invoked and the value is returned and immediately sent to the output stream. There are three parameters: `first`, `second`, and `third`. The three arguments are `one`, `two`, and `three`. Notice that the documentation on the function prototype is different from the documentation on the function definition.

Chapter 8: Prelab Assignment

Name _____ Date _____

Section _____

Read program `Scope` carefully and answer Exercises 1 through 6.

```cpp
// Program Scope demonstrates scope rules and lifetime
// classes.

#include <iostream>
#include <fstream>
using namespace std;

int   counter;
int   sum = 0;
int   number;

ifstream   inNums;

void  SumNumbers(ifstream&, int&);

int main ()
{
    inNums.open("Numeric.dat");
    {
        int   sum = 0;
        SumNumbers(inNums, sum);
        cout  << "Output from first call to SumNumbers"
               << endl;
        cout  << "Sum is "  << sum  << endl;

    }
    SumNumbers(inNums, sum);
    cout  << "Output from second call to SumNumbers"
           << endl;
    cout << "Sum is "  << sum  << endl;
    return 0;
}
//*************************************

void  SumNumbers(ifstream& inFile, int& answer)
{
    static int  counter = 1;
    while (counter <= 4)
    {
        inFile  >> number;
        answer = answer + number;
        counter++;
    }
}
```

Exercise 1: File `Numeric.dat` contains the following values: 10 20 30 40 10 20 30 40. What is printed?

Exercise 2: List the global identifiers.

Exercise 3: Circle each of the blocks in program `Scope` and number them from top to bottom.

Exercise 4: List the local identifiers and state the block(s) in which each is accessible.

Exercise 5: List the automatic local variables.

Exercise 6: List the static local variables.

Lesson 8–1: Check Prelab Exercises

Name _____ Date _____

Section _____

Exercise 1: Run program `Scope` to check your answers. Were your answers correct? If not, explain what you did wrong.

Exercise 2: `counter`, `sum`, `number`, `inNums`, and `SumNumbers`.

Exercise 3:

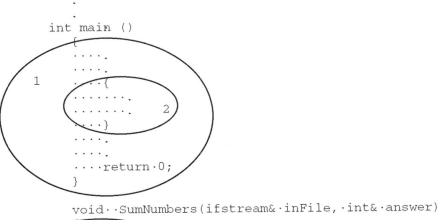

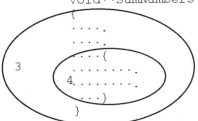

Exercise 4: Block 1 has no local identifiers. Block 2 has local identifier `sum`, which hides global identifier `sum`. Block 3 has three local identifiers: `inFile`, `answer`, and `counter`.

Exercise 5: automatic local variable: `sum` (local to 2). All parameters also are automatic variables.

Exercise 6: static local variable: `counter` (local to 3). All global variables also are static.

Lesson 8–2: Static and Automatic Variables

Name _____ Date _____

Section _____

Use program `Shell1` for Exercises 1 and 2.

```cpp
// Program Shell1 is for investigating the differences between
// automatic and static variables.

#include <iostream>
using namespace std;

void  TestLocals();

int main ()
{
    TestLocals ();
    TestLocals ();
    TestLocals ();
    return 0;
}

// *************************************

void  TestLocals()
{
    /* TO BE FILLED IN */
}
```

Exercise 1: Function `TestLocals` defines an automatic variable, `count`, and initializes it to 1. The contents of `count` are incremented and sent to the output stream. Write this code and run program `Shell1`. Record your output. Was it what you expected?

Exercise 2: Change function `TestLocals` so that variable `count` is a static variable. Rerun your program and show your output. Was it what you expected?

Exercise 3: Explain the difference between automatic and static variables.

Lesson 8–3: Value-Returning and Void Functions

Name _____ Date _____

Section _____

Exercise 1: Lesson 6–4, Exercise 1, contains a loop nested within a loop. The outer loop prompts for and inputs a digit. The inner loop sums the integers from zero through the digit. Rewrite your solution to this task so that the summing of the digits from zero through the input digit is done in an int function, SumDigits. The digit should be an input parameter. Rerun your changed version with the same data. The results should be the same.

Exercise 2: Write an int function, Minimum, that finds the minimum value on a file. Write a main function that calls Minimum and prints out the minimum value. Use file Numbers.dat. What is printed?

Exercise 3: In Exercise 2, did you access the file name globally or did you pass the file name as a parameter to function Minimum? If you passed the file name, you had a reference parameter to a value-returning function. Both accessing a variable globally and having a reference parameter to a value-returning function are bad style. Should this function have been a void function with two reference parameters? Justify your answer.

Exercise 4: Program Convert is an old friend. This version uses an int function to convert temperatures from Fahrenheit to Celsius or from Celsius to Fahrenheit. Examine program Convert carefully. The next exercises ask you to modify it.

```
// Program Convert converts a temperature from Fahrenheit to
// Celsius or a temperature from Celsius to Fahrenheit
// depending on whether the user enters an F or a C.

#include <iostream>
int  ConvertedTemp(int, char);

using namespace std;

int main ()
{
    char  letter;        // Place to store input letter
    int   tempIn;        // Temperature to be converted
```

```
        cout  << "Input Menu"  << endl  << endl;
        cout  << "F:  Convert from Fahrenheit to Celsius"  << endl;
        cout  << "C:  Convert from Celsius to Fahrenheit"  << endl;
        cout  << "Q:  Quit"  << endl;
        cout  << "Type a C, F,  or Q; then press return."  << endl;

        cin  >> letter;
        while (letter != 'Q')
        {
            cout  << " Type an integer number, and press return."
                  << endl;
            cin  >> tempIn;

            if (letter == 'F')
                cout << "Fahrenheit to Celsius"  << endl;
            else
                cout << "Celsius to Fahrenheit"  << endl;
            cout  << "Temperature to convert: "  << tempIn
                  << endl;
            cout  << "Converted temperature:  "
                  << ConvertedTemp(tempIn, letter)
                  << endl  << endl;
            cout  << "Type a C, F,  or Q; then press return."
                  << endl;

            cin  >> letter;
        }
return 0;
}


// ********************************************

int  ConvertedTemp(int tempIn, char letter)
{
    if (letter == 'C')
        return (9 * tempIn / 5) + 32;
    else
        return 5 * (tempIn - 32) / 9;
}
```

Run program Convert using the following data.

Code	Temperature	Result
C	0	_____
C	100	_____
c (lowercase)	100	_____
C	57	_____
C	6	_____
F	42	_____
F	212	_____
F	134	_____
Q		(terminate run)

Exercise 5: Enclose the menu in a void function with no parameters. Rerun your program to check that the results are the same.

Exercise 6: Did you notice that the wrong answer was returned when a lowercase *c* was input? Program `Convert` has no error checking. Incorrect input just produces an incorrect answer. Write a `Boolean` function, `Error`, that takes `letter` and returns `true` if `letter` is not an uppercase *C*, *F*, or *Q* and `false` otherwise. Use `Error` to check for bad data immediately after `letter` is read. If `letter` is not correct, write an error message and prompt again for `letter`. Run the original program and your revised version using lowercase *c* and uppercase *X* as inputs.

Show output from the original version.

Show output from the revised version.

Exercise 7: Restricting the input to uppercase letters in program `Convert` is unrealistic. Revise the program so that it accepts both uppercase and lowercase input. (Lesson 8–4, Exercise 1, asks you to write a test plan for the revised version of program `Convert`.)

Lesson 8–4: Test Plan

Name _____ Date _____

Section _____

Exercise 1: Design a test plan for program Convert as revised in Lesson 8–3, Exercise 7.

Reason for Test Case	Input Values	Expected Output	Observed Output

Exercise 2: Implement the test plan designed in Exercise 1. You may show the results in the chart in Exercise 1.

Lesson 8–5: Debugging

Name _____ Date _____

Section _____

Exercise 1: Function Swap takes two values as input and returns them in reverse order. This little utility routine is very useful. However, it doesn't seem to work correctly. Can you fix it? Program Driver is written to test function Swap. A program whose only purpose is to test a subprogram is called a *driver*. The driver reads in two values, calls Swap with the two input values, and writes out the result. Run Driver using 10 and 15 as the input values. What is printed?

Exercise 2: This answer looks correct but the program has a bug in it—take our word for it. Search until you find an error, correct it, and run the program again. What is printed?

Exercise 3: We bet there is still a problem with your program. Keep on trying. What error did you find this time?

Postlab Activities

Exercise 1: Along with eating a heart healthy diet, everyone should get regular exercise. You are attending an aqua jogging class. After you have been jogging for 15 minutes, the instructor stops the class and has everyone take his or her pulse for six seconds. (She times you.) She then asks if you are in your target zone. To help the class out, you decide to program a target-zone calculator. Each person's target zone is between 60 percent and 75 percent of his or her predicted maximal heart rate in beats per minute. A good approximation to this maximal heart rate is 220 less the person's age.

Write a function, `InTheZone`, that takes a person's age and the six-second pulse rate and returns `true` if the person is within his or her zone and `false` otherwise. Keep prompting for and reading an age and a pulse rate until the user enters a negative value. You must use at least one value-returning function in this assignment.

Exercise 2: Write a driver and a test plan for function `InTheZone`. Implement your test plan.

Exercise 3: In Postlab Exercise 6–6, you were asked to create a table comparing Celsius temperatures with the actual Fahrenheit equivalent and an approximated equivalent. Redesign that program and use `float` functions to calculate the actual value and the approximated value. Run your program with the same data.

Exercise 4: Add a column to the table in Exercise 3 that shows the difference between the actual Fahrenheit equivalent and the approximation. This change makes use of value-returning functions, as specified in Exercise 3, inappropriate. Rewrite the `float` functions as void functions and explain why value-returning functions are no longer appropriate.

Additional Control Structures

- To be able to convert a series of *if-then-else* statements to a *switch* statement.

- To be able to construct a *switch* statement to implement a specified task.

- To be able to convert a *while* loop to a *do-while* loop.

- To be able to construct a *do-while* loop to do a specified task.

- To be able to construct a *for* statement to do a specified task.

Chapter 9: Assignment Cover Sheet

Name _____ Date _____

Section _____

Fill in the following table showing which exercises have been assigned for each lesson and check what you are to submit: (1) lab sheets, (2) listings of output files, and/or (3) listings of programs. Your instructor or teaching assistant (TA) can use the Completed column for grading purposes.

Activities	Assigned: Check or list exercise numbers	Submit (1)	(2)	(3)	Completed
Prelab					
Review					
Prelab Assignment					
Inlab					
Lesson 9–1: Check Prelab Exercises					
Lesson 9–2: Multi-Way Branching					
Lesson 9–3: Additional Control Structures					
Lesson 9–4: Test Plan					
Lesson 9–5: Debugging					
Postlab					

Prelab Activities

Review

In preceding chapters, we covered four control structures: the sequence, the *if* statement, the *while* statement, and void and value-returning functions. In this chapter, we introduce five additional control structures that make certain tasks easier. However, they are the icing on the cake. You cannot do anything with them that you cannot do with the control structures that you already know.

break and continue

Both *break* and *continue* are statements that alter the flow of execution within a control structure. The *break* statement is used with the *switch* statement, the *while* statement, the *do-while* statement, and the *for* statement. (The *switch*, *do-while*, and *for* statements are defined below.) The *break* statement interrupts the flow of control by immediately exiting these statements. In contrast, the *continue* statement is used only with looping statements. It alters the flow of control by immediately terminating the current iteration. Note the difference between these two statements used in a loop: continue skips to the next iteration of the loop, and break skips to the statement following the loop.

The *break* statement is extremely useful with the *switch* statement but should be used with extreme caution with looping statements. Good style dictates that loops have only one entry and one exit except under very unusual circumstances. The *continue* statement is very seldom used; we only mention it for completeness.

Multi-Way Branching: *switch*

The *switch* statement is a selection statement that can be used in place of a series of *if-then-else* statements. Alternative statements are listed with a *switch label* in front of each. A switch label is either a *case label* or the word default. A case label is the word case followed by a constant expression. An integral expression called the *switch expression* is used to match one of the values on the case labels. The statement associated with the value that is matched is the statement that is executed. Execution then continues sequentially from the matched label until the end of the *switch* statement is encountered or a *break* statement is encountered.

```
switch (grade)
{
    case 'A' : cout  << "Great work!";
               break;
    case 'B' : cout  << "Good work!";
               break;
    case 'C' : cout  << "Passing work!";
               break;
    case 'D' :
    case 'F' : cout  << "Unsatisfactory work.";
               cout  << "See your instructor.";
               break;
    default  : cout  << grade  << " is not a legal grade";
               break;
}
```

`grade` is the switch expression; the letters beside the statements make up the case labels. The value in `grade` is compared with the value in each case label. When a match is found, the corresponding statement is executed. If the value of the switch expression does not match a value in any case label, the `default` label is matched by default. Because execution continues after a match until `break` is encountered, both 'D' and 'F' send the same message to the screen. What would happen if we forgot to put `break` after the statement associated with `case` 'B'? Every time `grade` contained a *B* both "Good work!" and "Passing work!" would be printed.

Looping: *do-while*

The *do-while* statement is a looping statement that tests the Boolean expression at the end of the loop. A statement (or sequence of statements) is executed while an expression is true. The *do-while* statement differs from the *while* statement in one major respect: The body of the loop is always executed at least once in the *do-while* statement. For example, the following loop reads and counts characters in stream `inFile` until a blank is found.

```
numberOfCharacters = 0;
inFile  >> character;

// assume first character is not a blank
do
{
    numberOfCharacters++;
    inFile >> character;
} while (character != ' ');
```

We may use the *do-while* statement to construct both count-controlled and event-controlled loops.

Looping: *for*

In contrast, the *for* statement is a looping construct designed specifically to simplify the implementation of count-controlled loops. The loop-control variable, the beginning value, the ending value, and the incrementation are explicitly part of the *for* heading itself. The following *for* statement reads and sums 10 values.

```
sum = 0;
for (counter = 1; counter <= 10; counter++)
{
    cin  >> value;
    sum = sum + value;
}
```

`counter`, the loop-control variable, is initialized to 1. While `counter` is less than or equal to 10, the block of code is executed, and `counter` is incremented by 1. The loop is executed with `counter` equal to the initial value, the final value, and all the values in between. The second expression in the *for* heading is the assertion that controls the loop. If the assertion is false initially, the body of the loop is not executed. Here are two *for* headings and what they mean.

`for (counter = limit; counter != 0; counter—)`: Initialize `counter` to the value stored in `limit`; if `counter` is not equal to 0, execute the body of the loop; decrement `counter` by 1 and go back to the test. If `limit` contains the value 10, this *for* loop is identical to the previous one: It executes 10 times.

`for (int counter = 1; counter <= limit; counter++)`: Define an `int` variable `counter` and initialize it to 1. If `counter` is less than or equal to the value stored in `limit`, execute the body of the loop. Increment `counter` by 1. The scope of `counter` is the body of the loop, not the block in which the *for* statement is enclosed.

The *for* statement in C++ is very flexible. Although designed to simplify count-controlled loops, it can be used for event-controlled loops. The first statement in the *for* header can be any statement—even a stream extraction or the null statement. The second statement is a test that occurs at the beginning of the loop. The third statement is one that is executed at the end of the loop. So the *for* heading

```
for (cin >> character; character != '.'; cin >> character)
```

is legal. In fact, no loop body (except the null statement—a semicolon) is needed here because everything is done in the heading. However, we recommend that the *for* statement be used only for count-controlled loops. That is what *for* statements are designed for. Most other uses fall into the category of tricky code and should be avoided. (How long did it take you to determine what this loop is doing?)

Loops constructed with the *while* statement and the *for* statement are called pretest loops because the expression is tested at the beginning of the loop before the body of the loop is executed the first time. Loops constructed with the *do-while* statement are called posttest loops because the expression is tested at the end of the loop.

Chapter 9: Prelab Assignment

Name _____ Date _____

Section _____

Read program Loops **carefully and answer Exercises 1 and 2.**

```
// Program Loops demonstrates various looping structures.
#include <iostream>
#include <fstream>
using namespace std;

int main ()
{
    ifstream  inData;
    int   value;
    inData.open("Loop.dat");

    {// while loop
        int   counter = 1;
        int   sum = 0;
        while (counter <= 4)
        {
            inData  >> value;
            sum = sum + value;
            counter++;
        }
        cout  << sum  << endl;
    }

    {// do-while loop
        int   counter = 1;
        int   sum = 0;
        do
        {
            inData  >> value;
            sum = sum + value;
            counter++;
        } while (counter <= 4);
        cout  << sum  << endl;
    }
```

```
{// for loop
    int  sum = 0;
    for (int counter = 1; counter <= 4; counter++)
    {
        inData  >> value;
        sum = sum + value;
    }
    cout  << sum  << endl;
}

    return 0;
}
```

Exercise 1: If file `Loop.dat` contains the following values, what is printed?

```
10 20 30 40 10 20 30 40 10 20 30 40
```

Exercise 2: Which of these loops are pretest loops? Which are posttest loops?

Examine program `Switches` **and answer Exercises 3 and 4.**

```
// Program Switches demonstrates the use of the Switch
// statement.

#include <iostream>
using namespace std;

int main ()
{
    char  letter;
    int   first;
    int   second;
    int   answer;

    cout  << "Enter an A for addition or an S for"
          << " subtraction, followed by two integer "  << endl
          << " numbers.  Press return.  Enter a Q to quit."
          << endl;
    cin  >> letter;
    while (letter != 'Q')
    {
        cin  >> first  >> second;

       switch (letter)
       {
           case 'A' : answer = (first + second);
                      cout << first  << " + "  << second
                           << " is "  << answer  << endl;
                      break;
           case 'S' : answer = (first - second);
                      cout << first  << " - "  << second
                           << " is "  << answer  << endl;
                      break;
       }
```

```
        cin  >> letter;
    }

    return 0;
}
```

_____

Exercise 3: What is printed if the following values are entered?

```
A   5   -7
A  -5   -8
S   7    7
S   8   -8
Q
```

Exercise 4: What happens if the _Q_ to quit is entered as a lowercase letter?

Lesson 9–1: Check Prelab Exercises

Name _____   Date _____

Section _____

Exercise 1: Run program `Loops` and check your answers. Were your answers correct? If not, do you understand your mistakes?

Exercise 2: *while* loops and *for* loops are pretest loops; the loop body is not executed if the ending condition is true initially. *do-while* loops are posttest loops; their bodies are always executed at least once.

Exercise 3: Run program `Switches` to check your answers. Were your answers correct? If not, do you understand your mistakes?

Exercise 4: If a lowercase *Q* is entered, the body of the *while* statement is executed again. The screen freezes while waiting for you to enter more values.

Lesson 9–2: Multi-Way Branching

Name _____ Date _____

Section _____

Exercise 1: As Prelab Exercise 4 demonstrated, program Switches is not very robust. Add the code necessary to allow the program to work properly with both lowercase and uppercase versions of the input letters. Run your program with the same data, but key the letters as lowercase.

Exercise 2: Program Switches is still not very robust. Add a default case that prints an error message and asks for the letter to be reentered. Test your program with the same data set, but add several letters that are not correct.

Exercise 3: Program Shell1 is the shell of a program that counts all the punctuation marks in a file.

```
// Program Shell1 counts punctuation marks in a file.

#include <iostream>
#include <fstream>
using namespace std;

int main ()
{
    ifstream  inData;
    char symbol;
    int   periodCt = 0;
    int   commaCt = 0;
    int   questionCt = 0;
    int   colonCt = 0;
    int   semicolonCt = 0;
    inData.open("switch.dat");
    /* FILL IN */
    return 0;
}
```

Fill in the missing code and run your program. Show the answers below.

Number of periods:	_____	Number of commas:	_____
Number of question marks:	_____	Number of colons:	_____
Number of semicolons:	_____		

Exercise 4: Add the code necessary for program Shell1 to count blanks as well. How many blanks are there in file switch.dat? If you did not get 12, go back and check your program.

Lesson 9–3: Additional Control Structures

Name _____ Date _____

Section _____

Use program Looping for Exercises 1, 2, and 3. This program reads and sums exactly 10 integers and then reads and sums integers until a negative value is read.

```
// Program Looping uses a count-controlled loop to read and
// sum 10 integer values and an event-controlled loop to
// read and sum values until a negative value is found.
// The data is on file Looping.dat.

#include <iostream>
#include <fstream>
using namespace std;

int main ()
{
    ifstream  inData;
    int   value;
    int   counter;
    int   sum;
    inData.open("Looping.dat");

    counter = 1;
    sum = 0;
    while (counter <= 10)
    {// ten values read and summed
        inData >> value;
        sum = sum + value;
        counter++;
    }
    cout << "The first sum is " << sum << endl;

    inData >> value;
    sum = 0;
    while (value >= 0)
    {// values are read and summed until a negative is read
        sum = sum + value;
        inData >> value;
    }
    cout << "The second sum is " << sum << endl;
    return 0;
}
```

Exercise 1: Compile and run program `Looping`.

First sum is _____.

Second sum is _____.

Exercise 2: Program `Looping` contains two loops implemented with *while* statements. Rewrite program `Looping`, replacing the *while* statements with *do-while* statements.

First sum is _____.

Second sum is _____.

Exercise 3: Can program `Looping` be rewritten using a *for* statement for each loop? Explain.

Rewrite program `Looping` using a *for* statement to implement the count-controlled loop.

First sum is _____.

Second sum is _____.

Exercise 4: Rerun your program using data file `Looping.d2`. Describe what happens.

If an error condition was generated, correct your program and rerun the program.

First sum is _____.

Second sum is _____.

Exercise 5: Yet another version of program `Convert` is shown on the next page. (Remember, this program converts Fahrenheit to Celsius or Celsius to Fahrenheit.)

```
// Program Convert converts a temperature from Fahrenheit to
// Celsius or a temperature from Celsius to Fahrenheit
// depending on whether the user enters an F or a C.
```

```cpp
#include <iostream>

void  PrintMenu();
int  ConvertedTemp(int, char);
using namespace std;

int main ()
{
    char letter;           // Place to store input letter
    int  tempIn;           // Temperature to be converted

    PrintMenu();
    cin  >> letter;

    while (letter != 'Q')
    {
        if (letter == 'R')
           PrintMenu();
        else
        {
            cout  << "Type an integer number "
                  << "and press return."
                  << endl;
            cin  >> tempIn;
            if (letter == 'F')
               cout  << "Fahrenheit to Celsius"  << endl;
            else
                cout  << "Celsius to Fahrenheit"
                      << endl;
            cout  << "Temperature to convert: "
                  << tempIn  << endl;
            cout  << "Converted temperature:  "
                  << ConvertedTemp(tempIn, letter)
                  << endl  << endl;
            cout  << "Type a C, F, R, or Q;"
                  << " press return."
                  << endl;
        }
        cin  >> letter;
    }
     return 0;
}

// ******************************************

int  ConvertedTemp(int tempIn, char letter)
{
    if (letter == 'C')
        return (9 * tempIn / 5) + 32;
    else
            return 5 * (tempIn - 32) / 9;
}
```

```
//***********************************************

void  PrintMenu()
{
    cout  << "Input Menu"  << endl  << endl;
    cout  << "F:  Convert from Fahrenheit to Celsius"
          << endl;
    cout  << "C:  Convert from Celsius to Fahrenheit"
          << endl;
    cout  << "R:  Reprint the menu"  << endl;
    cout  << "Q:  Quit"  << endl;
    cout  << "Type a C, F, R or Q; then press return."
          << endl;
}
```

Rewrite program Convert replacing the *if* statements with *switch* statements. Make your program as robust as possible. (Recall that robust is a descriptive term for a program that can recover from erroneous inputs and keep running.) Run your program using the following input data.

Code	Temperature	Result
C	0	_____
C	57	_____
R		menu printed
F	212	_____
R		menu printed
F	134	_____
Q		run terminated

Exercise 6: There is no error checking in program Convert, and only uppercase letters are accepted. Rewrite the solution to Exercise 5 with the following changes and rerun the program.

- The program accepts both uppercase and lowercase letters.
- If a letter that is not in the set of acceptable letters is entered, print an error message and ask for the letter to be re-entered. (Hint: Use the default case.)

Lesson 9–4: Test Plan

Name _____ Date _____

Section _____

Exercise 1: Design a test plan for program Convert as changed in Lesson 9–3, Exercise 6.

Reason for Test Case	Input Values	Expected Output	Observed Output

Lesson 9–5: Debugging

Name _____ Date _____

Section _____

Exercise 1: Program Bugs is supposed to sum the first ten values on a file and the second ten values on a file. The second ten values are a duplicate of the first ten, so the answers should be the same. The program checks to be sure that the file has been found and halts execution if the file is not found. Program Bugs compiles, says that the file cannot be found, but then the screen freezes. Can you find the problem? Describe it.

Exercise 2: Correct the problem and rerun the program. The file cannot be found, but now the program halts correctly. Correct the name of the file and rerun the program.

Exercise 3: What—the screen freezes again? Back to the drawing board. Describe the next error you find. Correct the program and run it again.

Exercise 4: Now you are getting output, but the answer is wrong for the second sum. When you find this last error, describe it, correct it, and rerun the program. What are the correct totals?

Postlab Activities

Exercise 1: Write a functional design and a program to analyze a sample of text. Count the instances of the following categories of symbols:

- Uppercase letters
- Lowercase letters
- Digits
- End-of-sentence markers (periods, explanation points, and question marks)
- Intrasentence markers (commas, semicolons, and colons)
- Blanks
- All other symbols

Use a *switch* statement in your processing. (If you are not using the ASCII character set, you need to use functions found in <cctype>.)

After collecting these statistics, use them to approximate the following statistics:

- Average word length
- Average sentence length

Exercise 2: Design and implement a test plan for the program in Exercise 1.

Exercise 3: Scoring a tennis game is different from scoring any other game. The following table shows how a tennis game is scored. The score is always given with the server's score first. In this table, Player 1 is the server.

Score	Player 1 Wins Point	Player 2 Wins Point
0/0	15/0	0/15
0/15	15/15	0/30
0/30	15/30	0/40
0/40	15/40	game
15/0	30/0	15/15
15/15	30/15	15/30
15/30	30/30	15/40
15/40	30/40	game
30/0	40/0	30/15
30/15	40/15	30/30
30/30	40/30	30/40
30/40	<u>30/30</u>	game
40/0	game	40/15
40/15	game	40/30
40/30	game	<u>30/30</u>

The two underlined scores (30/30) should actually be 40/40, but in tennis you have to win by 2 points, so 40/40 behaves like 30/30. (See what we mean about being strange?) Write a function that takes two scores and the player who won the point as input and returns the new scores. This function is more complex than any you have done so far. Treat it like a complete program. Begin with a top-down design that outlines your solution. There are 15 possibilities, but some can be combined. You must use at least at least one *switch* statement in your program.

Exercise 4: Write a test plan for the function written for Exercise 3. Implement your test plan.

Simple Data Types: Built-In and User-Defined

- To be able to determine the range of numeric types.

- To be able to work with character data.

- To examine the results of using floating point arithmetic.

- To be able to define and use enumeration data types.

- To be able to distinguish between widening and narrowing in type coercion.

Chapter 10: Assignment Cover Sheet

Name _____ Date _____

Section _____

Fill in the following table showing which exercises have been assigned for each lesson and check what you are to submit: (1) lab sheets, (2) listings of output files, and/or (3) listings of programs. Your instructor or teaching assistant (TA) can use the Completed column for grading purposes.

Activities	Assigned: Check or list exercise numbers	Submit (1) (2) (3)			Completed
Prelab					
Review					
Prelab Assignment					
Inlab					
Lesson 10–1: Check Prelab Exercise					
Lesson 10–2: Numeric Data Types					
Lesson 10–3: Char Data Types					
Lesson 10–4: Enumeration Data Types					
Lesson 10–5: Debugging					
Postlab					

Prelab Activities

Review

Simple Data Types   The built-in, simple data types in C++ are integral types, enumeration types, and floating types. The integral types are `char`, `short`, `int`, `long`, and `bool`. The floating types are `float`, `double`, and `long double`. All of these data types are called *simple* or *atomic* because they are composed of single, indivisible values.

The range of values that can be stored in a simple, integral data type depends on the number of bytes of storage assigned to the data type. C++ provides a unary operator, `sizeof`, that returns the number of bytes in its operand. C++ does not specify the number of bytes for any data type except `char`, which is defined to be one byte but guarantees that the following relationships are true.

```
1= sizeof(char)
<= sizeof(short)
<= sizeof(int)
<= sizeof(long)
```

and

```
1<= sizeof(bool)
<=  sizeof(long)
```

and

```
   sizeof(float)
<= sizeof(double)
<= sizeof(long double)
```

Recall that a data type is made up of a set of values and a set of allowable operations on those values. The operations on numeric data types are the arithmetic operators and the relational operators. The operations on Boolean values are the relational operators and the Boolean operators.

Numeric Constants   C++ allows three types of integral constants: decimal, octal, and hexadecimal. All of the integral constants we have used so far have been decimal. An octal constant begins with an explicit 0 (zero) and contains only the digits 0 through 7. A hexadecimal constant begins with an explicit 0 followed by either *x* or *X* and the digits in the number chosen from the set of digits 0 through 9 and the letters *A* through *F*, which represent the digits 0 through 15. For the rest of this manual, we use only decimal constants. Octal and hexadecimal constants are used in more advanced programming.

Floating point constants are assumed to be of data type `double`. If you want the constant to be of data type `float`? append an *f* or *F* to the end of the number.

Numeric Processing In a previous lesson, you wrote a program to convert temperatures from Fahrenheit to Celsius and from Celsius to Fahrenheit. Because the program uses integer values, some strange results occur. For example, the temperature 6 degrees Celsius is converted to 42 degrees Fahrenheit, but 42 degrees Fahrenheit is converted to 5 degrees Celsius. The temperature 57 degrees Celsius is converted to 134 degrees Fahrenheit, but 134 degrees Fahrenheit is converted to 56 degrees Celsius.

This strange behavior is caused by *truncation error.* The calculation is done using integer arithmetic. The / operator returns an integer quotient, and the remainder is thrown away. If the temperatures are stored in floating point variables, the results are more accurate.

There are also problems associated with floating point arithmetic. For example, we know that 1/3 + 1/3 + 1/3 should sum to 1. This is not true, however, when we are representing 1/3 in a computer. The real number 1/3 is a repeating fraction that never terminates. A repeating fraction represented in a computer, must terminate, leading to inaccuracies. For example, if a particular computer can represent only five decimal places in a real number, look what happens with the following code segment:

```
oneThird = 1.0 / 3.0;
one = oneThird + oneThird + oneThird;
if (one == 1.0);
        .
        .
else
        .
        .
```

Theoretically, the else branch is always taken because the value stored in one is 0.99999. If one is printed, however, it shows 1.0 because the displayed result is rounded, unless the number of decimal places you request in the field specification is the exact number that can be represented in your machine.

Char Constants Although data type char can be used to hold small integer values, its main purpose is to hold character data. Each character in a character set has two representations: an external and an internal. The external representation is what it looks like on an I/O device; the internal representation is the way in which it is encoded in memory. The external representation of the letter *B* is *B*; the internal representation is an integer value. The external representation of any character is the same in all character sets, but the internal representation is not. The internal representation of the letter *B* is 66 in ASCII and 194 in EBCDIC. When you send a variable to the output stream, how does it know whether to send the character or the number? If the variable is of data type char, the external representation is sent (printed). For any other integral type, a number is sent (printed).

There are two types of char constants: printable and nonprintable characters. The printable characters are listed in the text of a program enclosed in single quotes. The nonprintable characters, which are control characters used with hardware devices, are written in the program by their escape sequence. The escape sequence is one or more characters following a backslash (\). The most commonly used escape sequence is '\n' that forces a new line on an output device. In Chapter 6, an example of counting characters in lines of text used the expression (character != '\n') to control a loop. That is, the loop executed as long as the character read was not the newline character '\n'. Note that the escape sequence is enclosed within single quotes, not double quotes, because even though we represent it with two characters, it is actually just a single character.

Char Processing Because data type `char` is considered a numeric data type, we can apply all the numeric operators to values of type `char`. Because we *can* does not mean we *should*. If you are using `char` variables to hold alphanumeric characters, adding two of them doesn't make sense. However, using them in relational expressions does make sense: We are making statements about the relationship between the two characters in terms of their relative positions in the collating sequence of the machine.

Compound conditions involving characters can be a problem depending on the character set of the machine. For example, if you want to test to see if a character is an uppercase letter, the following expression works correctly on an ASCII machine but not on an EBCDIC machine.

```
if (character >= 'A' && character <= 'Z')
```

In ASCII, the letters are sequential, but in EBCDIC there are several gaps between letters that are used to represent nonprintable characters. Therefore, `character` could contain a nonprintable character rather than an uppercase letter and the expression would still return true. To ensure that your programs are portable to any machine, you should use the collection of functions provided in `<cctype>` when working with character data. A few of the most useful functions are listed below:

`isalpha(ch)`	Returns true if `ch` is a letter; false otherwise.
`isdigit(ch)`	Returns true if `ch` is a digit; false otherwise.
`iscntrl(ch)`	Returns true if `ch` is a control character; false otherwise.
`ispunct(ch)`	Returns true if `ch` is a nonblank printable character (i.e., not a letter or a digit); false otherwise.
`toupper(ch)`	Returns `ch` in uppercase regardless of original case.
`tolower(ch)`	Returns `ch` in lowercase regardless of original case.

Enumeration Types An *enumeration type* is a type in which the constant identifiers (called *enumerators)* are explicitly listed.

```
enum Birds {BLUEJAY, CARDINAL, ROBIN, SEAGULL, SWALLOW};
enum LetterGrade {A, B, C, D, F};

Birds   aBird;
LetterGrade  grade;
```

`aBird` can contain any of the enumerators (constants) listed in data type `Birds`. `grade` can contain any of the enumerators listed in data type `LetterGrade`. The enumerators of an enumeration type can be used in a program just like any other constant.

```
aBird = ROBIN;
grade = A;
if (grade == B)
```

Note that `grade` does not contain the character *A*. `grade` contains a value of the data type `LetterGrade`, the enumerator *A*. For obvious reasons, enumeration types are called *user-defined* data types.

Enumerators are ordered by the way in which they are listed. In a relational expression, enumerators are evaluated exactly as characters would be: whether one enumerator come before the other in the ordering of the enumerators.

Stream I/O is not defined for enumeration types. Printing out the values of an enumeration type must be done by converting the value from the enumeration type into a string that corresponds to the enumerator.

```
switch (aBird)
{
    case BLUEJAY : cout << "BlueJay";
                   break;
    case CARDINAL: cout << "Cardinal";
                   break;
    .
    .
    .
}
```

Values of an enumeration type cannot be read; they must be set in the program. However, the name of the enumeration type can be used to convert, or type cast, a number representing the position of an enumerator in the listing of the data type into the enumerator in that position. For example,

```
aBird = Birds(0)
```

stores BLUEJAY into variable aBird because BLUEJAY is in the 0th position of the enumerators. You can use this technique to input values of enumeration types. The user can be given a menu showing the enumerators and asked to key in the number representing the enumerator they wish to input. The number is read and type cast into the enumerator.

If you create an enumeration type that you might want to use again, you can store the definition in a file and use #include to access the file. Rather than putting the file name in angled brackets, you put it in double quotes. This tells the preprocessor to look for the file in your current directory.

More on Type Coercion and Type Conversion   Recall that *type coercion* is the implicit changing of a data type by C++ and *type conversion* is explicit type changing by the programmer. Type coercion occurs whenever values of different data types are used in arithmetic and relational expressions, assignment operations, parameter passing, and as return values from value-returning functions.

In arithmetic and relational expressions, values of char, short, or enum data types are changed to values of type int. If all the data types involved are now type int, the expression is evaluated. If they are not all the same, the "lower" ones are promoted to the "highest" data type in the expression, and the expression is evaluated. The data types are ordered as follows from lowest (int) to highest (long double):

int, unsigned int, long, unsigned long, float, double, long double

Converting one data type to another that is higher is called *promotion* or *widening*. Notice that no information is lost.

When coercion occurs in assignment operations, parameter passing, and returning values from a value-returning function, a value is being stored into a variable. If the data type of the value and the variable are not the same, the value is coerced into the data type of the variable. If the data type of the variable is higher, then no information is lost, but it may be lost if the data type of the variable is lower. For example, if the function type is int and the value returned is float, the value is truncated. Converting a value from a higher to a lower data type is called *demotion* or *narrowing*.

Type coercion is defined from an `enum` type to an `int` type but not the other way around. You must use type conversion (type casting) to change an integer value into an enumerator. Look at the following statement.

```
aBird = Birds(aBird + 1);
```

`aBird` is coerced to `int` and 1 is added. However, the result must be type cast back to the enumeration type to be stored.

Side Effects   C++ supplies a bewildering array of specialized operators that, like the control structures described in the last chapter, are nice to have but not necessary. We do not review them here, but we must take a few moments to review what we have called the basic *assignment operator*, a single equal sign, because all of the assignment operators behave in the same way.

A variable followed by an equal sign followed by an expression forms an *assignment expression*. Assignment expressions do two things: They calculate a value and (as a side effect) they store that value in the place named on the left of the equal sign. An assignment expression becomes an assignment statement when the expression is terminated by a semicolon. Because an assignment expression returns a value, it can be used within another expression. Thus,

```
if (value >= one = one + 1)
```

calculates the value of `one + 1` and compares `value` to the result. As a side effect, variable `one` has the incremented value stored back in it. We mentioned in Chapter 5 that an assignment is actually an expression in the context of explaining what happens when the equal sign is used when the double equal is meant.

We are not advocating that you use assignment expressions embedded within other expressions in your program. Quite the contrary. We just want you to be aware that this type of statement is legal and what it means if you encounter it. Because this feature is so complex, hard to understand, and unnecessary, we do not recommend its use.

Chapter 10: Prelab Assignment

Name _____ Date _____

Section _____

Exercise 1: Program `Gauge` reads `int` values and converts them to the appropriate constant in an enumeration type. The constants in the enumeration type are used as the case labels in a *switch* statement that controls which message is printed.

```cpp
// Program Gauge inputs pressure readings from file Gauge.dat
// and writes appropriate messages.

#include <iostream>
#include <fstream>
using namespace std;

enum  DecisionType {ERROR, NORMAL, HIGH, EVACUATE};

void  GetPressure(ifstream&, DecisionType&);
// Gets variable of DecisionType from a file.

int main ()
{
    ifstream  readings;
    DecisionType  pressure;
    readings.open("gauge.dat");
    do
    {
        GetPressure(readings, pressure);
        switch (pressure)
        {
            case ERROR    : cout  << "Error in input."
                                  << endl;
                            break;
            case NORMAL   : cout  << "Pressure in normal range."
                                  << endl;
                            break;
            case HIGH     : cout  << "Pressure on the high side."
                                  << endl;
                            break;
            case EVACUATE : cout  << "Evacuate plant!!!!"
                                  << endl;
                            break;
        }
    } while (pressure != EVACUATE);
    return 0;
}

/*************************************************************/
```

```
void GetPressure(ifstream& readings, DecisionType& pressure)
// Pre:   File readings has been opened.
// Post: An integer pressure has been read from file readings.
//       pressure is ERROR if a negative pressure was read.
//       pressure is NORMAL if the value was between 0 and 49.
//       pressure is HIGH if the value was between 50 and 99.
//       pressure is EVACUATE if the value was 100 or above.

{
    int  reading;

    readings  >> reading;
    if (reading < 0)
        pressure = ERROR;
    else if (reading < 50)
        pressure = NORMAL;
    else if (reading < 100)
        pressure = HIGH;
    else
        pressure = EVACUATE;
}
```

If file Gauge.dat has the following data values, what is printed?

10 1   49   50   99   -2   120

Lesson 10–1: Check Prelab Exercise

Name _____   Date _____

Section _____

Exercise 1: Run program `Gauge` and check your answer. Was your answer correct? If not, what did you calculate incorrectly?

Lesson 10–2: Numeric Data Types

Name _____ Date _____

Section _____

Exercise 1: Write a program that prints out the followings values:

```
INT_MAX
1 + INT_MAX
1 + (- INT_MAX)
1 - INT_MAX
1 - (- INT_MAX))
```

In order to access INT_MAX, you must include file <climits>. Did you get what you expected? Explain.

Exercise 2: Write a program that prints out the size in bytes of all of the numeric types, both integral and floating. Use the sizeof operator. Show your results.

Exercise 3: Run program `Problems`.

```cpp
// Program Problems demonstrates some problems associated
// with floating point arithmetic.

#include <iostream>
#include <iomanip>
using namespace std;

int main ()
{
    float   oneThird;
    float   one;

    cout  << fixed  << showpoint;

    oneThird = 1.0 / 3.0;
    cout  << " 1/3 "  << setprecision(5)  << setw(7)
          << oneThird  << endl;
    one = oneThird + oneThird + oneThird;
    cout  << " 1/3 + 1/3 + 1/3 "  << setw(7)
          << one  << endl;
    if (one == 1.0)
        cout  << "Result when used in test is 1.0."
              << endl;
    else
        cout  << "Result when used in test is NOT 1.0."
              << endl;
    return 0;
}
```

What was printed? What does this tell you about your C++ system?

Exercise 4: Rewrite program `Problems`, substituting 1.0/10.0 for 1.0/3.0. In decimal arithmetic, 1/10 added to itself 10 times is exactly 1.0. Is this true when calculated on a computer? Run the program and record the results.

Exercise 5: Examine the following program:

```cpp
// Program FactTest is a driver program that tests function
// Factorial.

#include <iostream>
using namespace std;

int  Factorial(int);
// Calculates factorial of an integer.

int main ()

{
    int  number;

    cout  << "Enter a nonnegative integer number. "
          << "Press return."  << endl;
    cin  >> number;
    while (number >= 0)
    {
        cout  << number  << " factorial is "
              << Factorial(number)  << endl;
        cout  << "To continue, enter another nonnegative "
              << "number; to quit, enter a negative number."
              << endl;
        cin  >> number;
    }
    return 0;
}

/**********************************************************/

int  Factorial(int  number)
// Pre: number is positive.
// Post: Return value is the factorial of number, calculated
//       iteratively.
{
    int  tempFact = 1;

    while (number > 1)
    {
        tempFact = tempFact * number;
        number = number - 1;
    }
    return tempFact;
}
```

The factorial of 0 is 1; the factorial of a positive integer is the product of the numbers from 1 up to and including the integer. For example, the factorial of 4 (written 4!) is 1*2*3*4, or 24. Program FactTest is a driver for function Factorial, which computes the factorial of an input value. Compile and run this program using increasing integer values beginning with zero. Record the input values along with the associated factorials until something strange happens.

Value	Factorial	Value	Factorial
_____	_____	_____	_____
_____	_____	_____	_____
_____	_____	_____	_____
_____	_____	_____	_____
_____	_____	_____	_____

Factorials build up very quickly. When the value being calculated gets too large to be stored in a memory location in your particular computer (greater than INT_MAX), overflow occurs. Each system handles it differently. Describe what happens on your system. Relate the results to the answers to Exercise 1.

Exercise 6: Change function Factorial to be of type long and rerun your program. What is the largest factorial that can be computed using type long?

Lesson 10–3: Char Data Types

Name _____ Date _____

Section _____

Exercise 1: Shell1 is the shell of a program designed to read characters and process them in the following way.

lowercase character	converts to uppercase and writes the character
uppercase character	writes the character
digit	writes the digit
blank	writes a blank
newline	writes newline
any other character	does nothing

```
// Program Shell1 reads characters from file DataIn and
// writes them to DataOut with the following changes:
//     All letters are converted to uppercase, digits are
//     unchanged, and all other characters except blanks and
//     newline markers are removed.

#include <iostream>
#include <cctype>
#include <fstream>
using namespace std;

int main ()
{
    ifstream   dataIn;
    ofstream   dataOut;
    char   character;

    dataIn.open("ReFormat.dat");
    dataOut.open("DataOut.dat");

    dataIn.get(character);     // priming read
    while (dataIn)
    {
        /* FILL IN THE Code to output the correct character */
        dataIn.get(character);
    }
    return 0;
}
```

You are to fill in the code to make the required conversions and create the output file. Run your program. List below the last three lines of output written on file DataOut.

Exercise 2: Write a program that prints out all of the characters in the character set that your C++ compiler uses. Describe what happens.

Exercise 3: If you are using a machine that has the ASCII character set, change the program in Exercise 2 to print the characters between ' ' and '~'. Describe what happens. Why are the outputs from Exercises 2 and 3 so different?

Exercise 4: If you are using a machine that has the EBCDIC character set, explain why Exercise 3 is not appropriate for you.

Lesson 10–4: Enumeration Data Types

Name _____ Date _____

Section _____

Exercise 1: Shell2 is the shell of a program that solves the problem in Lesson 10–3, Exercise 1, using an enumeration data type.

```cpp
// Program Shell2 reads characters from file DataIn and
// writes them to DataOut with the following changes:
//     all letters are converted to uppercase, digits are
//     unchanged, and all other characters except blanks and
//     newline markers are removed.

#include <iostream>
#include <cctype>
#include <fstream>
using namespace std;

enum CharType {LO_CASE, UP_CASE, DIGIT, BLANK_NEWLINE, OTHER};

CharType  KindOfChar(char);
// Gets the enumerator equivalent to its character input.

int main ()
{
    ifstream  dataIn;
    ofstream  dataOut;
    char  character;

    dataIn.open("ReFormat.dat");
    dataOut.open("DataOut.dat");

    dataIn.get(character);     // priming read
    while (dataIn)
    {
        switch (KindOfChar(character))
        {

          // FILL IN THE Code to output the correct character

        }
        dataIn.get(character);
    }
    return 0;
}

/**********************************************/
```

```
CharType  KindOfChar(char  character)
// Post: character has been converted to the corresponding
//       constant in the enumeration type CharType.
{
    if (isupper(character))
        return  // TO BE FILLED IN
    else if (islower(character))
        return  // TO BE FILLED IN
    else if (isdigit(character))
        return  // TO BE FILLED IN
    else if (character == ' ' || character == '\n')
        return  // TO BE FILLED IN
    else
        return  // TO BE FILLED IN
}
```

You are to fill in the code of function `KindOfChar` and the *switch* statement in the body of function `main`. Run your program. List below the last three lines of output written on file `DataOut`.

Lesson 10–5: Debugging

Name _____   Date _____

Section _____

Exercise 1: Program `EnumIO` compiles correctly, but the answers are wrong. Read the documentation carefully and correct the program. Describe the error.

Exercise 2: Program `Time` takes an Eastern standard time in hours, minutes, and seconds and prints it out in Eastern time, Central time, Mountain time, or Pacific time. Again, the program compiles, but the answer is wrong. Correct the program. Describe the error. (Hint: This bug is very subtle—you need a good test plan in order to find it.)

Postlab Activities

Exercise 1: Postlab Exercise 1 in Chapter 9 asked you to collect statistics on a sample of text. Rewrite your solution using an enumeration type to represent all of the items that you wish to count.

Exercise 2: Postlab Exercise 2 in Chapter 9 asked you to design and implement a test plan for the program in Exercise 1. Can you use the same test plan for your revised program? Explain.

Exercise 3: Postlab Exercise 3 in Chapter 9 asked you to score a tennis match. Recall that scoring a tennis game is different from scoring any other game. The following table shows how a tennis game is scored. The score is always given with the server's score first. In this table, Player 1 is the server.

Score	Player 1 Wins Point	Player 2 Wins Point
0/0	15/0	0/15
0/15	15/15	0/30
0/30	15/30	0/40
0/40	15/40	game
15/0	30/0	15/15
15/15	30/15	15/30
15/30	30/30	15/40
15/40	30/40	game
30/0	40/0	30/15
30/15	40/15	30/30
30/30	40/30	30/40
30/40	<u>30/30</u>	game
40/0	game	40/15
40/15	game	40/30
40/30	game	<u>30/30</u>

The two underlined scores (30/30) should actually be 40/40, but in tennis you have to win by 2 points, so 40/40 behaves like 30/30. (See what we mean about being strange?)

Write a function that takes two scores and the player who won the point as input and returns the new scores. Rewrite your solution making the players an enumeration type.

Structured Types, Data Abstraction, and Classes

- To be able to define a record data type.

- To be able to declare and use a record variable.

- To be able to declare and use a hierarchical record.

- To be able to declare a class data type.

- To be able to implement class member functions.

- To be able to define and use an instance of a class data type (a class object) in a client program.

- To be able to write class constructors.

Chapter 11: Assignment Cover Sheet

Name _____   Date _____

Section _____

Fill in the following table showing which exercises have been assigned for each lesson and check what you are to submit: (1) lab sheets, (2) listings of output files, and/or (3) listings of programs. Your instructor or teaching assistant (TA) can use the Completed column for grading purposes.

Activities	Assigned: Check or list exercise numbers	Submit (1) (2) (3)			Completed
Prelab					
Review					
Prelab Assignment					
Inlab					
Lesson 11–1: Check Prelab Exercise					
Lesson 11–2: Record Data Type					
Lesson 11–3: Hierarchical Records					
Lesson 11–4: Class Data Type					
Lesson 11–5: Header and Implementation Files					
Lesson 11–6: Class Constructors					
Lesson 11–7: Debugging					
Postlab					

Prelab Activities

Review

In addition to naming places and processes, an identifier can name a *collection of places*. When a collection of places is given a name, it is called a *composite data type* and is characterized by how the individual places within variables of the data type can be accessed. In this chapter, we look at records and classes. In the next chapter we look at arrays.

The *record* is a very versatile data type. It is a collection of components of any data type in which the components are given names. The components of a record are called *fields*. Each field has its own *field identifier* and data type. Hence, a record often contains variables of different types.

Structs

C++ has its own vocabulary in relation to the general concept of a record. Records are called *structures* (abbreviated to `struct`), fields are called *members*, and field identifiers are called *member names*. We use *record* when we are referring to the general concept and `struct` when we are referring to a specific C++ type or variable.

```
enum MediaType  {CD, TAPE, RECORD};

struct  Recording
{
    string    title;
    string    artist;
    MediaType medium;
    float     cost;
    int       quantity;
};

Recording  song;
```

`Recording` is a pattern for a group of five variables. `song` is a `struct` variable with five members: `title`, `artist`, `medium`, `cost`, and `quantity` are the member names. The accessing expression for members of a `struct` variable is the `struct` variable identifier followed by the member name with a period in between. This accessing expression is called the *member selector*.

`song.title` is a string variable.
`song.artist` is a string variable.
`song.medium` is a variable of type `MediaType`.
`song.cost` is a `float` variable.
`song.quantity` is an `int` variable.

The only aggregate operation defined on structures is assignment, but structures may be passed as parameters and they may be the return value type of a function.

Hierarchical Records   A member of a record can be another record. For example, we can define an additional member, date, of type DateType that is a struct containing members month, day, and year.

```
struct  DateType
{
    int   month;
    int   day;
    int   year;
};

struct  Recording
{
    string    title;
    string    artist;
    MediaType medium;
    float     cost;
    int       quantity;
    DateType  date;
};

Recording  song;
```

song.date.month accesses the month member of the date member of song.
song.date.day accesses the day member of the date member of song.

Initialization of Structs   You can initialize records by listing the values for the members. The following definition creates struct variable myFavorite, of type Recording (defined earlier), and initializes the members.

```
Recording  myFavorite =
{
    "La Vie En Rose",
    "Edith Piaf",
    TAPE,
    5.00,
    1,
    {
        10, 11, 1935
    }
};
```

Abstract Data Type   When you combine a variable or a collection of variables with the operations that create and manipulate them, you have an *abstract data type*. An abstract data type, often abbreviated ADT, is more than just a user-defined data type. An ADT has a specified set of properties, and the operations that create and manipulate the ADT must maintain these properties.

The operations for an ADT fall into one of the following four classes:

- *Constructors:* Operations that build or create new instances of an ADT.
- *Transformers:* Operations that build new values of an ADT based on one or more previous values of the ADT.
- *Observers:* Operations that report on the state of an instance of an ADT—for example, operations that tell how many values there are in an instance of an ADT or that tell if the structure is empty or full.
- *Iterators:* Operations that allow us to process all of the components sequentially.

Class Data Type The `class` data type is a C++ language feature that encourages good programming style by allowing the user to encapsulate both data and actions into a single object, making the `class` the ideal structure for representing an abstract data type.[1]

```
class MoneyType
{
public:
    void  Initialize(long, long);
    // Initializes dollars and cents.
    long  DollarsAre() const;
    // Returns dollars.
    long  CentsAre() const;
    // Returns cents.
private:
    long  dollars;
    long  cents;
};
MoneyType money;
```

`MoneyType` is a `class` data type. Like any type, it is a pattern for a structure. This pattern has two data items (member variables): `dollars` and `cents`; and three actions (member functions): `Initialize`, `DollarsAre`, and `CentsAre`. The word `public` means that the members defined in this section are accessible to anyone using the class (defining a variable of the class). The members defined following the word `private` are accessible only to the class's member functions. Member variables and functions defined between `public` and `private` form the interface between the class and its *clients*. A client is any software that declares variables of the class. Notice that member function prototypes, not definitions, are used in the class definition. This interface provides no information on how the member functions are implemented.

`money` is an instance of the `class` data type `MoneyType`; it is called a *class instance* or a *class object*. `money` has two member variables and three member functions. To apply a class instance's member functions, you append the function name to the instance of the data type separated by a period. For example, the following code segment instructs `money` to apply its member functions `Initialize`, `DollarsAre`, and `CentsAre` to itself.

```
money.Initialize(56, 23);
cout  << money.DollarsAre();
cout  << money.CentsAre();
```

---

[1]We put class in monospaced bold when we are referring to the C++ language construct (data type `class`), but leave it in regular type when we are referring to the general concept of an encapsulation of data and actions into one structure.

Member Function Definitions A member function is defined like any function with one exception: The name of the class type within which the member is declared precedes the member function name with a double colon in between (::). The double colon operator is called the *scope resolution operator.*

```
void  MoneyType::Initialize(long newDollars, long newCents)
// Post: dollars is set to newDollars; cents is set to
//       newCents.
{
    dollars = newDollars;
    cents = newCents;
}

long  MoneyType::DollarsAre() const
// Post: Class member dollars is returned.
{
    return dollars;
}

long  MoneyType::CentsAre() const
// Post: Class member cents is returned.
{
    return cents;
}
```

When the statement

```
money.Initialize(56, 23);
```

is executed, 56 is stored in `money.dollars` and 23 is stored in `money.cents`. Because `Initialize` is an action defined within class `MoneyType`, any invocation of `Initialize` is applied to a specific instance of `MoneyType`, in this case the variable `money`. The variable identifiers used in the body of the definition of function `Initialize` refer to those of the instance to which it is applied.

The following statement prints the data fields of `money`.

```
cout << "$"  << money.DollarsAre()
     << "."  << money.CentsAre();
```

Binary Operations When a binary operation is defined within a class type, one of the operands is passed as a parameter and the other is the class instance to which the member function is applied. For example, let's assume that a binary operation, `Add`, has been included as a member function in `MoneyType`. Here is its definition.

```
MoneyType  MoneyType::Add(MoneyType  value)
// Pre: Both operands have been initialized.
// Post: value + self is returned.
{
    MoneyType  result;
    result.cents = cents + value.cents;
    result.dollars = dollars + value.dollars;
    return result;
}
```

Given the following statement,

```
result = money.Add(value);
```

`cents` and `dollars` in the code of member function `Add` refer to those members in the class object to which `Add` has been applied—that is, to `money.cents` and `money.dollars`. The class object to which a member function is applied is often called *self*. Thus we say that `cents` and `dollars` without a variable appended refer to self.

Class Constructors   Because we use classes to encapsulate abstract data types, it is essential that class objects be initialized properly. We defined a member function, `Initialize`, to initialize the values of the member variables. What if the client forgets to apply member function `Initialize`? This can be such a serious problem that C++ provides a mechanism to guarantee that all class instances are properly initialized, called the *class constructor*. A class constructor is a member function with the same name as the class data type.

```
class MoneyType
{
public:
    void     Initialize(long, long);
    long     DollarsAre();
    long     CentsAre();
    MoneyType  Add(MoneyType  value) const;
    MoneyType();                      // class constructor
    MoneyType(long, long);            // class constructor
private:
    long    dollars;
    long    cents;
};

MoneyType   money;
MoneyType   myMoney(5000, 98);
```

There are two constructors: one with no parameters, called the default constructor, and one with two parameters. They look a little strange because there is no type identifier or `void` before them. They are invoked differently as well. A class constructor is invoked when a class instance is declared. In this example, `money` is initialized by the default class constructor (the one with no parameters), and `myMoney` is initialized with 5000 in member `dollars` and 98 in member `cents`. These constructors are defined as follows.

```
MoneyType::MoneyType(long initDollars, long initCents)
{
    dollars = initDollars;
    cents   = initCents;
}

MoneyType::MoneyType()
{
    dollars = 0;
    cents   = 0;
}
```

Notice that the class constructors do not make member function `Initialize` unnecessary. If you want to reinitialize a class object during run time, you must use member function `Initialize`. Class constructors are invoked implicitly when a class object is declared.

Packaging   Because classes are used to encapsulate abstract data types and because the separation of the logical properties of an ADT from the implementation details is so important, you should package the class declaration and the implementation of the member functions in different files. The class declaration should be in a file with a "`.h`" extension (called the specification file), and the implementation should be in a file with the same name but with a "`.cpp`" extension (called the implementation file). The implementation file must use the #`include` directive to access the specification file. Any client program must use the #`include` directive for the specification file (`.h` extension) to include your files in their source code.

Class Scope   In Chapter 8 we said there were four kinds of scope: local scope, namespace scope, global scope, and class scope. We defined the first three, but left the definition of class scope to this chapter. Class scope means that a member name is bound to the class or struct in which it is defined. That is, member names are not known outside of the struct or class in which they are defined.

Chapter 11: Prelab Assignment

Name _____ Date _____

Section _____

Read program `Cars` carefully.

```cpp
// Program Cars reads a record from a file and writes
// its contents back to another file with the price member
// increased by 10%.
#include <iostream>
#include <fstream>
#include <string>
using namespace std;

struct  DateType
{
    int  month;
    int  day;
    int  year;
};

struct  CarType
{
    float price;
    DateType purchased;
    string customer;
};

void  GetCar(ifstream&, CarType&);
// Reads a variable of CarType from a file.

void  WriteCar(ofstream&, CarType);
// Writes a variable of CarType on a file.

int main ()
{
    CarType  car;
    ifstream dataIn;
    ofstream dataOut;

    dataIn.open("cars.dat");
    dataOut.open("cars.out");
    cout  << fixed  << showpoint;

    GetCar(dataIn, car);
    while (dataIn)
    {
        car.price = car.price * 1.10;
        WriteCar(dataOut, car);
        GetCar(dataIn, car);
    }
```

```
        return 0;
}


//*****************************************************


void  GetCar(ifstream&  dataIn, CarType&  car)
// Pre: File dataIn has been opened.
// Post: The fields of car are read from file dataIn.
{
    dataIn >> car.customer;
    dataIn >> car.price  >> car.purchased.day
          >> car.purchased.month  >> car.purchased.year;
    dataIn.ignore(2, '\n');
}


//*****************************************************


void  WriteCar(ofstream&  dataOut, CarType  car)
// Pre: File dataOut has been opened.
// Post: The fields of car are written on file dataOut,
//       appropriately labeled.
{
    dataOut  << "Customer: "  << car.customer  << endl
            << "Price:    "  << car.price  << endl
            << "Purchased:"  << car.purchased.day  << "/"
            << car.purchased.month  << "/"
            << car.purchased.year  << endl;
}
```

Exercise 1: If file `Cars.dat` is as follows, what is written on file `Cars.out`?

```
TinyTim           55000   1 1 1985
MaryMurphay       12500   2 7 1995
BearBare          44444   9 6 1990
SallySale          7500   6 3 1970
BettyBye          18888   4 8 1988
AliceAlas         23005   6 6 1992
```

Use program `Money` **for Exercises 2, 3, 4, and 5.**

```
// Program Money manipulates instances of class MoneyType.

#include <iostream>
using namespace std;

class MoneyType
{
public:
    void  Initialize(long, long);
    long  DollarsAre() const;
    long  CentsAre() const;
    MoneyType  Add(MoneyType) const;
private:
    long  dollars;
    long  cents;
};
```

```
//***********************************************************

int main ()
{
    MoneyType  money1;
    MoneyType  money2;
    MoneyType  money3;
    money1.Initialize(10, 59);
    money2.Initialize(20, 70);
    money3 = money1.Add(money2);
    cout << "$"  << money3.DollarsAre() << "."
         << money3.CentsAre()  << endl;
    return 0;
}

//***********************************************************

void  MoneyType::Initialize(long newDollars, long newCents)
// Post: dollars is set to newDollars; cents is set to
//       newCents.
{
    dollars = newDollars;
    cents = newCents;
}

//***********************************************************

long  MoneyType::DollarsAre() const
// Post: Class member dollars is returned.
{
    return dollars;
}

//***********************************************************

long  MoneyType::CentsAre() const
// Post: Class member cents is returned.
{
    return cents;
}

//***********************************************************

MoneyType MoneyType::Add(MoneyType  value) const
// Pre: Both operands have been initialized.
// Post: value + self is returned.
{
    MoneyType  result;
    result.cents = cents + value.cents;
    result.dollars = dollars + value.dollars;
    return result;
}
```

Exercise 2: What is printed by program Money?

Exercise 3: Why does member function Add have only one parameter?

Exercise 4: The declaration and definition of class MoneyType are included in program Money. Circle and label the part of the program that should be in file money.h (the specification file), circle and label the part that should be in file money.cpp (the implementation file), and label the parts that should be in the client program Money.

Exercise 5: What is missing from the definition of class MoneyType?

Lesson 11–1: Check Prelab Exercise

Name _____ Date _____

Section _____

Exercise 1: Run program `Cars` to check your answers. Were they correct? If not, describe your error.

Exercise 2: Run program `Money` to check your answer to Exercise 2. Was your answer correct? If not, do you understand where you made your mistake?

Exercise 3: The second parameter for the `Add` operation is the object to which the member function is being applied. It is often referred to as "self"–in this example, `money1`.

Exercise 4: Program `Money` on the disk is documented to show what should be in the `money.h` file, what should be in the `money.cpp` file, and what is the client code.

Exercise 5: No constructors have been supplied with class `MoneyType`.

Lesson 11–2: Record Data Type

Name _____ Date _____

Section _____

Exercises 1, 2, and 3 use the declarations in file `Shell.cpp`.

`DistanceType` is defined as a record type with three fields: `feet`, `yards`, and `miles`. The following four operations (functions) are defined on variables of `DistanceType`:

- `AddDistance`: Adds two variables of type `DistanceType` and leaves the result in a third variable of type `DistanceType`. For example, 2 feet, 1750 yards, 2 miles + 2 feet, 10 yards, 0 miles = 1 foot, 1 yard, 3 miles.
- `ConvertFeet`: Converts feet into a variable of type `DistanceType`. For example, 6002 feet is converted to 2 feet, 240 yards, 1 mile.
- `ConvertYards`: Converts yards into a variable of type `DistanceType`. For example, 5230 yards is converted to 0 feet, 1710 yards, 2 miles.
- `PrintDistance`: Prints a variable of type `DistanceType`.

```cpp
const int FEET_IN_YARDS = 3;
const int YARDS_IN_MILES = 1760;

struct  DistanceType
{
    long   feet;
    long   yards;
    long   miles;
};

DistanceType  AddDistance(DistanceType, DistanceType);
DistanceType  ConvertYards(long);
DistanceType  ConvertFeet(long);
void  PrintDistance(DistanceType);

//********   DistanceType Operations *******************

DistanceType  AddDistance
    (DistanceType  distance1, DistanceType  distance2)
// Pre: distance1 and distance2 contain valid data.
// Post: Returns distance1 + distance2.
{
    // FILL IN Code to add two variables of DistanceType.
}

//********************************************************
```

```
DistanceType  ConvertYards(long  yards)
// Post: yards has been converted into a variable of
//         DistanceType.
{
    // FILL IN Code to convert yards to a variable of
    // DistanceType.
}
//********************************************************

DistanceType  ConvertFeet(long  feet)
// Post: feet has been converted into a variable of
//         DistanceType.
{
    // FILL IN Code to convert feet to a variable of
    // DistanceType.
}

//********************************************************

void  PrintDistance(DistanceType  Distance)
// Post: A vriable of DistanceType is printed as feet,
//         yards, and miles.
{
    // FILL IN Code to print a variable of DistanceType.
}
```

Exercise 1: Fill in the missing code in these operations.

Exercise 2: Write a driver (function `main`) that tests the operations with the data used in the description of the operations. Describe any bugs in your implementation and correct them.

Exercise 3: Write a function that takes a variable of type `DistanceType` and a time (in minutes) and calculates miles per hour. Convert the variable of type `DistanceType` to `miles` (a `float` variable) before performing the calculation. The result should be a `float` value representing miles per hour rather than a value of `DistanceType`. Your function heading should be as shown below.

```
float  MilesPerHour
          (DistanceType  distance,    // distance traveled
           long  time)                // time in minutes
```

Use your function to calculate miles per hour where the distance is (15,000 feet + 12,000 yards + 37 miles) and the time is 45 minutes.

Miles Per Hour Traveled ___62,2121___ .

0 feet ; 1160 yrds ; 46 mi

Lesson 11–3: Hierarchical Records

Name _____ Date _____

Section _____

This lesson works with program `Cars` defined in the Prelab assignment.

Exercise 1: Augment `CarType` in program `Cars` with the following two members:

`sold`   a Boolean variable
`soldDate`   if (`sold`), then `soldDate` contains the date of sale;
            otherwise `soldDate` is undefined.

Function `GetCar` should initialize `sold` to `false`. Write a function, `CarSold`, that takes variables of `DateType` and `CarType` and records that the car has been sold and the date. Before invoking `WriteCar`, write the car owner's name on the screen and ask if it has been resold. If it has, call function `CarSold` and then write the car to file `dataSold` rather than file `dataOut`. Run your program using file `cars.dat`. Let Betty's and Alice's cars be resold.

Exercise 2: Rewrite `CarType` so that `soldDate` and the new owner's name are encapsulated into a `struct` member `soldTo`. If the car has been resold, prompt for and read the new owner's name. Run your program again using `cars.dat`. Let Betty's car be sold to John and Alice's car be sold to Cliff.

Lesson 11–4: Class Data Type

Name _____ Date _____

Section _____

Exercise 1: Add a member function, `Normalize`, to class `MoneyType` that normalizes the cents to between 0 and 99 and adjusts the dollar amount accordingly. Apply function `Normalize` to `money3` before printing it. Run the revised program `Money`. What is printed?

Exercises 2, 3, and 4 use the declarations and definitions in file `Shell2`.

`DistanceType` is defined as a class with three data members: `feet`, `yards`, and `miles`.

Eight member functions are defined within class `DistanceType`:

- `FeetAre`: Returns the `feet` data member.
- `YardsAre`: Returns the `yards` data member.
- `MilesAre`: Returns the `miles` data member.
- `AddDistance`: Returns the result of adding two variables of type `DistanceType`. For example, 2 feet, 1,750 yards, 2 miles + 2 feet, 10 yards, 0 miles = 1 foot, 1 yard, 3 miles.
- `ConvertFeet`: Returns the result of converting feet into a variable of type `DistanceType`. For example, 6002 feet is converted to 2 feet, 240 yards, 1 mile. Returns a variable of `DistanceType`.
- `ConvertYards`: Returns the result of converting yards into a variable of type `DistanceType`. For example, 5230 yards is converted to 0 feet, 1710 yards, 2 miles.
- `PrintDistance`: Prints a variable of type `DistanceType`.
- `Initialize`: Initializes feet, yards, and miles to its parameters.

```
// File Shell2

const int FEET_IN_YARDS = 3;
const int YARDS_IN_MILES = 1760;

class DistanceType
{

    // TO BE FILLED IN.

}

//*********** Member functions for DistanceType ********

long  DistanceType::FeetAre() const
// Post: Member feet is returned.
{
    // TO BE FILLED IN.
}
```

```
long  DistanceType::YardsAre() const
// Post: Member yards is returned.
{
   // TO BE FILLED IN.
}

long  DistanceType::MilesAre()
// Post: Member miles is returned.
{
    // TO BE FILLED IN.
}

DistanceType  DistanceType::AddDistance
    (DistanceType  distance1) const
// Post: Result of adding two instances of DistanceType
//       is returned.
{
    // FILL IN Code to add two variables of DistanceType.

}

DistanceType  DistanceType::ConvertYards (int  conYards)
// Post: Yards has been converted into a distance in feet,
//       yards, and miles.
{
    // FILL IN Code to convert from yards to variable
    // of type DistanceType.

}

DistanceType  DistanceType::ConvertFeet (int  conFeet)
// Post: feet has been converted into a distance in feet,
//       yards, and miles.
{
    // FILL IN Code to convert from feet to variable
    // of type DistanceType.

}

void  DistanceType::PrintDistance()
// Post: Distance has been printed on the screen as feet,
//       yards, and miles.

{

    // FILL IN Code to print a variable of DistanceType.

}
```

Exercise 2: Fill in the missing code in these operations.

Exercise 3: Write a driver that tests the operations with the data used in the description of the operations. Describe any bugs in your implementation and correct them.

Exercise 4: Add a member function that takes a time (in minutes) as a parameter and calculates miles per hour. Convert the variable of type `DistanceType` to `miles` (a `float` variable) before performing the calculation. The result should be a `float` value representing miles per hour rather than a value of `DistanceType`. Your function heading should be as shown below.

```
float  MilesPerHour(long  time) const; // time in minutes
```

Use your function to calculate miles per hour where the distance is (15,000 feet + 12,000 yards + 37 miles) and the time is 45 minutes.

Miles Per Hour Traveled _____.

Exercise 5: Write a paragraph comparing and contrasting the implementation of `DistanceType` as a `struct` and as a `class`. Which do you think is more appropriate? Justify your answer.

Lesson 11–5: Header and Implementation Files

Name _____ Date _____

Section _____

Exercise 1: Take program Money and reorganize it into three files: money.h, money.cpp, and UseMoney.cpp. UseMoney.cpp is the client program that uses class MoneyType. Run program UseMoney. The results should be the same.

Exercise 2: Exercises 2 and 3 use the following FracType.h and FracType.cpp.

```cpp
// Header file FracType.h declares class FracType.

class FracType
{
public:
    FracType  Add(FracType  frac1) const;
    // Pre: frac1 and self have been initialized.
    // Post: self + frac1 is returned.

    FracType  Sub(FracType  frac1) const;
    // Pre: frac1 and self have been initialized.
    // Post: self - frac1 is returned.

    FracType  Mult(FracType  frac1) const;
    // Pre: frac1 and self have been initialized.
    // Post: self * frac1 is returned.

    FracType  Div(FracType  frac1) const;
    // Pre: frac1 and self have been initialized.
    // Post: self / frac1 is returned.

    int  NumIs() const;
    // Pre: self has been initialized.
    // Post: Numerator of frac1 is returned.

    int  DenomIs() const;
    // Pre: self has been initialized.
    // Post: Denominator of frac1 is returned.

    void  Set(int  num, int  denom);
    // Post: self has been set to num / denom.

    void  Set(int  num, int  denom);
    // Post: self has been set to num / denom.

private:
    int  numerator;
    int  denominator;
};
```

```cpp
// Implementation file FracType.cpp implements the member
// functions of class FracType.

#include "FracType.h"

FracType  FracType::Add(FracType  frac1) const
// Pre: frac1 and self have been initialized.
// Post: frac1 + self is returned in reduced form.
{
    // FILL IN Code.
}


FracType  FracType::Sub(FracType  frac1) const
// Pre: frac1 and self have been initialized.
// Post: self - frac1 is returned in reduced form.are
{
    // FILL IN Code.
}


FracType  FracType::Mult(FracType  frac1) const
// Pre: frac1 and self have been initialized.
// Post: frac1 * self is returned in reduced form.
{
    // FILL IN Code.
}


FracType  FracType::Div(FracType  frac1) const
// Pre: frac1 and self have been initialized.
// Post: frac1 is inverted and Mult is called.
{
    // FILL IN Code.
}

int  FracType::NumIs() const
// Pre: self has been initialized.
// Post: numerator member of self is returned.
{
    // FILL IN Code.
}


int  FracType::DenomIs() const
// Pre: self has been initialized.
// Post: denominator member of self is returned.
{
    // FILL IN Code.
}

void  Set(int  num, int  denom);
// Post: numerator has been set to num;
//       denominator has been set to denom.
{
    // FILL IN Code.
}
```

Exercise 2: Read the documentation of the header file and the implementation file carefully. Compare the documentation in the two files. How are they alike? How are they different?

Exercise 3: Fill in the missing code in the implementation file, and compile `FracType.cpp`. Were there many bugs in your file? Describe any problems that you had.

Exercise 4: Write a driver that uses class `FracType` to do the following calculations:

```
1/2 + 1/4
1/2 - 1/4
1/2 * 1/2
1/2 / 1/2
```

Write the output clearly labeled.

Lesson 11–6: Class Constructors

Name _____ Date _____

Section _____

Exercise 1: Add class constructors to `class MoneyType`. One should have parameters, and one should be parameterless setting `dollars` and `cents` to zero. Initialize `money1` and `money2` using the parameterized class constructor. Initialize `money3` using the default constructor. Write out the value of `money3` before the call to member function `Add`. Show your results.

Exercise 2: Add class constructors to class `DistanceType`. Describe your constructors. Run a test case and show the results.

Exercise 3: Add class constructors to class `FracType`. Describe your constructors. Run a test case and show the results.

Exercise 4: We have chosen to make the writing of class constructors a separate activity to emphasize its importance. From now on, you should always include class constructors in every class that you define. Explain why.

Lesson 11–7: Debugging

Name _____ Date _____

Section _____

Exercise 1: Program Mystery (file Mys.cpp) is a version of one of the programs that you have been working with in this lesson. Unfortunately, it is buggy. Debug and run the program. Describe the bugs you found.

Exercise 2: MysteryType is an alias for which type?

Postlab Activities

Exercise 1: You have an extensive music collection. You decide to write a program to create a file containing information on each individual recording. Use the `Recording` data type described in the Review. Write an interactive program that prompts the user to enter the data for each recording. Run your program entering at least five recordings.

Exercise 2: Add error checking to your program (if you did not include it originally) from Exercise 1. After an entry has been entered, print it back to the screen and ask the user if the entry should be saved or discarded.

Exercise 3: Write a program that takes the data file created in Exercise 1 and calculates the value of your record collection.

Exercise 4: Write a test plan for class `FracType`.

Exercise 5: Write a command-driven driver to implement the test plan written for Exercise 4. A command-driven program is one in which the user enters the operation to be tested followed by the values to use in the test. For example, to test if the `Add` member function correctly adds 1/2 and 3/4, the user might input

+ 1 2 3 4

The operation is invoked with the appropriate data, and the result is written on the screen. The user is prompted to enter another operation or quit.

Exercise 6: Generating test data is a time-consuming process, as you probably noticed. Write a program that uses a random number generator to generate a file of integers. The program should be interactive. The user enters the number of integers to generate, the range of the numbers, and the file to which they should be written. `int` function `rand` returns a random integer ranging from zero up to RAND_MAX. `rand` should be initialized by a call to `srand(seed)` where `seed` is a nonnegative integer. `rand`, `srand`, and RAND_MAX are available in `<cstdlib>`.

Arrays

Objectives

- To be able to define a one-dimensional array data type with integer indexes.

- To be able to declare a one-dimensional array variable with integer indexes.

- To be able to use a one-dimensional array variable with integer indexes.

- To be able to define a one-dimensional array data type with enumeration indexes.

- To be able to declare a one-dimensional array variable with enumeration indexes.

- To be able to use a one-dimensional array variable with enumeration indexes.

- To be able to pass arrays as parameters.

- To be able to apply subarray processing.

- To be able to use an array where the indexes have semantic content.

- To be able to define a two-dimensional array data type.

- To be able to read, store, and print values in a two-dimensional array variable.

- To be able to find the minimum value and the maximum value in a two-dimensional array variable.

- To be able to sum the individual rows of a two-dimensional array variable.

Chapter 12: Assignment Cover Sheet

Name _Shang-Yeu Chang_   Date _5-17-04_

Section _____

Fill in the following table showing which exercises have been assigned for each lesson and check what you are to submit: (1) lab sheets, (2) listings of output files, and/or (3) listings of programs. Your instructor or teaching assistant (TA) can use the Completed column for grading purposes.

Activities	Assigned: Check or list exercise numbers	Submit (1) (2) (3)			Completed
Prelab					
Review					
Prelab Assignment					
Inlab					
Lesson 12–1: Check Prelab Exercises					
Lesson 12–2: One-Dimensional Array Data Types with Integer Indexes					
Lesson 12–3: One-Dimensional Array Data Types with Enumeration Indexes					
Lesson 12–4: Two-Dimensional Arrays					
Lesson 12–5: Multidimensional Arrays					
Lesson 12–6: Debugging					
Postlab					

Prelab Activities

Review

In the last chapter we examined two heterogeneous data types, the record and the class. In this Chapter we introduce the array, a homogenous data type where each element in the structure must be of the same data type.

One-Dimensional Array Data Type   A *one-dimensional array* is a structured data type in which a collection of places is given a name and the individual places are accessed by their position within the collection. There are two types associated with the array data type: the type of the items to be stored in the individual places in the structure and the type of the index used to specify the individual places within the structure. In C++, the type of the index must be an integral type.

```
const int MAX_ITEMS = 100;

int  dataValues[MAX_ITEMS];
int  index;
```

dataValues is an array variable that contains 100 int variables. Giving the name of the array variable followed by its position (index) accesses an individual int variable within the array. For example, dataValues[0] accesses the first variable in the collection; dataValues[1] accesses the second variable in the collection; and dataValues[MAX_ITEMS-1] accesses the last variable in the collection. Notice that the items in the collection are indexed from zero through the number in the collection minus one. The following code segment would set all of the variables in the array variable dataValues to zero.

```
for (index = 0; index < MAX_ITEMS; index++)
    dataValues[index] = 0;
```

The index type can be any integral type. For example, we can define an array where the indexes are of an enumeration type Birds and the contents of the array are of type int.

```
const int MAX_BIRDS = 5;
enum  Birds {BLUEJAY, CARDINAL, ROBIN, SEAGULL, SWALLOW};

int  birdsSighted[MAX_BIRDS];
Birds  aBird;
int  index;
```

The following code segment sets all places in the array to zero.

```
for (aBird=BLUEJAY; aBird<=SWALLOW; aBird = Birds(aBird + 1))
    birdsSighted[aBird] =  0;
```

If the individual `int` values have all been set to zero, the following code segment reads and counts different types of birds until `cin` goes into the fail state (no more data).

```
cout  << "Enter a number between 0 and 4 representing a bird."
      << endl;
cin  >> index;
while (cin)
{
    aBird = Birds(index);
    birdsSighted[aBird] = birdsSighted[aBird] + 1;
    cout  << "Enter a number between 0 and 4"
          << " representing a bird."
          << endl;
    cin  >> index;
}
```

Notice that we read the value entered in the input stream as an `int` value and used the name of the enumeration type to convert it to an enumerator in that type. What would happen if the person at the keyboard accidentally keyed in the number 5? Unfortunately, the contents of what would be `birdsSighted[5]` (if it existed) probably would be accessed and incremented. The address of the first element in an array is called the *base address* of the array. To access a place in an array, the compiler generates the code to add the value of the index to the base address. If this calculation gives an out-of-bounds array index, the program does not notice and continues as if the reference were correct.

This type of error is hard to detect because it usually surfaces later in the program when a variable unrelated to an array reference has a wrong value. The moral here is to be very careful with array indexing expressions. The type of an index may be any integral type, but its value at run time must be between zero and the number of elements in the array minus one. If the index type is an enumeration type, the value must be a legitimate enumerator of the type.

There are no aggregate operations defined on arrays, but any operation that is defined on the component data type may be applied to items stored in an array.

Arrays as Parameters Simple variables can be passed by value or by reference. Arrays are *always* passed by reference, so the ampersand indicating pass-by-reference is never used. The programmer passes the base address and the number of elements to the function. Let's define a void function, `PrintBirds`, which takes array variable `birdsSighted` and prints out the number of each type sighted.

```
void PrintBirds(/* in */ int  birdsSighted[],
                /* in */ int  numOfTypes)
{
    int  i;

    for (i = 0; i < numOfTypes; i++)

        switch (Birds(i))
        {
            case BLUEJAY : cout << "Bluejays seen: "
                                << birdsSighted[BLUEJAY]  << endl;
                           break;
```

```
        case CARDINAL: cout << "Cardinals seen: "
                            << birdsSighted[CARDINAL]  << endl;
                            break;

                .
                .
                .

        }
}
```

The call to function `PrintBirds` would be

```
PrintBirds(birdsSighted, MAX_BIRDS);
```

The brackets on the parameter list alert the compiler that the argument in that slot is to be the base address of an array variable. The processing within function `PrintBirds` uses the second parameter to determine how many items in the array are to be processed. It is up to the caller of the function to be sure that the parameters and arguments are consistent—that is, that argument for `numOfTypes` is the number of items in the argument for `birdsSighted`.

For simple variables, we use value parameters when the argument is not to be changed. How can we protect incoming-only arrays from inadvertent changes if they are always reference parameters? If we insert the word `const` before the data type on the formal parameter list, the compiler does not let the code of the function change the array parameter.

```
void PrintBirds(/* in */ const int birdsSighted[],
                /* in */ int numOfTypes)
```

Because the processing is controlled by the second parameter, it can be the size of the array if all the elements are used or the number of data values that are actually stored if fewer values are stored than the size calls for. The latter type of processing is called *subarray* processing.

Initialization of Arrays   Just as we can initialize values within the definition of a simple variable, we can initialize array variables. The following declarations initialize each item in the array `birdsSighted` to zero.

```
const int MAX_BIRDS = 5;
enum  Birds {BLUEJAY, CARDINAL, ROBIN, SEAGULL, SWALLOW};

int  birdsSighted[MAX_BIRDS] = {0, 0, 0, 0, 0};
```

If this declaration is within a function other than `main`, `birdsSighted` is initialized each time the function is called. If `birdsSighted` is declared within a function and has the reserved word `static` before the `int`, it is initialized only once.

Two-dimensional Array Data Type   A *two-dimensional array* is a collection of components of the same type that is structured in two dimensions. Individual components are accessed by their position within each dimension. Three types are associated with a two-dimensional array data type: the type of the items to be stored in the individual places in the structure, the type of the index for the first dimension, and the type of the index for the second dimension. In C++ the type of both indexes must be integral.

```
const int MAX_ROWS = 10;
const int MAX_COLUMNS = 5;

float   twoDimAry[MAX_ROWS][MAX_COLUMNS];
```

twoDimAry is an array variable that has 10 rows and 5 columns. Each row and column entry is of type float. The following code fragment sets all the entries in twoDimAry to zero.

```
for (int column = 0; column < MAX_COLUMNS; column++)
    for(int row = 0; row < MAX_ROWS; row++)
        twoDimAry[row][column] = 0.0;
```

Two-dimensional Array Processing   The number of rows and columns in the two-dimensional array variable is fixed at compile time. The number of rows and columns that contain valid data items can vary as the program executes. Therefore, each dimension should have a parameter associated with it that contains the number of rows or columns actually used.

Processing a two-dimensional array variable requires two loops: one for the rows and one for the columns. If the outer loop is the index for the column, the array is processed by column. If the outer loop is the index for the row, the array is processed by row. The preceding loop processes twoDimAry by columns.

Multidimensional Arrays   You have seen one-dimensional and two-dimensional arrays. In C++, arrays may have any number of dimensions. To process every item in a one-dimensional array, you need one loop. To process every item in a two-dimensional array, you need two nested loops. The pattern continues to any number of dimensions. To process every item in an *n*-dimensional array, you need *n* nested loops.

Passing Arrays as Parameters   In the section on one-dimensional arrays, we said that the programmer passes the base address of an array and the number of elements in the array as parameters. The function does not need to know the actual size of the array. For arrays of more than one dimension, the function must know the sizes of all of the dimensions except the first. For example, if a function is defined to set the first num values of each row in twoDimAry to a specific value, the prototype might look like this:

```
void SetSomeVals(/* out */ ItemType twoDimAry[][MAX_COLUMNS],
                 /* in */   int rowsUsed,
                 /* in */   int num,
                 /* in */   ItemType initialValue);
```

Any argument must have exactly the same number of elements specified for the second dimension. If it does not, the program continues but does not initialize the correct locations. It is safer to define a type using a *typedef* statement, put the type name on the formal parameter list, and define the actual array to be of that type. Here is an example of how this could be done.

```
const int MAX_ROWS = 10;
const int MAX_COLUMNS = 5;
typedef char ItemType;

typedef char TwoDType[MAX_ROWS][MAX_COLUMNS];

void SetSomeVals(/* out */ TwoDType twoDimAry,
                 /* in */   int rowsUsed,
                 /* in */   int num,
                 /* in */   ItemType initialValue);
```

Any array to be passed to SetSomeVals should be defined to be of type TwoDType. Although this example is of a two-dimensional array, this pattern of defining a type and using the type name can be used for arrays of any number of dimensions.

Chapter 12: Prelab Assignment

Name _Shang-Yeu Chang_   Date _5-17-04_

Section _____

Exercise 1: Read program `Arrays` carefully.

```
// Program Arrays manipulates values in an array.

#include <iostream>
using namespace std;

int main ()
{
    const int MAX_ARRAY = 5;
    int   numbers[MAX_ARRAY];
    int   index;
    int   sum;

    // Stored values in the array.
    for (index = 0; index < MAX_ARRAY; index++)
        numbers[index] = index * index;

    // The values in the array are summed.
    sum = 0;
    for (index = 0; index < MAX_ARRAY; index++)
        sum = sum + numbers[index];
    cout << "Sum is "  << sum  << endl;
    return 0;
}
```

Describe what is written on the screen.

Exercise 2: What would happen if the *for* loop headings were changed as follows?

```
for (index = 0; index <= MAX_ARRAY; index++)
```

Exercise 3: What does the following code segment print if `MAX_ROWS` is 10 and `MAX_COLS` is 10? Fill in the table shown below the code.

```
rowsUsed = 5;
colsUsed = 5;
int   row;
int   column;

char   items[MAX_ROWS][MAX_COLS];

for (column = 0; column < MAX_COLS; column++)
    for (row = 0; row < MAX_ROWS; row++)
        items[row][column] = '*';

for (row = 0; rowsUsed; row < MAX_ROWS; row++)
    for (column = colsUsed; column < MAX_COLS; column++)
        items[row][column] = '+';

for (column = 0; column < colsUsed; column++)
    for (row = 0; row < rowsUsed; row++)
        items[row][column] = '-';
```

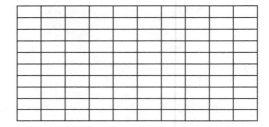

Exercise 4: Is the first nested *for* loop in Prelab Exercise 1 processing the chart by row or by column?

Is the second nested *for* loop processing the chart by row or by column?

Is the third nested *for* loop processing the chart by row or by column?

Lesson 12–1: Check Prelab Exercises

Name _____ Date _____

Section _____

Exercise 1: Run program `Arrays` to check your answer. Was your answer correct? If not, do you understand what you did wrong?

Exercise 2: C++ doesn't define what happens if you store more values than there are places in the array. Each system handles this differently. For example, on one system, the program may work correctly while on another system the program may crash. The moral is: Don't do it.

Exercise 3: Run program `Charts` to see the output. Was your diagram correct? If not, do you understand what you did wrong?

Exercise 4: The first loop is processing by column; the second by row; the third by column.

Lesson 12–2: One-Dimensional Array Data Types with Integer Indexes

Name _____ Date _____

Section _____

This lesson uses the following program shell.

```cpp
// Program Reverse reads numbers into an array
// and prints them out in reverse order.

#include <iostream>
#include <fstream>
using namespace std;

const int MAX = 10;

int main ()
{
    int   numbers[MAX];
    ifstream  inData;
    int   value;
    int   index;

    inData.open("reverse.dat");
    for (index = 0; index < MAX; index++)
    {
        // FILL IN Code to read value
        // FILL IN Code to store value into numbers
    }

    for (index = MAX - 1; index >= 0; index--)
        // FILL IN Code to write numbers on the screen
    return 0;
}
```

Exercise 1: Complete the missing code in program Reverse and run it. What is printed on the screen?

Exercise 2: Exercise 1 asked you to fill in the body of the first *for* loop with two statements. Replace these two statements with a single statement and rerun your program; your answer should be the same. If it is not, correct your code and rerun the program. Describe any problems that you had.

Exercise 3: Extend the program in Exercise 2 to print the sum of the values stored in numbers. What is the sum?

Lesson 12–3: One-Dimensional Array Data Types with Enumeration Indexes

Name _____   Date _____

Section _____

This lesson uses program `Favorit`.

```cpp
// Program Favorit determines the favorite soft drink.
#include <iostream>
using namespace std;

enum  DrinksType {COKE, PEPSI, SPRITE, DR_PEPPER};
void Prompt();

int main ()
{
    int   sums[4];
    int   number;
    DrinksType  index;

    for (index = COKE; index <= DR_PEPPER; index =  DrinksType(index+1))
      // FILL IN Code to set sums to zero

    Prompt();
    cin >> number;
    while (number != 4)
    {
        // FILL IN Code to increment the proper drink
      Prompt();
      cin >> number;
    }

    // FILL IN THE Code to write out the totals
    return 0;
}

/********************************************************/

void Prompt()
{
    cout  << "Enter a 0 if your favorite is a Coke."  << endl;
    cout  << "Enter a 1 if your favorite is a Pepsi." << endl;
    cout  << "Enter a 2 if your favorite is a Sprite."
          << endl;
    cout  << "Enter a 3 if your favorite is a DrPepper."
          << endl;
    cout  <<"Enter a 4 if you wish to quit the survey."
          << endl;
}
```

Exercise 1: Complete program `Favorit` and run it. What data did you use? What did the program write?

Exercise 2: Add a function to program `Favorit` that sums the number of responses to the survey. Pass the array `sums` as a parameter. Print the number of responses on the screen. Run the program with the same data you used in Exercise 1. How many responses were there?

Exercise 3: Add a function that takes the array `sums` as a parameter and prints the percentage of responses each drink received. Run your program on the same data. Show the results.

Lesson 12–4: Two-Dimensional Arrays

Name _____ Date _____

Section _____

This lesson uses program TwoDim.

```cpp
// Program TwoDim manipulates a two-dimensional array
// variable.

#include <iostream>
#include <fstream>
using namespace std;

const int ROW_MAX = 8;
const int COL_MAX = 10;

typedef int ItemType;

typedef ItemType ChartType[ROW_MAX][COL_MAX];

void  GetChart(ifstream&, ChartType, int&, int&);
// Reads values and stores them in the chart.

void  PrintChart(ofstream&, const ChartType, int, int);
// Writes values in the chart to a file.

int  main ()
{
    ChartType  chart;
    int  rowsUsed;
    int  colsUsed;
    ifstream  dataIn;
    ofstream  dataOut;

    dataIn.open("twod.dat");
    dataOut.open("twod.out");
    GetChart(dataIn, chart, rowsUsed, colsUsed);
    PrintChart(dataOut, chart, rowsUsed, colsUsed);
    return 0;
}

//*************************************************

void  GetChart(ifstream&  data, ChartType  chart,
               int&  rowsUsed, int&  colsUsed)
// Pre:  rowsUsed and colsUsed are on the first line of
//       file data; values are one row per line
//       beginning with the second line.
// Post: Values have been read and stored in the chart.
```

```
{
    ItemType  item;
    data  >> rowsUsed >> colsUsed;

    for (int row = 0; row < rowsUsed; row++)
        for (int col = 0; col < colsUsed; col++)

            // FILL IN Code to read and store the next value.
}

//*****************************************************

void  PrintChart(ofstream&  data, const ChartType  chart,
                 int  rowsUsed, int  colsUsed)
// Pre: The chart contains valid data.
// Post: Values in the chart have been sent to a file by row,
//       one row per line.
{

    // FILL IN Code to print chart by row.

}
```

Exercise 1: Read the documentation carefully and complete program `TwoDim`. Show what is printed.

2	3	2	4	6
7	1	4	3	3
2	8	8	5	8
4	2	7	7	4

Exercise 2: Add a function that prints the largest value in array variable `chart`. Rerun the program.

Largest value ____8____.

Exercise 3: Add a function that prints the smallest value in array variable `chart`. Rerun the program.

Smallest value ____1____.

Exercise 4: Add a function that sums the values in a column of array variable `chart`. Pass the column you want to sum as a parameter. Call your function to print the sum of each column appropriately labeled.

Sum of Column 1 __15__.   Sum of Column 2 __14__.

Sum of Column 3 __21__.   Sum of Column 4 __19__.

Sum of Column 5 __21__.

Exercise 5: The specifications on the data have been changed. The data is to be entered one column per line instead of one row per line. In addition, the order of rowsUsed and colsUsed has been reversed; that is, colsUsed is the first value on the first line and rowsUsed is the second value. Rewrite function GetChart to input chart using the new specifications. Run your program using twodalt.dat.

Smallest value   _2_ .

Largest value   _8_ .

Sum of Column 1   _12_ .

Sum of Column 2   _16_ .

Sum of Column 3   _21_ .

Sum of Column 4   _15_ .

Sum of Column 5   _10_ .

Lesson 12–5: Multidimensional Arrays

Name _____ Date _____

Section _____

Exercise 1: Write a void function, SetThreeDi, that sets all the cells in a three-dimensional array to a value that is passed as a parameter. You may access the dimension sizes nonlocally.

Exercise 2: Write a void function, PrintThreeD, that prints the values in the three-dimensional array.

Exercise 3: Write a driver that defines a three-dimensional array, declares a variable of that kind, passes it to function SetThreeDi to set the array to all zeros, and passes it to PrintThreeDi to print the values. What is written?

Lesson 12–6: Debugging

Name _____ Date _____

Section _____

Exercise 1: Program ReadData reads data into a two-dimensional array. The data is input as described in Lesson 12–4, Exercise 1. The data file is shown below:

```
3   4
1   2   3   4
5   6   7   8
9   8   7   6
```

Unfortunately, program ReadData contains an error. Can you find and fix it? Describe the error.

Exercise 2: Unless you found two errors at once in Exercise 1, there is still an error lurking in program ReadData. Correct the error and rerun the program. Describe the error.

Postlab Activities

Exercise 1: Write a program to grade a set of true/false tests. There are 15 true/false questions. True is represented by *T*, and false is represented by *F*. The key to the quiz is on file `Quiz.dat` followed by the student responses. Each student's name (maximum of 15 characters) immediately follows the student's last answer. For each student, write out the name followed by the number answered correctly and the number missed. Use stream failure to terminate processing.

Exercise 2: An organization that your little cousin belongs to is selling low-fat cookies. If your cousin's class sells more cookies than any other class, the teacher has promised to take the whole class on a picnic. Of course, your cousin volunteered you to keep track of all the sales and determine the winner.

Each class has an identification number. Each sales slip has the class identification number and the number of boxes sold. You decide to create two arrays: one to hold the identification numbers and one to record the number of boxes sold. The identification numbers range from 1 through 10. Here is a sample of the data.

Id. Number	Boxes Sold
3	23
4	1
2	13
2	7
4	5
1	6
10	16
.	
.	

The first time an identification number is read, store it in the next free slot in the array of identification numbers and initialize the corresponding position in the array of boxes sold to the number sold on the sales slip. Each subsequent time an identification number is read, add the number of boxes sold to the corresponding position in the array of boxes sold. You may assume that each class sold at least one box of cookies—the homeroom mothers had to buy one.

When there are no more sales slips, scan the array of boxes sold for the largest value. The identification number in the corresponding position in the array of identification numbers is the class that wins.

Write your program and run it using data file `Boxes.dat`. Which class won and how many boxes of cookies did they sell?

Exercise 3: In Exercise 2, the class identification numbers range from 1 through 10. If they ranged from 0 through 9, the identification number could be used as an index into the array of boxes sold. Using this scheme, you need only one array to hold the boxes sold. Rewrite your program implementing this scheme. You can use the same data file by always subtracting one from the identification number on input and adding one to the identification number on output. Run your program using `Boxes.dat`. You should get the same results as in Exercise 2. Did you?

Exercise 4: Write test plans for Exercises 2 and 3. Can these test plans be the same, or must they be different? Explain.

Exercise 5: If an index has meaning beyond simply indicating the place in the collection, we say that it has *semantic content*. Exercise 3 is an example of processing in which the array indexes have semantic content. Explain.

Exercise 6: Two-dimensional arrays are good structures to represent boards in games. Write a function that takes a two-dimensional array as input and marks the array as a checkerboard. Put an asterisk in the black squares and a blank in the white squares. Write a second function that prints the checkerboard on the screen. Because a checkerboard is a fixed size, the dimensions of the board may be set as constants and accessed nonlocally.

Exercise 7: Write a program that keeps track of stock prices for five stocks for one week. Choose any five stocks on the New York Stock Exchange. Use actual stock prices for one week as your data. Include the clippings from the paper with your program.

Your program should be interactive. Prompt the user to enter the names of the five stocks. Then prompt the user to enter a week's worth of prices for each stock. The program should print a table, showing the input in tabular form, and a table showing the average price of each stock for the week, and the average value of all five stocks for each day. You may assume that you have 100 shares of each stock.

Exercise 8: A two-dimensional array is the ideal structure to represent a matrix. Write the following functions, which implement the matrix operations add and subtract. In order to test your operations, you need a function to read values from a file and store them in a matrix and a function to write the values in a matrix on a file. Let your matrices be 5 by 4.

Add	Takes two matrices (A and B) as input and returns a matrix (Result) in which each position is the sum of the corresponding positions in A and B.
Sub	Takes two matrices (A and B) as input and returns a matrix (Result) in which each position is the corresponding position in A minus the corresponding position in B.
Write	Takes a file name and a matrix as input and writes the matrix by row, one row per line on the file.
GetMat	Takes a file name and a matrix as input and reads values from the file and stores them into the matrix.

Exercise 9: Write and implement a test plan for the matrix operations you wrote in Exercise 8.

Array-Based Lists

- To be able to define the data type list.

- To be able to implement the operations on the data type *unsorted* list.

- To be able to implement the operations on the data type *sorted* list.

- To be able to declare and use C strings (arrays of characters).

Chapter 13: Assignment Cover Sheet

Name _____   Date _____

Section _____

Fill in the following table showing which exercises have been assigned for each lesson and check what you are to submit: (1) lab sheets, (2) listings of output files, and/or (3) listings of programs. Your instructor or teaching assistant (TA) can use the Completed column for grading purposes.

Activities	Assigned: Check or list exercise numbers	Submit (1) (2) (3)			Completed
Prelab					
Review					
Prelab Assignment					
Inlab					
Lesson 13–1: Check Prelab Exercises					
Lesson 13–2: Linear (Unsorted) List Operations					
Lesson 13–3: Sorted List Operations					
Lesson 13–4: C Strings					
Lesson 13–5: Debugging					
Postlab					

Prelab Activities

Review

An array data type gives a name to a collection of data values and lets us access individual items by their position within the collection. Arrays are ideal structures to represent *lists* of items.

Lists   Lists occur as naturally in programming as they do in real life. We manipulate guest lists, grocery lists, class lists, things-to-do lists. . . . The list of lists is endless. Three properties characterize lists: The items are homogeneous, the items are linear, and lists have varying length. By linear we mean that each item except the first has a unique component that comes before it and each item except the last has a unique component that comes after it. For example, if there are at least three items in a list, the second item comes after the first and before the third.

A set of operations that manipulates lists must include at least initializing the list, putting an item on the list, removing an item from the list, searching for an item in a list, determining if the list is empty, and displaying the items in the list.

Array-Based Lists   An array data type is the structure that is often used to represent items in a list. The first item in the list is stored in the first place in the array, the second item in the list is stored in the second place in the array, and so on. The number of positions in an array is fixed at compile time, but the number of items in a list varies as a program executes. Therefore, when an array is used to implement a list, there must be a *length* parameter associated with the list. Let's examine a simple general declaration that defines a length and an array of items. (The comments must be replaced with actual values before the declarations can be used.)

```
const int MAX_LENGTH = /* some value */;
typedef /* type of item on the list */ ItemType;
typedef ItemType List[MAX_LENGTH];

List  list;
int   length;
```

The first statement defines an `int` constant, `MAX_LENGTH`, that is the maximum number of elements that might be in the list. The next statement defines data type `ItemType`. Whenever `ItemType` appears in the program, the actual type filled in when the declaration is used is substituted for `ItemType`. The next statement defines a data type `List` that is an array of `MAX_LENGTH` items of type `ItemType`. The next two statements define an array variable `list` of data type `List` and an `int` variable `length`. Notice that there are `MAX_LENGTH` places in the array variable `list`, but `length` is used to tell us how many of these places contain actual list items.

Distinction between the Array and the List   If `/* some value */` is replaced with 100, and `/* type of item on the list */` is replaced with `char,` the array variable `list` has 100 slots, each of which can contain one character. At the logical level, the length of an empty list is zero. As each successive item is entered into the list, the item is stored into the array variable at the position indexed by `length`, and `length` is incremented. All processing of the logical list is done from the zeroth position in the array variable `list` through the `length-1` position.

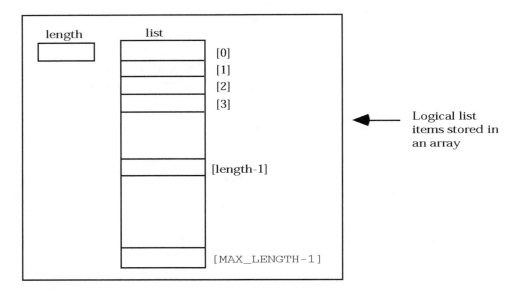

Logical list items stored in an array

Sorted and Unsorted Lists   Lists can be categorized into two classes: sorted and unsorted. In an unsorted list, the component that comes before or after an item has no semantic relationship with it. In a sorted list, the items are arranged in such a way that the component that comes before or after an item has a semantic relationship with that item. For example, a grade list can be a random list of numbers or sorted by value. The following diagrams show an unsorted list of grades and a sorted list of grades.

Unsorted List

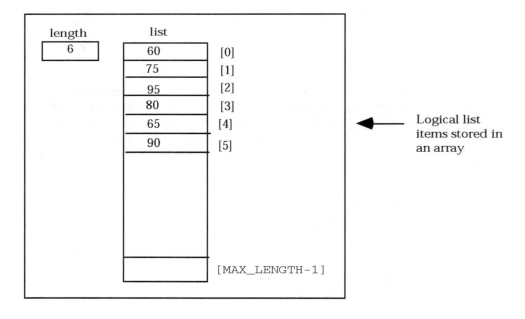

Logical list items stored in an array

Sorted List

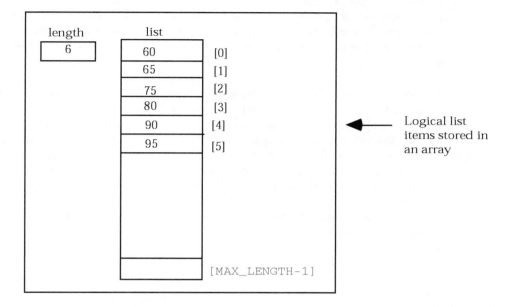

length

list

| 6 |

| 60 | [0]
| 65 | [1]
| 75 | [2]
| 80 | [3]
| 90 | [4]
| 95 | [5]

Logical list
items stored in
an array

[MAX_LENGTH-1]

List Algorithms In the following algorithms, we use *list* and *length* in their logical meaning. That is, they are not program variables but logical entities.

Storing an item in an unsorted list: The item is stored in the length position and length is incremented.

Inserting an item in a sorted list: Find the position where the item should be inserted (use one of the sorted searches below), move the items in the array from that point to the end down one position, store the item, and increment the length.

Linear search in an unsorted list: To search for an item in an unsorted list, loop through the items in the list examining each one until you find the item you are searching for or you run out of items to examine.

Linear search in a sorted list: If the list items are sorted, the loop can terminate when the item is found or when the place where the item would be if it were in the list is passed. For example, if you are searching for the grade 70, you can terminate the search when the value 75 is encountered.

Binary search: A binary search is only possible if the list is sorted. Rather than looking for the item starting at the beginning of the list and moving forward, you begin at the middle in a binary search. If the item for which you are searching is less than the item in the middle, continue searching between the beginning of the list and the middle. If the item for which you are searching is greater than the item in the middle, continue searching between the middle and the end of the list. If the middle item is equal to the one for which you are searching, the search stops. The process continues with each comparison cutting in half the portion of the list left to be searched. The process stops when the item is found or when the portion of the list left to be searched is empty.

Sorting: Sorting a list converts it from unsorted to sorted. One algorithm for doing so is as follows. Define the current item to be the first in the list (the value in the zeroth position). Find the minimum value in the rest of the list and exchange it with the value in the current position. Increment the current position and repeat the process. When the current position is equal to the length minus two, the process stops and the list is sorted.

Implementing the ADT List   For illustrative purposes, our earlier example used two separate variables to represent a list: an array and an integer. In Chapter 11 we introduced the concept of an abstract data type: a set of values and the operations that manipulate the values in the set. A list fits this definition. A list is a set of values, and the algorithms discussed in the previous section are examples of the operations that manipulate the values in the set. Therefore, the abstract data type list should be encapsulated in a class. The array of elements and the length are the data members, and the operations on the values are the member functions.

There are many possible list definitions, depending on how the list elements are to be manipulated. Here is one definition. The items being stored in the list are of type ItemType.

```
class ListType
{
public:
    void Store(ItemType item);
    // Pre:  item is not in the list.
    //       The list is not full.
    // Post: item is in the list.
    void PrintList();
    // Post: List elements are printed on the screen.
    int Length();
    // Post: return value is the number of items in the list.
    bool IsEmpty();
    // Post: returns true if list is empty; false otherwise.
    bool IsFull();
    // Post: returns true if there is no more room in the
    //       list; false otherwise.
    ListType();
    // Constructor
    // Post: Empty list is created.
private:
    int length;
    ItemType values[MAX_ITEMS];
}
```

C Strings   In Chapter 2, we introduced the data type string, available in the Standard Library. The implementations of the operations on variables of type string are hidden within the string class as member functions. Here we introduce another type of string that is built into the C++ language. We call these strings "C strings" to distinguish them from objects of the string class.

C strings are one-dimensional arrays where the component type is char. A special character is appended following the last character in the array to signal the end of the C string. In other words, C strings are lists of characters. But rather than having a separate variable that contains the number of items in the list, a special symbol, the *null character*, is used to signal the end of the list. The null character is the escape sequence \0 (backslash zero). When declaring an array for a C string, the array size must be one more than the number of characters in the C string in order for there to be a slot for the null character.

Like other arrays, C strings can be initialized in their declaration statement. For example, the following statement declares a C string and initializes it.

```
char greeting[7] = "Hello!";
```

`greeting` is stored in memory as follows.

```
greeting
  'H'
  'e'
  'l'
  'l'
  'o'
  '!'
  '\0'
```

Like other arrays, C strings cannot be assigned to one another; they must be copied character by character.

C strings have certain properties that arrays do not have. For example, we can declare C string constants and C strings can be sent to the output stream as a whole rather than having to send them character by character. Both the extraction operator (>>) and the function `get` from `<iostream>` can be used with C strings. If `title` is defined as a `char` array of 21 characters, then

```
cin >> title;
```

extracts characters from `cin` one at a time and stores them in `title` until whitespace is encountered. The null character is stored in the position immediately following the last character stored. Therefore, an array size of 21 provides room for 20 input characters plus the null character. The extraction operation terminates when whitespace is encountered, and the next extraction operation is positioned at the whitespace.

When function `get` is used to input a C string, it requires two parameters: first, the name of the C string variable and second, an `int` expression that is one more than the number of characters to be read. Characters are stored one at a time, including whitespace characters, until the proper number has been stored or the newline character ('\n') is encountered. The next extraction operation is positioned to read the newline character if it is what stopped the previous operation.

The parameter to function `open` in file `<fstream>` is a C string. In previous chapters we used a literal string as a parameter, but a C string variable also can be used. Being able to use a C string variable means that you can read in the file name, thus changing the data file without having to change the program.

C++ provides a set of C string-handling functions in file `<cstring>`. Three useful ones are shown below.

`strlen(s)`	Returns the number of characters in `s` (excluding '\0').
`strcmp(s1, s2)`	Returns a negative integer if `s1` comes before `s2`; returns zero if `s1` is equal to `s2`; and returns a positive integer if `s2` comes before `s1`.
`strcpy(s1, s2)`	Copies `s2` into `s1`; the previous contents of `s1` are destroyed.

Comparison of C Strings and the String Class C strings are arrays of characters. They are subject to the limitations of arrays: There are no aggregate C string operations other than input and output, and the maximum number of characters must be fixed when the C string is declared. On the other hand, the Standard Library `string` class provides strings of any length, aggregate assignment and comparison, and concatenation. Because there are certain operations that require a C string, the `string` class provides a member function `c_str` that converts a `string` object into a C string. Be careful: The C string must be large enough to hold the `string`.

Chapter 13: Prelab Assignment

Name _____ Date _____

Section _____

Read program `FloatLst` carefully.

```cpp
#include <iostream>
#include <fstream>
using namespace std;

const int MAX_LENGTH = 50;

class FloatList
{
public:
    void GetList(ifstream&);
    void PrintList();
    FloatList();
private:
    int length;
    float values[MAX_LENGTH];
};

int  main ()
{
    ifstream  tempData;
    FloatList  list;

    cout  << fixed  << showpoint;

    tempData.open("real.dat");

    // Input and print a list
    list.GetList(tempData);
    list.PrintList();
    return 0;
}

//*******************************************

FloatList::FloatList()
{
    length = 0;
}

//*******************************************
```

```
void  FloatList::GetList(ifstream&  data)
{
    float  item;
    data  >> item;
    while (data)
    {
        values[length] = item;
        length++;
        data  >> item;
    }
}

//***********************************************************

void  PrintList()
{
    int  index;

    for (index = 0; index < length; index++)
        cout  << values[index]  << endl;
}
```

Exercise 1: Document the program heading.

Exercise 2: Document the prototypes of the member functions of FloatLst.

Exercise 3: Document the definitions of the member functions of FloatLst.

Lesson 13–1: Check Prelab Exercises

Name _____   Date _____

Section _____

In order to be able to write documentation, you must thoroughly understand the code. Run program `FloatLst`. What were the last four values printed?

The version of program `FloatLst` on the disk is documented.

Exercise 1: Check the documentation for the program heading. Did you understand what the program was doing? If not, describe what you did not understand.

Exercise 2: Check the documentation for the prototypes of the member functions of `FloatLst`. Did you understand what the functions were doing? If not, describe what you did not understand.

Exercise 3: Check the documentation for the definitions of the member functions of `FloatLst`. Did you understand how the functions were being implemented? If not, describe what you did not understand.

Lesson 13–2: Linear (Unsorted) List Operations

Name _____ Date _____

Section _____

Use the following declaration on file `ListType.h` for Exercises 1 through 3. Read the documentation on the member function declarations carefully.

```
const int MAX_ITEMS = 20;
typedef int ItemType;

class ListType
{
public:
    void Store(ItemType item);
    // Pre: The list is not full;
    // Post: item is in the list.
    void PrintList();
    // Post: If the list is not empty, the elements are
    //       printed on the screen; otherwise "The list
    //       is empty" is printed on the screen.
    int Length();
    // Post: return value is the number of items in the list.
    bool IsEmpty();
    // Post: returns true if list is empty; false otherwise.
    bool IsFull();
    // Post: returns true if there is no more room in the
    //       list; false otherwise.
    ListType();
    // Constructor
    // Post: Empty list is created.
private:
    int length;
    ItemType values[MAX_ITEMS];
}
```

Exercise 1: Write the definitions for the member functions. There is nothing in the documentation for the member functions that indicates order. Therefore, implement `Store` by putting each new value in the next space in the array. Save the code in file `ListType.cpp`.

Exercise 2: Write a driver program that reads values from file `int.dat`, stores them in the list, and prints them on the screen. What are the last four values in the file?

Exercise 3: Add a member function `IsThere` to class `ListType` that returns `true` if its parameter is in the list and `false` otherwise.

Exercise 4: Add a member function `RemoveItem` that removes a value from the list. The precondition is that the value is in the list.

Exercise 5: Add a member function `WriteList` that writes the values in the list to a file passed as a parameter.

Exercise 6: Write a test driver that tests the member functions added in Exercises 3 through 5 using the data on file `int.dat`. Have your driver complete the following activities:

- Read and store the values into the list.
- Print the values to a file.
- Search for a value that is there (10) and print the results.
- Search for a value that is not there (5) and print the results.
- Delete a value (10) and print the list with the value removed.

Write your driver so that it prompts for and reads the names of the input and output files.

Lesson 13–3: Sorted List Operations

Name _____ Date _____

Section _____

Use the following declaration on file `SLstType.h` for Exercises 1 through 3. Read the documentation on the member function declarations carefully.

```
const int MAX_ITEMS = 20;
typedef int ItemType;

class SListType
{
public:
    void Insert(ItemType item);
    // Pre: The list is not full;
    // Post: item is in the list; list is stored in
    //       increasing order.
    void PrintList();
    // Post: If the list is not empty, the elements are
    //       printed on the screen in increasing order;
    //       otherwise "The list is empty" is
    //       printed on the screen.
    int Length();
    // Post: return value is the number of items in the list.
    bool IsEmpty();
    // Post: returns true if list is empty; false otherwise.
    bool IsFull();
    // Post: returns true if there is no more room in the
    //       list; false otherwise.
    SListType();
    // Constructor
    // Post: Empty list is created.
private:
    int length;
    ItemType values[MAX_ITEMS];
}
```

Exercise 1: Write the definitions for the member functions. Save the code in file `SLstType.cpp`.

Exercise 2: Write a driver program that reads values from file `int.dat`, stores them in the list, and prints them on the screen. Be sure that your driver adheres to the preconditions on the member functions. What are the last four values in the file?

Exercise 3: Add a member function `IsThere` to class `SListType` that returns `true` if its parameter is in the list and `false` otherwise.

Exercise 4: Add a member function `RemoveItem` that removes a value from the list. The precondition is that the value is in the list.

Exercise 5: Add a member function `WriteList` that writes the values in the list to a file passed as a parameter.

Exercise 6: Write a test driver that tests the member functions added in Exercises 3 through 5 using the data on file `int.dat`. Have your driver complete the following activities:

- Read and store the values into the list.
- Print the values to a file.
- Search for a value that is there (10) and print the results.
- Search for a value that is not there (5) and print the results.
- Delete a value (10) and print the list with the value removed.

Write your driver so that it prompts for and reads the names of the input and output files.

Exercise 7: Were you able to use any of the member functions you wrote in Lesson 13–2 for Exercises 1 through 6? Explain.

Lesson 13–4: C Strings

Name _____ Date _____

Section _____

√ Exercise 1: Write a function, GetFileName, that prompts for and reads a file name from cin. Did you encapsulate the code to do this task in Lessons 2 and 3 into a function? If so, this exercise is already completed.

√ Exercise 2: Program Shell1 is a driver for function Compare that compares two C strings. The return value type of function Compare is CompareType (LESS, EQUAL, GREATER). Complete this program.

```cpp
// Program Shell1 is a driver for function Compare.
#include <iostream>
#include <cstring>
using namespace std;

typedef  char String20[21];
enum  CompareType {LESS, EQUAL, GREATER};
CompareType  Compare(const String20, const String20);

int  main ()
{
    String20  str1;
    String20  str2;

    cout  << "Enter a string of up to 20 characters."
          << " Do not include whitespace."  << endl;
    cin  >> str1;
    cout  << "Enter a string of up to 20 characters."
          << " Do not include whitespace."  << endl;
    cin  >> str2;
    switch (Compare(str1, str2))
    {
        // FILL IN Code to write out which string
        // comes first alphabetically
    }
    return 0;
}

//*************************************************

CompareType Compare(const String20 str1, const String20  str2)
{
    int  result;
    result = strcmp(str1, str2);

    // FILL IN Code to return the appropriate enumerator

}
```

Test this program as many times as it takes to test function `Compare`. Show your data and your results.

Exercise 3: Enclose the body of function `main` in program `Shell1` in a loop that continues until `Quit` is entered for `str1`. Test your program. Show your data and your results.

Exercise 4: Rewrite the solution to Exercise 3 so that the data are on file `StringPr.dat` as pairs of C strings separated by whitespace. Run your program and list the results of the last three pairs of C strings.

Exercise 5: Function `Compare` used the built-in C string function `strcmp`. Outline the algorithm you would have to use if `strcmp` were not available.

Lesson 13–5: Debugging

Name _____ Date _____

Section _____

Exercise 1: Program `ListEr` is a slight variation on program `FloatLst`. Note, however, that `MAX_LENGTH` has been changed in `ListEr`. Run program `ListEr` and check the results against the output from program `FloatLst`. Describe what happens.

Exercise 2: In Lesson 12–1, Exercise 2, we said that C++ does not define what happens when you store more values into an array than there are places defined. Because an error of this type happens so frequently, we want you to see what happens on at least one system. If you have an opportunity to use another C++ system, try the same experiment and record what happens.

There are two important lessons to be learned here. The first is that you should be very careful about storing values in an array. The second is that a program with an error might run correctly on one system but not on another.

Postlab Activities

Exercise 1: In Postlab Exercise 2 in Chapter 12, you wrote a program to keep track of low-fat cookie sales for your cousin. Rewrite the program using the sorted list operations you wrote for this chapter. Can you keep both lists sorted? Can you keep one or the other sorted but not both? Write a justification for the data structures you use.

Exercise 2: Write and implement a test plan for your program in Exercise 1.

Exercise 3: A clothing manufacturer wants to keep track of how many copies of each item are sold over a period of a week. The information on the sales slip includes the item identification number, the number of copies sold, the unit price, and the total amount of the sale. How is the problem similar to judging a cookie contest (Postlab Exercise 2, Chapter 12)? How is the problem different? What changes would be necessary if the manufacturer asked you to include a total sales figure at the end of the week?

Exercise 4: Write a program to implement the problem described in Exercise 3, including the total sales figure.

Exercise 5: Postlab Exercises 4 and 5 in Chapter 6 were simulations of a children's game to determine who would be "it." Rewrite your solution to Exercise 4 using a list of children's names. Print out the name of the child who is it rather than the position that the child occupies in the original grouping.

Exercise 6: Rewrite your solution to Exercise 5 using the altered form described in Postlab Exercise 5 in Chapter 6.

Object–Oriented Software Development

- To be able to define a descendant class from an existing class data type.

- To be able to declare and use descendant-class objects.

- To be able to define a class data type in which a private member is of an existing class data type.

- To be able to define a class data type with a dynamically bound (virtual) member function.

- To be able to declare and use a class object with a dynamically bound member function.

- To be able to relate object-oriented terminology to C++ constructs.

Chapter 14: Assignment Cover Sheet

Name _____ Date _____

Section _____

Fill in the following table showing which exercises have been assigned for each lesson and check what you are to submit: (1) lab sheets, (2) listings of output files, and/or (3) listings of programs. Your instructor or teaching assistant (TA) can use the Completed column for grading purposes.

Activities	Assigned: Check or list exercise numbers	Submit (1) (2) (3)			Completed
Prelab					
Review					
Prelab Assignment					
Inlab					
Lesson 14–1: Check Prelab Exercises					
Lesson 14–2: Classes					
Lesson 14–3: Classes with Inheritance					
Lesson 14–4: Virtual Methods					
Lesson 14–5: Debugging					
Postlab					

Prelab Activities

Review

Object-Oriented Terminology The vocabulary of object-oriented programming (OOP) has its roots in the programming languages Simula and Smalltalk and can be very bewildering. Such phrases as "sending a message to," "methods," and "instance variables" are sprinkled throughout the OOP literature. Don't panic! These are just synonyms for C++ constructs you already know. First of all, an object is a class object or class instance. A method is a public member function, and an instance variable is a private data member. Sending a message is a call to a public member function. In order for you to become more comfortable with object-oriented terminology, we mix these terms with their C++ counterparts in the rest of this Review.

Objects may be related to one another in one of two ways. An object may be a descendant of another object and inherit the ancestor's properties, or it may include another object as a member. The first is called *inheritance*, and the second is called *composition* or *containment*.

Inheritance In C++, `class` data types can inherit data and actions from another `class` data type. For example, to extend our `MoneyType` defined in Chapter 11 to include a currency name, we define a data type that inherits from `MoneyType`.

```
#include <string>
class MoneyType
{
public:
    void  Initialize(long, long);
    long  DollarsAre() const;
    long  CentsAre() const;
    void  Print() const;
    MoneyType  Add(MoneyType  value) const;
    MoneyType();
    MoneyType(long, long);
private:
    long  dollars;
    long  cents;
};

class ExtMoneyType : public MoneyType
{
public:
    string  CurrencyIs();
    void  Initialize(long, long, const string);
    void  Print() const;
    ExtMoneyType();
    ExtMoneyType(long, long, const string);

private:
    string  currency;
};

ExtMoneyType  extMoney;
```

The colon followed by the words `public` and `MoneyType` (a class identifier) says that the new class being defined (`ExtMoneyType`) is inheriting the members of class `MoneyType`. `MoneyType` is called the *base* class or *superclass* and `ExtMoneyType` is called the *derived* class or *subclass*.

extMoney has three member variables: one of its own (`currency`) and two that it inherits from `MoneyType` (`dollars` and `cents`). extMoney has five member functions: two of its own (`Initialize` and `CurrencyIs`) and three that it inherits from `MoneyType` (`Initialize`, `DollarsAre`, and `CentsAre`). `ExtMoneyType` also has two constructors, and extMoney is defined using the default constructor.

Although extMoney inherits the private member variables from its base class, it does not have direct access to them. extMoney must use the public member functions of `MoneyType` to access its inherited member variables.

```
void   ExtMoneyType::Initialize
  (long newDollars, long newCents, string newCurrency)
{
    currency = newCurrency;
    MoneyType::Initialize(newDollars, newCents);
}

string ExtMoneyType::CurrencyIs() const
{
    return currency;
}

void ExtMoneyType::Print() const
{
    MoneyType::Print();
    cout  << currency  << endl;
}

ExtMoneyType::ExtMoneyType()
{
    currency = "dollars";
}

ExtMoneyType::ExtMoneyType()
  (long newDollars, long newCents, const string newCurrency)
    : MoneyType(newDollars, newCents)
{
    currency = newCurrency;
}
```

There are several points to notice about the syntax of these constructor and member function definitions. The first is that the scope resolution operator (`::`) is used between the type `MoneyType` and the member functions `Initialize` and `Print` in the definition of these member functions. Because there are now two member functions named `Initialize` and two named `Print`, you must indicate the `class` in which the one you mean is defined. (That's why it's called the scope resolution operator.) If you do not, the compiler assumes you mean the most recently defined one.

There are two constructors. The parameterless constructor sets the member `currency` to a default value of "dollars". What about the inherited member variables? The default constructor for the base class automatically sets them. The other constructor takes three values, one for its own member and two for its inherited members. But note that the inherited member variables are not set in the body of the function but by a call to the base class's parameterized constructor. A colon separates the function heading and the call to the constructor before the body of the function.

Virtual Methods   In the previous section we defined two methods with the same name, `Initialize`. The statements

```
money.Initialize(20, 66);
extMoney.Initialize(20, 66, "francs");
```

are not ambiguous, because the compiler can determine which `Initialize` to use by examining the type of the object to which it is applied. There are times, however, when the compiler cannot make the determination of which member function is intended, and the decision must be made at run time. If the decision is to be left until run time, the word *virtual* must precede the member function heading in the base class definition and a class object passed as a parameter to a virtual function must be a reference parameter.

Class Objects as Parameters   If the parameter for a function is of the base class, you may pass an argument of the base class or any class derived from it. If the parameter is a reference parameter, all is fine. If the parameter is a value parameter, only those members defined in the base class are actually passed to the function.

Chapter 14: Prelab Assignment

Name _____ Date _____

Section _____

Read the following header files and driver carefully. The implementation files are not shown.

```
// Money.h is the header file for class MoneyType with
// constructors.
#include <string>
using namespace std;

class MoneyType
{
public:
    void    Initialize(long, long);
    long    DollarsAre() const;
    long    CentsAre() const;
    void    Print() const;
    MoneyType Add(MoneyType) const;
    MoneyType();                        // constructor
    MoneyType(long, long);              // constructor
private:
    long    dollars;
    long    cents;
};

// This is the header file for class ExtMoneyType
// (file ExtMoney.h)

#include "money.h"

class ExtMoneyType : public MoneyType
{
public:
    void    Print() const;
    string  CurrencyIs() const;
    void    Initialize(long, long, string);
    ExtMoneyType();
    ExtMoneyType(long, long, string);
private:
    string  currency;
};
```

```
// Program UseMny manipulates objects of class ExtMoneyType.

#include <iostream>

#include "extMoney.h"

int main ()
{
    MoneyType   money;
    cout  << "initialized by default constructors"  << endl;
    money.Print();
    ExtMoneyType   extMoney1;
    extMoney1.Print();
    cout  << "initialized by parameterized constructors"
          << endl;
    ExtMoneyType   extMoney2(3000, 88, "forints");
    extMoney2.Print();
    cout  << "initialized at run time"  << endl;
    extMoney1.Initialize(5000, 99, "pounds");
    extMoney1.Print();
    return  0;
}
```

Exercise 1: What is printed?

Exercise 2: Why did we not show the implementation files?

Exercise 3: Fill in the C++ names or constructs for the following object-oriented concepts.

Object-Oriented	*C++*
Object	
Instance variable	
Method	
Message Passing	

Lesson 14–1: Check Prelab Exercises

Name _____ Date _____

Section _____

Exercise 1: Run program `UseMny.cpp` to check your answers. Were they correct? Explain.

Exercise 2: You do not need to see the implementation files to understand what a program is doing. The information for the user (the client program) is in the header files.

Exercise 3:

Object-Oriented	C++
Object	Class object or class instance
Instance variable	Private data member
Method	Public member function
Message Passing	Invoking a public member function

Lesson 14–2: Classes

Name _____ Date _____

Section _____

Exercise 1: Define a class `myInt` made up of one `int` data member called `value`. There should be an observer function for `value`, a print function, an initializer, a parameterized constructor, and a default constructor. Place this definition in a header file.

Exercise 2: Write the implementation file for the header file in Exercise 1. Let the default constructor set the value to 0.

Exercise 3: Write a driver program that tests the files in Exercises 1 and 2. Show your input data and the results.

Exercise 4: Write a program that reads items of the type defined above, stores them in a list, and then prints out the list. Run your program using file `int.dat`. List the last three values. Use the list you implemented in Lesson 13–2.

Exercise 5: Substitute the list you implemented in Lesson 13–3 and rerun the program. List the last three values.

Exercise 6: The advantage of representing the list in a `class` data type is that client programs cannot access the elements in the list. This protection is both good news and bad news. The client program cannot change the items in the list except through the member functions provided: That is good news. However, each time a client program needs to access each individual item to process it in some way, a new member function must be added to the class. This is bad news because it contradicts the whole idea of encapsulation.

There are two solutions. We can make the items in the list public, which is bad style, or we can add an iterator to the list. This exercise asks you to provide an iterator for `ListType`, the unsorted list ADT implemented in Lesson 13–2. The iterator requires a new instance variable, `nextItem`, and two member functions, `Reset` and `GetNext`. `Reset` sets `nextItem` to 0, and `GetNext` returns the item at the `nextItem` position in the list and increments `nextItem`. The client program can then use member functions `Length`, `Reset`, and `GetNext` to iterate through the items in the list.

Use file `int.dat` to test your program by having the driver iterate through the items in the list and print each one.

Lesson 14–3: Classes with Inheritance

Name _____ Date _____

Section _____

Exercise 1: Derive a new class from myInt, the one defined in Exercise 1 in the last lesson. This new class has a binary member function, Compare, with one parameter that returns {LESS, EQUAL, GREATER} depending on whether value is less than, equal to, or greater than the parameter. Change the declaration of ListType as modified in Exercise 6 in the last lesson so that ItemType is your new derived class. Derive a new class from ListType that has a member function that goes through the items in the list and prints out how many values in it are greater than a given value, equal to a given value, and less than a given value. Pass the value to be tested against as a parameter. Test your function using value 678. Show the results.

Exercise 2: Define type HiPriorityType that inherits from ListType and has the member function Priority that returns the maximum value in the list. Run your program using file int.dat.

Priority item is _____.

Exercise 3: Define type LoPriorityType that inherits from ListType and has the member function Priority that returns the minimum value in the list. Run your program using file int.dat.

Priority item is _____.

Lesson 14–4: Virtual Methods

Name _____ Date _____

Section _____

Exercise 1: To both `LoPriorityType` and `HiPriorityType` from Lesson 14–3, add a member function, `PrintList`, that prints the priority item (appropriately labeled) and then prints the entire list using the member function `PrintList` defined in `ListType`. Test these functions using file `int.dat`.

You are going to add the following function to a client program that uses `ListType`, `HiPriorityType`, and `LoPriorityType`.

```
void  Print(ListType&  list)
{
    cout << "The list is: "  << endl;
    list.PrintList();
}
```

Exercise 2: Can the compiler tell which member function `PrintList` to use in the following statements?

```
ListType  list;

HiPriorityType  list1;

LoPriorityType  list2;

int main ()
{
    Print(list);
    Print(list1);
    Print(list2);
    return 0;
}
```

Explain.

Exercise 3: No, the compiler cannot determine. Therefore, member function `PrintList` must be a virtual method. Describe the changes to the following definitions:

`ListType`:

`HiPriorityType`:

`LoPriorityType`:

Exercise 4: Implement these changes and run your program applying function `Print` to an instance of `ListType`, an instance of `HiPriorityType`, and an instance of `LoPriorityType`. Run your program using `int.dat`. Show your output.

Lesson 14–5: Debugging

Name _____ Date _____

Section _____

Exercise 1: Program UsePart is a client program that uses PartsType (file Parts.h) and ExtPartsType (file ExtParts.h). The .cpp files for these classes don't even compile! There is one syntax error in file Parts.h and two syntax errors in ExtParts.h. Find these errors and correct them. Describe the errors.

Exercise 2: Look at your output carefully. You are missing some values! Correct the logic, recompile, and rerun your program. Describe the error.

Exercise 3: Some of the missing output is now showing, but not all of it! Keep looking. When you find this error, correct it and rerun the program. The output should now be correct. Describe the error.

Postlab Activities

Your music collection is getting quite a reputation. Friends are always calling you and asking if you have such-and-such recording. Create an ADT MusicCollection. The set of operations must include at least the following functionality.

- List the song titles alphabetically within `MediaType`.
- Given a song title as input, determine whether you have a recording of the song.
- Add new recordings to your list.
- Delete recordings.

Design your classes carefully. Make your function `main` just a driver that uses the classes that you have defined.

Exercise 1: Write a design document showing your classes and how they interact.

Exercise 2: Write the header files for your classes.

Exercise 3: Write the implementation files for your classes.

Exercise 4: Write test plans for each class and implement them.

Exercise 5: Write a command-driven driver that lets the user determine the operations to apply. Write a test plan for integrating all the classes. Use the command-driven driver to implement your integration test plan. (An integration test is one that tests the interactions among different classes.)

Pointers, Dynamic Data, and Reference Types

■ To be able to define pointer types.

■ To be able to create dynamic variables, read values into them, and print them.

■ To be able to manipulate dynamic variables.

■ To be able to distinguish between shallow copying and deep copying.

Chapter 15: Assignment Cover Sheet

Name _____ Date _____

Section _____

Fill in the following table showing which exercises have been assigned for each lesson and check what you are to submit: (1) lab sheets, (2) listings of output files, and/or (3) listings of programs. Your instructor or teaching assistant (TA) can use the Completed column for grading purposes.

Activities	Assigned: Check or list exercise numbers	Submit (1) (2) (3)			Completed
Prelab					
Review					
Prelab Assignment					
Inlab					
Lesson 15–1: Check Prelab Exercises					
Lesson 15–2: Pointer Variables					
Lesson 15–3: Dynamic Data					
Lesson 15–4: Classes and Dynamic Data					
Lesson 15–5: Debugging					
Postlab					

Prelab Activities

Review

Pointer Types The *pointer* type is a simple data type that contains the address (or otherwise indicates the location) of a variable of a given type.

```cpp
#include <iostream>
using namespace std;

char*  charPtr;
int    *intPtr;
char*  aString;

char   letter = 'B';
int    value = 1066;
char   myName[10] = "Nell";
```

charPtr is a pointer that can point to a location in memory that can contain an alphanumeric character. intPtr is a pointer that can point to a location in memory that can contain an integer. Note that the asterisk (*) that indicates a pointer can go either to the right of the type or to the left of the variable. If it is appended to the type, and more than one variable is being defined, the * only applies to the first variable in the list. We consistently use the asterisk as a postfix operator on the type and define only one variable at a time. aString is a pointer that can point to a location in memory that can contain a character. letter and value are variables of types char and int. myName is a C string, an array of char.

Now look at the following three assignment statements.

```cpp
charPtr = &letter;
intPtr  = &value;
aString = myName;
```

The prefix operator ampersand (&) means "address of." So &letter means the address in memory assigned to the variable letter; &value means the address of the variable value; and myName without a subscript means the base address of the C string variable myName. These three assignments are legal, because the identifiers on the left of the assignment operator are pointers to the appropriate type.

To access the location that the pointer points to, you use the dereferencing operator: a prefix asterisk (*). For example, the next three lines write what is shown below them.

```cpp
cout  << aString;
cout  << " "  << *charPtr  << ". ";
cout  << *intPtr  << endl;
```

```
Nell B. 1066
```

If we send `*aString` to the output stream rather than `aString`, the first letter is sent to the output stream rather than to the entire string.

Pointers to Structures In the last chapter we defined a class `MoneyType`. Let's use it to define a pointer to an instance of `MoneyType`.

```
#include "money.h"
MoneyType*  moneyPtr;
```

`moneyPtr` is a pointer to an instance of class `MoneyType`, and `*moneyPtr` is the class variable pointed to by `moneyPtr`. We access the member functions of the class with `(*moneyPtr).DollarsAre()` and `(*moneyPtr).CentsAre()`. The parentheses are necessary in each case because the dot operator has higher precedence than the dereferencing operator (the asterisk). For this reason, C++ supplies the arrow operator made up of a hyphen and a greater-than sympol (->). This operator both dereferences the pointer and accesses the member field. That is, the following pairs of expressions are equivalent.

```
(*moneyPtr).CentsAre()  and  moneyPtr->CentsAre()
```

```
(*moneyPtr).DollarsAre()  and  moneyPtr->DollarsAre()
```

Dynamic Variables In the previous discussion, we created a variable and stored its address in a pointer variable. By now, you should be asking, *but why?* Why would you go to this much trouble if it is only an alternative way to do something you can already do? Just be patient. The ability to store and manipulate the addresses of variables allows us to create a new kind a variable: *dynamic*. In Chapter 8, we described two kinds of data: static and automatic. Static variables exist for the lifetime of the program. Automatic variables are created when control reaches their declaration and deleted when control exits the block in which they are declared. Dynamic variables, in contrast, are created and destroyed as needed by the program itself. `new` is an operator that allocates a dynamic variable; `delete` is an operator that deallocates it.

```
#include <iostream>
#include <cstring>
using namespace std;

char*   charPtr;
int*    intPtr;
char*   aString;

charPtr = new char;
intPtr  = new int;
aString = new char[10];

*charPtr = 'B';
*intPtr  = 1066;
strcpy(aString, "Nell");

cout << aString ;
cout << " "  << *charPtr  << "." ;
cout << *intPtr   << endl;

delete  charPtr;
delete  intPtr;
delete  aString;
```

This code segment produces the same output as the previous example, but there is one major difference. In the first example, the variables `letter`, `value`, and `myName` exist for as long as the program that includes the code segment is running. In the second example, the variables created by `new` to hold the same data exist only from the execution of `new` to the execution of `delete`. The locations that were allocated for them can now be allocated for some other variables. Here, we are talking about three variables, so space is not important. However, when you graduate to writing very large programs, this technique of using space only during the time that you need it becomes important.

The variables generated by `new` are called dynamic variables because they are created at run time. Dynamic variables are used just like any other variables of the same type, but pointer variables should only be assigned to one another, tested for equality, and dereferenced. Other operators are defined on pointer variables, but their application is outside the scope of this manual.

Pointer Constants   There is only one literal pointer constant in C++: the value zero. Zero is called the *null* pointer and points to nothing. Logically, a pointer that points to memory address zero does point to something, so we define a constant `NULL` and use it in our programs to make this logical distinction clear. The definition can be found in file `<cstddef>`.

An array variable without index brackets is a constant pointer expression whose value is the base address of the array.

Reference Types   Reference variables, like pointer variables, can contain the address of another variable. A reference variable is defined in the same way that a pointer variable is defined, but the operator ampersand (`&`) is used rather than the asterisk (`*`). That is, the operator may be a postfix operator on the type identifier or a prefix operator on the variable being defined. If more than one variable is being defined, the ampersand operator on the type only applies to the first in the list. There is no dereferencing operator for reference variables because the compiler dereferences them automatically.

You used reference variables before when you declared a parameter to be a reference parameter. The address of the argument is sent to a function if the parameter is a reference parameter. The code within the function uses the name of the parameter, and the compiler automatically accesses the place pointed to.

Copying Structures with Pointer Variables   It is very important to make the distinction between a pointer and what the pointer points to. If you assign a `struct` variable or `class` variable to another `struct` or `class` variable and the structure contains a pointer variable, the pointers themselves are copied, not what the pointers point to. Let's redefine class `ExtMoneyType` slightly and show what we mean.

```
class MoneyType
{
public:
    void    Initialize(long, long);
    long    DollarsAre() const;
    long    CentsAre() const;
    MoneyType  Add(MoneyType  value) const;
    MoneyType();
    MoneyType(long, long);
private:
    long    dollars;
    long    cents;
};
```

```
typedef char String10[11];

class ExtMoneyType : public MoneyType
{
public:
    char*   CurrencyIs();
    Initialize(long, long, const String10);
    ExtMoneyType();
    ExtMoneyType(long, long, const String10);
private:
    char*   currency;
};
```

We have made `currency` a pointer to an array of `char` rather than a `string` and changed the parameters to C strings. Of course, the corresponding appropriate changes must be made to the definition of the member functions themselves. Now look what happens after the following statements.

```
ExtMoneyType   extMoney1;
ExtMoneyType   extMoney2 = (5000, 99, "pounds");
extMoney1 = extMoney2;
extMoney2.Initialize(300, 77, "francs");
cout << "extMoney1 "  << extMoney1.CurrencyIs()  << endl;
cout << "extMoney2 "  << extMoney2.CurrencyIs()  << endl;
```

What do you think is printed? We would expect the `currency` member of `extMoney1` to be "pounds" and the `currency` member of `extMoney2` to be "francs." But it isn't; here is the output.

```
extMoney1 francs
extMoney2 francs
```

How can this be? The assignment statement `extMoney1 = extMoney2` copies `extMoney2` into `extMoney1`, so `extMoney1.currency` points to "pounds." When `extMoney2` is reinitialized in the next statement, what `extMoney2.currency` points to is changed. `extMoney1.currency` is still the same pointer, so it now points to "francs" as well.

When copying occurs and one or more of the member data variables are pointers, we need a *deep copy* operation. A deep copy copies what a pointer points to, not the pointer itself. The copying that occurred in the assignment statement above is called *shallow copying*: the pointer was copied, not what the pointer pointed to.

When working with classes in which one or more of the member variables is a pointer, the class should provide a class destructor, a deep copy operation, and a class copy-constructor.

Recall that when an automatic object goes out of scope, its memory locations automatically go back to be used again. However, if a member is a pointer, its location is returned, but what it points to is not. A destructor is a function that is called automatically when an object goes out of scope. The function prototype for the destructor for `ExtMoneyType` would be

```
~ExtMoneyType();
```

and the following code would be in the body of the destructor.

```
delete [] currency;
```

A class copy-constructor has the following pattern:

```
TypeName(const TypeName& newData);
```

If a class copy-constructor is present, it overrides the default method of initialization and is used implicitly when a class object is initialized by another in its declaration, is passed by value to a function, or is the result of a value-returning function.

Summary of New Operators

Operator	Where placed	Meaning
*	postfix on a type or prefix on a variable in a pointer variable declaration	declare a variable that is a *pointer to* a place that can contain a variable of the type; must be dereferenced to access the place pointed to
*	prefix on a pointer variable in an expression	dereferencing operator; accesses *place pointed to*
&	postfix on a type or prefix on a variable in a reference variable declaration	declare a variable that is a *pointer to* a place that can contain a variable of the type; is dereferenced automatically by the compiler
&	prefix on a variable	*address of* variable
->	infix between a pointer variable to `struct` or `class` and member name	dereferences a pointer variable and accesses a member

Chapter 15: Prelab Assignment

Name _____ Date _____

Section _____

Read program Pointer carefully.

```cpp
// Program Pointer reads in three variables, assigns
// pointers to them, adds them, and prints the result.

#include <iostream>
using namespace std;

int  main ()
{
    int   one;
    int   two;
    int   three;
    int   result;
    int*  ptrOne;
    int*  ptrTwo;
    int*  ptrThree;

    cout  << "Enter three integer numbers separated"
          << " by blanks; press return."  << endl;
    cin  >> one  >> two  >> three;
    ptrOne = &one;
    ptrTwo = &two;
    ptrThree = &three;
    cout  << endl  << *ptrOne  << " + "  << *ptrTwo
          << " + "  << *ptrThree  << " = ";
    result = *ptrOne + *ptrTwo + *ptrThree;
    cout  << result  << endl;
    return 0;
}
```

Exercise 1: If the three input values are 20, 10, and 30, what is printed by the first output statement?

Exercise 2: What is printed by the second output statement?

Exercise 3: What is the lifetime of the variables in this program?

Lesson 15–1: Check Prelab Exercises

Name _____ Date _____

Section _____

Exercise 1: Run program `Pointer` to check your answer to Exercise 1. Was your answer correct? If not, explain where you made your error.

Exercise 2: Was your answer correct? If not, explain where you made your error.

Exercise 3: The variables in program `Pointer` exist as long as the program is running.

Lesson 15–2: Pointer Variables

Name _____ Date _____

Section _____

Exercise 1: Extend program `Pointer` by adding the code to print the three input values in ascending order using the pointers to them. Show your output.

Exercise 2: Write a program that is the mirror image of program `Pointer` but the values that are read in are strings of length ten rather than integer values. That is, read in three strings, write them out, concatenate them (the string equivalent of addition), and print the result. Show your input data and your output.

Lesson 15–3: Dynamic Data

Name _____ Date _____

Section _____

Exercise 1: File `AltPtr.cpp` contains a shell of a program that does exactly what program `Pointer` does (Exercise 1, Lesson 15–2), but it uses dynamic variables. Fill in the code and run the program.

```cpp
// Program AltPtr reads in three variables, assigns
// pointers to them, adds them, and prints the result.
#include <iostream>
using namespace std;

int  main ()
{
    int*  one;
    int*  two;
    int*  three;
    int  result;

    // FILL IN THE Code to create dynamic variables
    // *one, *two, *three.

    cout  << "Enter three integer numbers separated"
          << " by blanks; press return."  << endl;

    // FILL IN THE Code to read the values into the
    // dynamic variables.

    // FILL IN THE Code to print the values that are to
    // be summed.

    // FILL IN THE Code to add the three values and store
    // the answer in result.

    cout  << result  << endl;

    // FILL IN THE Code to deallocate the dynamic data.
    return 0;
}
```

Show the output. It should be the same as Exercise 1, Lesson 15–2.

Exercise 2: Alter the program in Exercise 1 so that it reads strings of length ten rather than integers. That is, read in three strings, write them out, concatenate them, and print the result. Show your input data and your output.

Exercise 3: The outputs from Exercises 1 and 2 in this lesson are identical to the outputs from Exercises 1 and 2 in the previous lesson. The lifetime of the variables involved, however, is different. Explain.

Lesson 15–4: Classes and Dynamic Data

Name _____ Date _____

Section _____

Exercise 1: The header file for MoneyType is shown below.

```
// Header file for class MoneyType with constructors.

#include <iostream>
using namespace std;

class MoneyType
{
public:
    void  Initialize(long, long);
    long  DollarsAre() const;
    long  CentsAre() const;
    void  Print() const;
    MoneyType  Add(MoneyType) const;
    MoneyType();
    MoneyType(long, long);
private:
    long  dollars;
    long  cents;
};
```

Does class MoneyType need either a copy-constructor or a deep-copy operation? Explain.

Exercise 2: Class ExtMoneyClass as defined in this chapter is changed as shown below.

```
typedef char String10[11];

class ExtMoneyType : public MoneyType
{
public:
    char*  CurrencyIs();
    Initialize(long, long, const String10);
    ExtMoneyType();
    ExtMoneyType(long, long, const String10);
private:
    String10  currency;
};
```

Does class `ExtMoneyType` need either a copy-constructor or a deep-copy operation? Explain.

Exercise 3: The header file for the original class `ExtMoneyClass` is shown below.

```
class ExtMoneyType : public MoneyType
{
public:
    string  CurrencyIs();
    void  Initialize(long, long, const string);
    void  Print() const;
    ExtMoneyType();
    ExtMoneyType(long, long, const string);
private:
    string  currency;
};

ExtMoneyType  extMoney;
```

Does class `ExtMoneyType` need either a copy-constructor or a deep-copy operation? Explain.

Exercise 4: How is the version of `ExtMoneyType` shown in the Prelab Review different from the ones shown above? Discuss the impact of the differences on the concept of determining if either a copy-constructor or a deep-copy operation is necessary.

Lesson 15–5: Debugging

Name _____ Date _____

Section _____

Exercise 1: Program `UseParts` from the last chapter has been altered to add a part name to class `ExtPartsType`. It seems to compile but gives the wrong answer. Can you find the bug? Describe it.

Exercise 2: The output is still wrong! Keep looking until you find another bug. Describe it, correct it, and rerun the program.

Postlab Activities

Exercise 1: In Exercise 5, Lesson 14–2, you wrote a program that read in class objects, stored them in a list class object, and then printed them out again. Rewrite the program so that the items in the list are pointers to the class objects rather than the class objects themselves. Test your program using the same data.

Exercise 2: The algorithm for *insertion sort* is given below. Add a member function to your list class object in Exercise 1 that implements this algorithm. That is, the sort function transforms an unsorted list into a sorted list. Note that the algorithm sorts values in an array, and your function should sort pointers to values in an array.

```
FOR Index  ←  0 TO List.Length-1 DO
  Item ←  List.Items[Index ]
  Index2 ← Index - 1
  PlaceFound ←  False
  WHILE  NOT  PlaceFound  AND  Index2 >= 0
      IF  Item  <  List.Items[Index2]
          THEN
              List.Items[Index2 + 1] ←  List.Items[Index2]
              Index2 ←  Index2 - 1
          ELSE
              PlaceFound ←  True
      List.Items[Index2 + 1] ←  Item
```

Exercise 3: The algorithm for *selection sort* is given below. Write a member function that implements this algorithm. Again, the algorithm sorts values, not pointers to values.

```
FOR Index  ←  0 TO List.Length - 2 DO
  FOR Index2  ←  Index  TO Length-1 DO
    Find  Minimum  Value
  Swap  Minimum  Value  with  List.Items[Index]
```

Exercise 4: The algorithm for *bubble sort* is given below. Write a member function that implements this algorithm.

```
FOR Index  ←  0 TO List.Length - 2 DO
  FOR Index2  ←  List.Length-1 DOWNTO Index + 1
    IF  List.Items[Index2]  <  List.Items[Index2 - 1]
        THEN
            Swap  (List.Items[Index2],  List.Items[Index2 - 1])
```

Exercise 5: Bubble sort is unique among sorting algorithms because it has the capability of knowing when the list is already sorted. If no swap occurs for one iteration of the outer loop, the list is already sorted and the algorithm can stop. Add a member function that implements this improved version of bubble sort.

Exercise 6: Compare the performance of the four sorting algorithms. Postlab Exercise 6 in Chapter 11 asked you to write a program to generate test data. Use that program to generate data. If your system has built-in routines for timing the execution of a program, use them in your experiment. Otherwise, put a statement in your code that counts the number of times a swap is made. Fill in the following chart with either run times or number of swaps. Notice that the chart calls for the data to be in random order, in sorted order, and sorted in reverse order.

Number of Items	Insertion	Selection	Bubble	Modified Bubble
10				
random				
in order				
in reverse				
100				
random				
in order				
in reverse				
1000				
random				
in order				
in reverse				
10000				
random				
in order				
in reverse				

Exercise 7: Write a report comparing the four sorting algorithms based on your test results.

Linked Structures

- To be able to define and declare a linked list structure.

- To be able to create an unordered linked list of data values.

- To be able to process data values in an unordered linked list.

- To be able to create and process an unordered linked list of objects.

- To be able to create and process an ordered linked list of data values.

Chapter 16: Assignment Cover Sheet

Name _____ Date _____

Section _____

Fill in the following table showing which exercises have been assigned for each lesson and check what you are to submit: (1) lab sheets, (2) listings of output files, and/or (3) listings of programs. Your instructor or teaching assistant (TA) can use the Completed column for grading purposes.

Activities	Assigned: Check or list exercise numbers	Submit (1) (2) (3)			Completed
Prelab					
Review					
Prelab Assignment					
Inlab					
Lesson 16–1: Check Prelab Exercises					
Lesson 16–2: Unordered Linked Lists					
Lesson 16–3: Linked Lists of Objects					
Lesson 16–4: Sorted Lists of Objects					
Lesson 16–5: Debugging					
Postlab					

Prelab Activities

Review

Linked Structures Dynamic variables can be linked together to form dynamic lists. We define a record (called a *node*) that has two members: `next` (a pointer to the next node in the list) and `component` (the type of the items on the list). For example, let's assume that our list is a list of integers.

```
typedef int ComponentType;
struct NodeType;                  // forward declaration
typedef NodeType* NodePtr;
struct NodeType
{
    ComponentType  component;
    NodePtr  next;
};

NodePtr  listPtr;                 // external pointer
NodePtr  newNodePtr;              // extra pointer
NodePtr  currentNodePtr;          // extra pointer
```

Because an identifier must be declared before it can be used, we have to tell the compiler that `NodeType` is going to be a `struct`. We do this with a forward declaration that has the type name following the word `struct`. The forward declaration is similiar in use to a function prototype.

To form dynamic lists, we link variables of `NodeType` together to form a chain using the `next` member. We get the first dynamic list node and save its address in an *external pointer*. The external pointer is the name of the pointer to the first node in the list. We then get another node and store its address in the `next` member of the first node.

```
listPtr = new NodeType;           // external pointer
newNodePtr = new NodeType;
listPtr->next = newNodePtr;
```

We get a third node and store its address in the `next` member of the second node. This process continues until the list is complete. The pointer constant NULL (defined in `<cstddef>`) is a pointer that indicates the end of a list. The following code fragment reads and stores integer numbers into a list until the input stream fails.

```
#include <iostream>
#include <cstddef>                // to access NULL
using namespace std;
ComponentType  tempValue;
listPtr = new NodeType;
cin >> listPtr->component;        // assumes at least one value
currentNodePtr = listPtr;
cin >> tempValue;
```

```
while (cin)
{
    newNodePtr = new NodeType;
    newNodePtr->component = tempValue;
    currentNodePtr->next = newNodePtr;
    currentNodePtr = newNodePtr;
    cin >> tempValue;
}

currentNodePtr->next = NULL;
```

We read the first value outside the loop so that we can store it in the node pointed to by listPtr, the external pointer to the list. currentNodePtr is then set to point to listPtr. Within the loop we continue to get a node (newNodePtr), store a value in it, put the node's address in the next member of currentNodePtr, make currentNodePtr point to newNodePtr, and lastly read a new value. When all the values have been read and stored, NULL is placed in the next member of the last node in the list (the node pointed to by currentNodePtr).

Lists of dynamic variables are traversed (nodes accessed one by one) by beginning with the first node (the one pointed to by the external pointer) and accessing each node until the next member of a node is NULL. The following code fragment prints out the values in the list whose external pointer is listPtr.

```
currentNodePtr = listPtr;
while (currentNodePtr != NULL)
{
    cout << currentNodePtr->component << endl;
    currentNodePtr = currentNodePtr->next;
}
```

currentNodePtr is initialized to listPtr, the first node. If listPtr is NULL, the list is empty and the loop is not entered. If there is at least one node in the list, we enter the loop, print the member component of currentNodePtr, and update currentNodePtr to point to the next node in the list. currentNodePtr is NULL when the last component has been printed, and we exit the loop.

Because the component type of a list node can be any data type, we can create an infinite variety of lists. Pointers also can be used to create very complex data structures such as stacks, queues, and trees that are the subject of more advanced computer science courses.

Chapter 16: Prelab Assignment

Name _____ Date _____

Section _____

Read program `RealList` carefully and answer Exercises 1 through 4.

```cpp
// Program RealList creates a linked list of values from a
// file and prints the list.

#include <iostream>
#include <cstddef>          // to access NULL
#include <fstream>
using namespace std;

typedef float ComponentType;

struct NodeType;                    // forward declaration
typedef NodeType* NodePtr;
struct NodeType
{
    ComponentType  component;
    NodePtr  next;
};

int main ()
{
    NodePtr  listPtr;                   // external pointer
    NodePtr  newNodePtr;                // extra pointer
    NodePtr  currentNodePtr;            // extra pointer
    ComponentType  tempValue;
    ifstream  data;

    cout << fixed << showpoint;
    data.open("real.dat");
    listPtr = new NodeType;
    data >> listPtr->component;
    if (data)
    {   // read in values
        currentNodePtr = listPtr;
        data >> tempValue;
        while (data)
        {
            newNodePtr = new NodeType;
            newNodePtr->component = tempValue;
            currentNodePtr->next = newNodePtr;
            currentNodePtr = newNodePtr;
            data >> tempValue;
        }
        currentNodePtr->next = NULL;
    }
```

```
    else
        listPtr = NULL;

    // print out values
    currentNodePtr = listPtr;
    while (currentNodePtr != NULL)
    {
        cout << currentNodePtr->component  << endl;
        currentNodePtr = currentNodePtr->next;
    }
    return 0;
}
```

Exercise 1: Draw a picture of the structure when the data file contains the values 11.1, 22.2, 33.3, and 44.4. Use a slash (/) to represent NULL.

Exercise 2: What is printed?

Exercise 3: Draw a picture of the structure when the data file is empty.

Exercise 4: What is printed?

Lesson 16–1: Check Prelab Exercises

Name _____ Date _____

Section _____

Exercise 1:

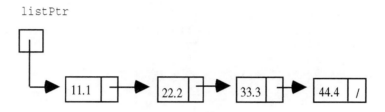

Exercise 2: Run program `RealList` to check your answer. Were you answers correct? If not, can you explain the difference?

Exercise 3:

Exercise 4: Nothing is printed.

Lesson 16–2: Unordered Linked Lists

Name _____ Date _____

Section _____

This lesson uses class `ListType`.

```
// Header file for class ListType
// The user must provide a file "DataDefn.h" that includes a
// definition of ItemType, the type of the items in the list.

#include "DataDefn.h"                // to access ItemType

struct  NodeType;                    // forward declaration

class  ListType
{
public:
    ListType();
    // Post: List is the empty list.

    ListType(const ListType& otherList);
    // Copy-constructor for ListType.

    bool  IsThere(ItemType  item) const;
    // Post: If item is in the list IsThere is
    //       True; False, otherwise.

    void  Insert(ItemType  item);
    // Pre: item is not already in the list.
    // Post: item is in the list.

    void  Delete(ItemType  item);
    // Pre: item is in the list.
    // Post: item is no longer in the list.

    void  Print() const;
    // Post: Items on the list are printed on the screen.

    int  Length() const;
    // Post: Length is equal to the number of items in the
    //       list.

    ~ListType();
    // Post: List has been destroyed.

private:
    NodeType* listPtr;
};
```

```
// This is the implementation file for class ListType

#include <iostream>
#include <cstddef>            // to access NULL
#include "ListType.h"
using namespace std;

typedef NodeType* NodePtr;

struct NodeType
{
    ItemType item;
    NodePtr  next;
};

ListType::ListType()
// Post: listPtr is set to NULL.
{
    // FILL IN Code.
}


//*************************************************************


ListType::ListType(const ListType&  otherList)
// Copy-constructor for ListType.
{
    // FILL IN Code.
}


//*************************************************************


bool  ListType::IsThere(ItemType  item) const
// Post: If item is in the list IsThere is
//       True; False, otherwise.
{
    // FILL IN Code.
}


//*************************************************************


void  ListType::Insert(ItemType  item)
// Pre: item is not already in the list.
// Post: item is the first item in the list.
{
    // FILL IN Code.
}


//*************************************************************


void  ListType::Delete(ItemType  item)
// Pre: item is in the list.
// Post: item is no longer in the list.
{
    // FILL IN Code.
}


//*************************************************************
```

```
void  ListType::Print() const
// Post: Items on the list are printed on the screen.
{
    // FILL IN Code.
}


//*************************************************************


int  ListType::Length() const
// Post: Number of items have been counted; result returned.
{
    // FILL IN Code.
}


//*************************************************************


ListType::~ListType()
// Post: All the components are deleted.
{
    // FILL IN Code.
}
```

Exercise 1: Read the internal documentation for class `ListType` carefully. Fill in the missing code in the implementation file, taking advantage of the preconditions. (`ItemType` is defined to be `int` in file `DataDefn.h`.) Compile your program.

Exercise 2: Write a simple driver that reads values from file `int.dat`, inserts them into the list, prints the length of the final list, and prints the items. Be sure that your driver checks for the preconditions on the member functions of class `ListType` before calling them. How many items are in the list? If your answer is not 11, your driver did not adhere to the preconditions. Correct your driver and rerun your program.

Exercise 3: Add code to your driver to test the remaining member functions. Delete –47, 1926, and 2000 and print the list to be sure they are gone. How do you test the copy-constructor and the destructor?

Exercise 4: Add member functions to class `ListType` that find the minimum and maximum values in the list. Rerun your program.

Minimum value is _____.

Maximum value is _____.

Lesson 16–3: Linked Lists of Objects

Name _____ Date _____

Section _____

Exercise 1: Define a `class` data type, `StringType`, that contains one data field, a C string of 10 characters. There should be four member functions: `Initialize`, `GetString`, `PrintString`, and `CompareString`. `Initialize` stores a value in an instance of `StringType`; `GetString` returns as a parameter the value stored in an instance of `StringType`; and `PrintString` prints the value in an instance of `StringType` on the screen. Do you need a copy-constructor, a destructor, and a deep copy function? Explain.

Exercise 2: What changes are necessary to class `ListType` (in Lesson 16–2) to convert `ItemType` into `StringType`—that is, to make the list a list of C strings rather than a list of integers?

Describe the changes necessary in the specification file.

Fill in the chart below, indicating which member function implementations must be changed and which could be changed.

Member Function	Not changed	Must be changed	Could be changed
IsThere			
Insert			
Delete			
Print			
Length			
MinValue			
MaxValue			
Constructor			
Destructor			

Describe the changes necessary in the driver program.

Exercise 3: Make the changes necessary and run your program, deleting *Dove* and *sandpiper* from file `char.dat`.

Minimum value is _____.

Maximum value is _____.

Exercise 4: Examine your output from Exercise 3 carefully. Notice that *sandpiper* is printed as the maximum although *Wren* is logically the maximum. We tend to ignore the difference between uppercase and lowercase letters when we are looking for the one closest to the beginning of the alphabet (minimum) or closest to the end of the alphabet (maximum). Unfortunately, the computer does not. Add the code to your program to convert the strings to all uppercase letters before you store them in the list. Rerun your program.

Minimum value is _____.

Maximum value is _____.

Lesson 16–4: Sorted List of Objects

Name _____ Date _____

Section _____

Exercise 1: Class `ListType` puts each new item at the front of the list because that is the most efficient algorithm if the list is unordered. However, searching for an item requires that the entire list be searched in order to determine that an item is not in the list. If the list is ordered, the search can stop when the place is passed where the item would be if it were in the list. Specify an ordered list class. Fill in the following chart, showing which algorithms can remain the same, which must change, and which can be changed to make them more efficient. Note that we have gone back to the original member functions defined for `ListType`.

Member Function	Not changed	Must be changed	Could be changed
IsThere			
Insert			
Delete			
Print			
Length			
Constructor			
Destructor			

Exercise 2: Write the implementation for the specification in Exercise 1. If you said that only member function `Insert` must to be changed, you are correct. However, `IsThere` and `Delete` can be made more efficient.

Exercise 3: Write a driver program to test your new sorted list, using file `Char.dat`.

Lesson 16–5: Debugging

Name _____ Date _____

Section _____

Exercise 1: Program IntList reads values into a linked list and prints the list. However, the list is always empty. Can you find the errors? Describe them, correct them, and rerun the program.

Postlab Activities

Exercise 1: The Postlab for Chapter 14 required you to design and implement the ADT MusicCollection. You kept the recordings as an array-based list because that was the only list implementation structure that you knew. Now you realize that a linked list is a better structure to use because your collection is continuing to grow. Rewrite your program once again, changing the array-based list to a linked list.

Exercise 2: Can you use the same test plan you used for the previous version? Explain.

Exercise 3: The program to manipulate information about your music collection takes a long time to run. You decide to improve its performance by keeping the list ordered by title. Which operations have to be changed? Which ones do not?

Exercise 4: Arrays and linked structures are two implementations of the abstract data type list. Can one implementation always be substituted for the other? Are there types of problems for which one is more efficient than the other? Discuss the relative merits of array-based lists and linked lists using concrete examples.

Templates and Exceptions

- To be able to use the C++ template mechanism for defining generic functions.

- To be able to instantiate and use a template function.

- To be able to use the C++ template mechanism for defining generic data types.

- To be able to instantiate and use a template class.

- To be able to use the C++ exception handling mechanism.

Chapter 17: Assignment Cover Sheet

Name _____ Date _____

Section _____

Fill in the following table showing which exercises have been assigned for each lesson and check what you are to submit: (1) lab sheets, (2) listings of output files, and/or (3) listings of programs. Your instructor or teaching assistant (TA) can use the Completed column for grading purposes.

Activities	Assigned: Check or list exercise numbers	Submit (1) (2) (3)			Completed
Prelab					
Review					
Prelab Assignment					
Inlab					
Lesson 17–1: Check Prelab Exercises					
Lesson 17–2: Generic Data Types					
Lesson 17–3: Generic Functions					
Lesson 17–4: Exception Handling					
Lesson 17–5: Test Plan					
Postlab					

Prelab Activities

Review

Generic Data Types   A *generic data type* is a data type for which the operations are defined but the types of the items being manipulated are not. Some programming languages have a built-in mechanism for defining generic data types; some do not. C++ does. The mechanism is called a *template*. A template allows us to write a description of a class type with "blanks" left in the description to be filled in by the client code. Just as variables are the parameters to functions, types are the parameters to templates.

In the `ListType` class in Chapter 13, we defined the item on the list to be of type `ItemType` and used a *typedef* statement to equate `ItemType` with a built-in type. The following code crates a *class template*, a pattern for a class type in which `ItemType` is the *template parameter*.

```
template<class ItemType>
class ListType
{
public:
    void Store(ItemType item);
    // Pre: item is not in the list.
    //       The list is not full.
    // Post: item is in the list.
    void PrintList();
    // Post: List elements are printed on the screen.
    int Length();
    // Post: return value is the number of items in the list.
    bool IsEmpty();
    // Post: returns true if list is empty; false otherwise.
    bool IsFull();
    // Post: returns true if there is no more room in the
    //       list; false otherwise.
    ListType();
    // Constructor
    // Post: Empty list is created.
private:
    int length;
    ItemType values[MAX_ITEMS];
}
```

Everything looks the same except for the statement

```
template<class ItemType>
```

but this statement has a powerful effect on the following class definition. The definition is no longer a pattern for stamping out objects, but a pattern for stamping out individual class data types. To instantiate the class and subsequently create an object of this class, we have to provide a type as an argument.

```
ListType<int> myList, myList2;
ListType<float> yourList;
ListType<string> theirList;
```

The type in angle brackets is the *template argument*. Everywhere `ItemType` appears in the class template, it is replaced by the template argument when the class template is instantiated. It's as if we had written three distinct class definitions: `ListInt`, where `ItemType` is `int`, `ListFloat`, where `ItemType` is `float`, and `ListSring`, where `ItemType` is `string`.

```
ListInt myList, myList2;
ListFloat yourList;
ListString theirList;
```

In effect, that is exactly what the compiler does. When the compiler instantiates a class template, it literally substitutes the argument for the formal parameter throughout the class template, just as we would do a search-and-replace operation in a word processor or text editor. After the class template has been instantiated, an object of the class is created. An instantiated class template is called a *template class*. Note that, although the class template uses the word *class*, the argument can be any type, built-in or user defined.

We must write the member functions as *function templates* so that the compiler can associate each one with the proper template class. For example, we code the `Insert` function as the following function template:

```
template <class ItemType>
void ListType<ItemType>::Store(ItemType item)
// Pre:   item is not in the list.
//        The list is not full.
// Post: item is added at the end of the list.
//        length has been incremented.
{
    values[length] = item;
    length++;
}
```

The template statement must be immediately above each function definition in the implementation file. To associate each function with the appropriate template class, `<ItemType>` must be appended to the class name everywhere it appears in the member functions. When the functions are instantiated, the compiler substitutes the template argument for `ItemType` throughout the function bodies.

Generic Functions   There are times when we want to make a function generic, that is, not a class member. For example, sorting is a very common activity; it is the process of changing an unsorted list into a sorted list. Here is a generic function that takes an unsorted array and the number of items and sorts the items in the array into ascending order. Chapter 15, Postlab Exercise 3, gives the algorithm for the selection sort used here.

```
template<class ItemType>
void SelectSort(ItemType values[], int numValues)
// Pre:  < is defined on ItemType.
// Post: The elements in the array values are sorted in
//       ascending order using the selection sort algorithm.
```

```
{
    int endIndex = numValues-1;
    int indexOfMin;
    ItemType temp;
    for (int current = 0; current < endIndex; current++)
    {
        indexOfMin = current;
        for (int index = current+1; index <= endIndex; index++)
            if (values[index] < values[indexOfMin])
                indexOfMin = index;

        // Swap values[current] and values[indexOfMin]
        temp = values[current];
        values[current] = values[indexOfMin];
        values[indexOfMin] = temp;
    }
}
```

To instantiate the function template, we use a template argument to tell the compiler what type to substitute for template parameter `ItemType`.

```
SelectSort<int>(intList, length);        // sorts integers
SelectSort<AdrType>(adrList, length);    // sorts AdrType objects
SelectSort(floatList, length);           // sorts floats
```

The first statement sorts an array of `int` values; the second sorts an array of `AdrType` values; and the third sorts an array of—what? If the template argument is missing, the compiler deduces the template argument by looking at the function argument list. Most programmers use the default and do not bother to insert the template argument.

There is one more thing you should notice about this function template. The precondition states that the relational operator < is defined on `ItemType`. All built-in types automatically have the relational operators defined. This precondition alerts the client: If the template argument is a user-defined type, the < operator must be redefined using *operator overloading*. Operator overloading is beyond the scope of this manual, but we mention it to alert you to interesting features yet to come.

File Organization with Templates We have been putting class declarations in `.h` files and member function code in the `.cpp` files. This allows the class to be compiled independently of any client code. However, the use of templates poses a problem with this configuration. The compiler cannot compile a function template until it knows the template argument, which is defined in the client code. To get around this dilemma, include the corresponding `.cpp` file as the last statement in the `.h` file and include the `.h` file in the client code. This way all of the code is compiled together. For example, #include "ListType.cpp" would be the last statement in the `ListType.h` file.

If you are using an IDE (integrated development environment), you need to be careful when using templates. With most IDEs you are asked to create a project and include the `.cpp` files in the project. These file are automatically compiled separately. When using templates, the `.cpp` file containing templates cannot be compiled separately and should *not* be included in the project. The #include "ListType.h" in the client code brings the files in to be compiled with the client code.

Exceptions Exceptions are just what the name implies: exceptional situations. They are situations that, when they occur, the flow of control of the program must be altered, usually resulting in a premature program termination. An exception may be handled at any place in the software hierarchy—from the place in the program where the exception is first detected through the top level of the program. Where in an application an exception *should* be handled is a design decision; however, exceptions should be handled at a level that knows what the exception means.

The exception-handling mechanism is made up of the *try-catch* and *throw* statements that allow us to detect an exception (*try* code with a possible exception), to alert the system to an exception (*throw* the exception), and to handle an exception (*catch* the exception). The code that may cause an exception and the code to detect it are embedded in the body of the *try* clause. If an exception is detected, the *throw* statement is used to alert the system that the exception has occurred. Associated with each *try* clause is one or more *catch* clauses. The body of the *catch* clause contains the exception handler, the code to handle the exception. If an exception is not thrown, execution continues with the statement immediately following the *try-catch* statement.

Let's examine the following concrete example that reads and sums positive values from a file. An exception occurs if a zero or negative value is encountered. If this happens, we want to write a message to the screen and stop the program.

```
string msg = "Negative value";
try
{
    infile >> value;
    do
    {
        if (value <= 0)
            throw msg;  // Exception is a string
        sum = sum + value;
    }while (infile);
}

catch (string message)
// Parameter of the catch is type string
{
    // Code that handles the exception
    cout << message << " found in file. Program aborted."
    return 1;
}
// Code to continue processing if exception not thrown.
cout << "Sum of values on the file: " << sum << endl;
```

A values is read. If it is less than or equal to zero, a string is thrown. Otherwise, the value is added to the sum. If a string is thrown, control jumps to the closest `catch` with a string parameter. The argument to the `catch` parameter (`message`) is the exception that is thrown. The exception handler prints the parameter and exits. If all the values are greater than zero, execution continues with the statement below the `catch` block.

If there is more than one `throw` in a `try` block and the thrown exceptions are of different types, there must be a `catch` for each type. The type of the exception thrown is matched against the parameter of each `catch` to find the appropriate exception handler.

In this example, the exception handler has a *return* statement that transfers control to another part of the program. If the exception handler doesn't transfer control elsewhere, control is passed to the first statement immediately following the *try-catch* statement.

The *throw* statement is followed by an expression. In this example, a string is thrown. A value or a variable of any data type, built-in or user-defined, can be thrown. In practice, it is more common to embed the exception handler in a class or struct and throw an object of this class or struct.

Chapter 17: Prelab Assignment

Name _____ Date _____

Section _____

Read the following class declaration in file "SListType.h" carefully and answer Exercises 1 and 2.

```cpp
// File SListType.h contains the class declaration for a
//    sorted list.
const int MAX_ITEMS = 20;
typedef int ItemType;

class SListType
{
public:
    void Insert(ItemType item);
    // Pre:  The list is not full;
    // Post: item is in the list; list is stored in
    //       increasing order.
    void PrintList();
    // Post: If the list is not empty, the elements are
    //       printed on the screen in increasing order;
    //       otherwise "The list is empty" is
    //       printed on the screen.
    int Length();
    // Post: return value is the number of items in the list.
    bool IsEmpty();
    // Post: returns true if list is empty; false otherwise.
    bool IsFull();
    // Post: returns true if there is no more room in the
    //       list; false otherwise.
    SListType();
    // Constructor
    // Post: Empty list is created.
private:
    int length;
    ItemType values[MAX_ITEMS];
}
```

Exercise 1: Make the changes necessary on the text of this declaration to make it a class template.

Exercise 2: Write the headers for the function definitions. Do not include the documentation or the function bodies.

Read the following code segment carefully and answer Exercises 3, 4, and 5.

```
string msg1 = "Negative value";
string msg2 = "Zero value";
try
{
    infile >> value;
    do
    {
        if (value < 0)
            throw msg1;  // Exception is a string
        else if (value == 0)
            throw msg2;  // Exception is a string
        sum = sum + value;
    }while (infile);
}

catch (string message)
// Parameter of the catch is type string
{
    // Code that handles the exception
    cout << message << " found in file. Program aborted."
         << endl;
    return 1;
}
// Code to continue processing if exception not thrown.
cout << "Sum of values on the file: " << sum << endl;
```

Exercise 3: What is printed by the code segment if the data is as follows:
5, 6, 0, -1

Exercise 4: What is printed by the code segment if the data is as follows:
5, 6, -1, 0

Exercise 5: What is printed if the return statement is removed and the data is as shown in Exercise 4?

Lesson 17–1: Check Prelab Exercises

Name _____   Date _____

Section _____

Exercise 1: Additional statements are in bold.

```
// File SListType.h contains the class declaration for a
//    sorted list.
const int MAX_ITEMS = 20;

template<class ItemType>
class SListType
{
public:
  √ void Insert(ItemType item);
     // Pre:  The list is not full;
     // Post: item is in the list; list is stored in
     //        increasing order.
  √ void PrintList();
     // Post: If the list is not empty, the elements are
     //        printed on the screen in increasing order;
     //        otherwise "The list is empty" is
     //        printed on the screen.
  √ int Length();
     // Post: return value is the number of items in the list.
  √ bool IsEmpty();
     // Post: returns true if list is empty; false otherwise.
  √ bool IsFull();
     // Post: returns true if there is no more room in the
     //        list; false otherwise.
  √ SListType();
     // Constructor
     // Post: Empty list is created.
private:
    int length;
    ItemType values[MAX_ITEMS];
}
#include "SListType.cpp"
```

Exercise 2:

```
template<class ItemType>
void SListType<ItemType>::Insert(ItemType item);
template<class ItemType>
void SListType<ItemType>::PrintList();
template<class ItemType>
int SListType<ItemType>::Length();
template<class ItemType>
```

```
bool SListType<ItemType>::IsEmpty();
template<class ItemType>
bool SListType<ItemType>::IsFull();
template<class ItemType>
SListType<ItemType>::SListType();
```

Exercise 3: "Zero value found in file. Program aborted."

Exercise 4: "Negative value found in file. Program aborted."

Exercise 5: "Negative value found in file. Program aborted."

"Sum of values on the file: 11"

Lesson 17–2: Generic Data Types

Name _____ Date _____

Section _____

Exercise 1: Complete the implementation file for the SListType class template in the Prelab Exercise 1. Class SListType was used in Lesson13–3. Can the function bodies written for this lesson be used here? Explain.

Exercise 2: Exercise 2 in Lesson 13–3 asked you to write a driver. How must you change that driver to execute with SListClass as written in Exercise 1 above?

Exercise 3: Make the changes outlined in Exercise 2 and run your program with int.dat. Your answers should be the same.

Exercise 4: Change your driver and run the program using data file real.dat. What changes did you have to make in the driver?

Exercise 5: Lesson 16–2, Exercise 1 asks you to fill in the missing code in class ListType, a linked implementation of a list. This implementation has ItemType defined in a file DataDefn.h. Take your solution and change it so that ItemType is a template parameter. Hint: Both ListType and NodeType must be templated.

Exercise 6: Take the driver you wrote in Lesson 16–2, Exercise 2 and run it with the class template defined in Exercise 5. Your answers should be the same.

Lesson 17–3: Generic Functions

Name _____ Date _____

Section _____

Exercise 1: *Merging* is the process of taking two sorted lists and combining them into one sorted list. Here is the algorithm for merging two array-based lists with no duplicates into one array-based list with no duplicates. The input parameters are the two arrays containing the list items (`values1` and `values2`) and the number of elements in each (`numElements1` and `numElements2`). The output parameters are the array `valuesOut` and the number of items in `valuesOut` (`numValues`). Study this algorithm carefully, using sample data until you are sure you understand it.

```
Set index1 to 0 // index for first array
Set index2 to 0 // index for second array
Set index3 to 0 // index for result
WHILE (index1 < numElements1 AND index2 < numElements2) DO
    IF (values1[index1] < values2[index2])
            THEN // item in values1 is the smallest
                    Set valueOut[index3] =  values1[index1]
                    Set index1 to index1 + 1
                    Set index3 to index3 + 1
    ELSE IF (values1[index1] == values2[index2])
            THEN // items are equal; only one copy goes into the result
                    Set valueOut[index3] to values1[index1]
                    Set index1 to index1 + 1
                    Set index2 to index2 + 1
                    Set index3 to index3 + 1
    ELSE // item in values2 is the smallest
            Set valuesOut[index3] to values2[index2]
            Set index2 to index2 + 1
            Set index3 to index3 + 1

// One or both arrays have been processed
// Move any unprocessed items into result
WHILE (index1 < numElements1)
    // does not execute if all values1 has been processed
    Set valueOut[index3] =  values1[index1]
    Set index1 to index1 + 1
    Set index3 to index3 + 1
WHILE (index2 < numElements2)
    // does not execute if all values2 has been processed
    Set valuesOut[index3] to values2[index2]
    Set index2 to index2 + 1
    Set index3 to index3 + 1

Set numValues to index3
```

Exercise 2: Implement the merge algorithm in Exercise 1 as generic function `Merge`.

Exercise 3: Write a driver that instantiates two lists of class `SListType`, calls function `Merge`, and prints the results. Use files `charOne.dat` and `charTwo.dat`. Function argument is `char`. What is printed?

Exercise 4: If the values in the data files represent items in a set, what set operation does the `Merge` function implement?

Exercise 5: By removing four statements in this algorithm, you can implement another very common set operation. What four statements would you remove and what common set operation would the changed algorithm implement?

Lesson 17–4: Exceptions

Name _____ Date _____

Section _____

✓

Exercise 1: Class `SListType` uses a precondition to guarantee that the list is not full before an insertion is made. Change function `Insert` so that it throws a string exception if the list is full when the function is called. Have the driver catch the exception and print an error message. Run your program using `realTwo.dat`. What is printed? (Did you remember to change the documentation in `SListType`?)

✓

Exercise 2: Create a class template `SList2Type` that is just like `SListType` except that duplicates are not allowed. Here is the documentation for the `Insert` function. How much of the code from Exercise 1 can you use for this exercise?

```
void Insert(ItemType item);
// Post: If the list is full, a string exception is thrown.
//       Otherwise if item is already in the list, a string
//       exception is thrown; otherwise, item is inserted
//       into list. The list is stored in increasing order.
```

Exercise 3: Write a driver for class `SList2Type`. Have the driver print any exceptions and continue processing. Lesson 17–5 asks you to write a test plan for this class.

Lesson 17–5: Test Plan

Name _____ Date _____

Section _____

Exercise 1: Write a test plan for generic function `Merge` implemented in Lesson 17–3.

Reason for Test Case	Input Values	Expected Output	Observed Output

Exercise 2: Implement the test plan written in Exercise 1.

Exercise 3: Write a test plan for class `SList2Type`.

Reason for Test Case	Input Values	Expected Output	Observed Output

Exercise 4: Implement the test plan written in Exercise 3.

Postlab Activities

Exercise 1: Lesson 12, Postlab Exercise 8 asked you to implement a matrix with the following functions for a 5-by-4 matrix. Rewrite this program as a template class, where the template argument is either `int` or `float`.

Add	Takes two matrices (A and B) as input and returns a matrix (`Result`) in which each position is the sum of the corresponding positions in A and B.
Sub	Takes two matrices (A and B) as input and returns a matrix (`Result`) in which each position is the corresponding position in A minus the corresponding position in B.
Write	Takes a file name and a matrix as input and writes the matrix by row, one row per line on the file.
GetMat	Takes a file name and a matrix as input, reads values from the file, and stores them into the matrix.

Exercise 2: Can you use the same test plan you used for the previous version? Explain.

Exercise 3: We pointed out that the merge operation can be used to implement set operations. Take the basic algorithm and rewrite it to answer each of the following questions, where A and B are sets. A is the first list and B is the second list.

- Is A a subset of B?
- Is B a subset of A?
- Are A and B identical sets?

Exercise 4: Implement the algorithms designed in Exercise 3.

Exercise 5: Write and implement a test plan for Exercise 4.

Recursion

- To be able to write a recursive value-returning function to solve a problem involving simple variables.

- To be able to write a recursive void function to solve a problem involving simple variables.

- To be able to write a recursive value-returning function to solve a problem involving structured variables.

- To be able to write a recursive void function to solve a problem involving structured variables.

Chapter 18: Assignment Cover Sheet

Name _____ Date _____

Section _____

Fill in the following table showing which exercises have been assigned for each lesson and check what you are to submit: (1) lab sheets, (2) listings of output files, and/or (3) listings of programs. Your instructor or teaching assistant (TA) can use the Completed column for grading purposes.

Activities	Assigned: Check or list exercise numbers	Submit (1) (2) (3)			Completed
Prelab					
Review					
Prelab Assignment					
Inlab					
Lesson 18–1: Check Prelab Exercises					
Lesson 18–2: Simple Variables					
Lesson 18–3: Structured Variables					
Lesson 18–4: Debugging					
Postlab					

Prelab Activities

Review

When a function invokes itself, the call is known as a *recursive* call. Recursion—the ability of a function to call itself—is an alternative control structure to repetition (looping). Rather than use a *while* statement, *do-while* statement, or *for* statement to execute a segment of code again, the program uses a selection statement (*if* or *switch* statement) to determine whether to repeat the code by calling the function again or to stop the process.

Each recursive solution has at least two cases: the *base case* and the *general case*. The base case is the one to which we have an answer; the general case expresses the solution in terms of a call to itself with a smaller version of the problem. Because the general case solves a smaller and smaller version of the original problem, eventually the program reaches the base case, where an answer is known and the recursion stops.

Simple Variables Associated with each recursive problem is some measure of the size of the problem. The size must get smaller with each recursive call. The first step in any recursive solution is to determine the *size factor*. If the problem involves a numerical value, the size factor might be the value itself. For example, a classic recursive problem is the factorial. The factorial of a number is defined as the number times the product of all the numbers between itself and 0: $N! = N * (N-1)!$. The factorial of 0 is 1. The size factor is the number for which we are calculating the factorial. We have a base case, Factorial(0) is 1, and we have a general case, Factorial(N) is $N *$ Factorial(N-1). An *if* statement can evaluate N to see if it is 0 (the base case) or greater than 0 (the general case). Because N is clearly getting smaller with each call, the base case is reached.

```
long Factorial(long n)
// Pre: n is not negative.
{
    if (n == 0)
       return 1;                      // base case
    else
       return n * Factorial(n-1);     // general case
}
```

What happens if n is a negative number? The function just keeps calling itself until the runtime support system runs out of memory. This situation is called infinite recursion and is equivalent to an infinite loop. If infinite recursion occurs, the program may crash with a message such as "RUN-TIME STACK OVERFLOW" or the program (and the screen) may just freeze.

Structured Variables If we are working with structures rather than single values, the size is often the number of items in the structure. For example, if we want to count the number of items in a list, the base case is when the list is empty: there are no items in an empty list. In a nonempty list, the number of items is one plus the number of items in the rest of the list.

```
int  NumItems(NodePtr  listPtr)
{
    if (listPtr == NULL)
       return  0;
    else
       return  (1 + NumItems(listPtr->next));
}
```

When using recursion with structured variables, the base case can be a "do nothing" case. For example, the following function prints the values in a linked list in reverse order.

```
void  RevPrint(NodePtr  listPtr)
{
    if (listPtr != NULL)
    {
        RevPrint(listPtr -> next);
        cout  << listPtr -> component  << endl;
    }
}
```

Notice that there is no `else` branch. When `listPtr` is NULL, the function simply returns to the previous call.

Recursion is a very powerful and elegant tool. However, not all problems can easily be solved recursively, and not all problems that have an obvious recursive solution should be solved recursively. But there are many problems for which a recursive solution is preferable. If the problem statement logically falls into two cases, a base case and a general case, you should consider a recursive solution.

Chapter 18: Prelab Assignment

Name _____ Date _____

Section _____

Exercise 1: Fill in the following chart showing the value of the variable n at the beginning of each execution of function Factorial, starting with the nonrecursive call Factorial(5). Fill in the third column with the function value returned at the completion of the execution of that call.

Call	n	Function Value Returned
Nonrecursive Call		
1st Recursive Call		
2nd Recursive Call		
3rd Recursive Call		
4th Recursive Call		
5th Recursive Call		

Exercise 2: Fill in the chart showing the value of the variable listPtr at the beginning of each execution of function NumItems where listPtr is as shown below. Refer to listPtr by an arrow → to the value in the node. For example, →3 refers to the node containing the value 3. Fill in the third column with the function value returned at the completion of the execution of that call.

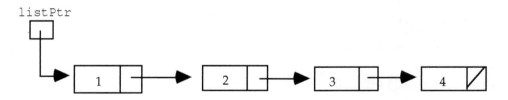

Call	listPtr	Function Value Returned
Nonrecursive Call		
1st Recursive Call		
2nd Recursive Call		
3rd Recursive Call		
4th Recursive Call		

Lesson 18–1: Check Prelab Exercises

Name _____ Date _____

Section _____

Exercise 1:

Call	n	Function Value Returned
Nonrecursive Call	5	120
1st Recursive Call	4	24
2nd Recursive Call	3	6
3rd Recursive Call	2	2
4th Recursive Call	1	1
5th Recursive Call	0	1

Exercise 2:

Call	listPtr	Function Value Returned
Value Returned		
Nonrecursive Call	→ 1	4
1st Recursive Call	→ 2	3
2nd Recursive Call	→ 3	2
3rd Recursive Call	→ 4	1
4th Recursive Call	NULL	0

Note that the function return value gets assigned at the end of the execution of each call.

Lesson 18–2: Simple Variables

Name _____ Date _____

Section _____

Exercise 1: C++ does not have an exponential operator. Write the recursive value-returning function `Power` that takes two parameters (`number` and `exponent`) and returns `number` multiplied by itself `exponent` times. That is, `Power` returns the result of numberexponent. Run a driver program that calls `Power(7, 3)` and prints the result.

What is printed?

Exercise 2: The Fibonacci numbers are defined as the following sequence:

0 1 1 2 3 5 8 13 21 34 55 ... *89 144 233 377 610 987 1597 2584 4181*

Notice that, except for the first two numbers, each number is the sum of the two preceding numbers. Write a recursive value-returning function, `Fib`, which returns the *N*th Fibonacci number where N is a parameter. Test your program with `Fib(5)`, `Fib(10)`, and `Fib(20)`.

Show your output.

Exercise 3: Write an iterative version of function `Fib` and test it with the same values.

Exercise 4: You have just demonstrated that the Fibonacci numbers can be generated recursively and iteratively. If you need them in a program, which version do you use? Justify your answer.

Lesson 18–3: Structured Variables

Name _____ Date _____

Section _____

Exercise 1: Write a recursive void function that prints out the values in a linked list.

Exercise 2: Is Exercise 1 a good use of recursion? In the Chapter Review, we wrote a function to print the values in a linked list in reverse order. Was that a good use of recursion? Explain your answers.

Exercise 3: Write a recursive int function that returns the position of a given value in a linked list. If the value is not in the list, return 0. For example, given the following list and a value of 4, the function would return 2.

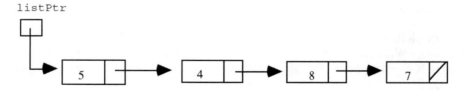

Exercise 4: Write a test driver for your function in Exercise 3. Use the list shown above. Run your driver, asking for the positions of 5, 4, 8, 7, and 10. Record the results.

Lesson 18–4: Debugging

Name _____ Date _____

Section _____

Exercise 1: In order to practice writing recursive processes, you decide to write a recursive function to sum the values in a file. Program SumTest is the result, but it isn't working. Debug it.

List the errors found and what you did to correct them. (Hint: There are two.)

Postlab Activities

Exercise 1: How many possible bridge hands are there? This question is a specific case of the general question, "How many combinations of X items can I make out of Y items?" In the case of the bridge hand, X is 13 and Y is 52. The solution is given by the following formula:

Combinations(Y, X) =

Y	if $X = 1$
1	if $X = Y$
(Combinations(Y–1, X–1) + Combinations(Y–1, X))	if $Y > X > 1$

Write a recursive function that calculates the number of combinations of X items that can be made from Y items. Write a driver and answer the original questions.

Exercise 2: Write a recursive void function that prints the contents of an array-based list in reverse order.

Exercise 3: Write and implement a test plan for Exercise 2 above. Is Exercise 2 a good use of recursion? Justify your answer.

Exercise 4: Write a recursive `bool` function, `IsThere`, that searches an array-based list for a value and returns `true` if the value is there and `false` otherwise. Use the binary search algorithm.

Exercise 5: Write and implement a test plan for Exercise 4 above. Is Exercise 4 a good use of recursion? Justify your answer.

Exercise 6: In Chapter 13, we described the binary search algorithm. This algorithm is an inherently recursive algorithm, though it is often implemented iteratively. Take the code for class `SlistType` as developed in Lesson 13–3, Exercises 1 through 5. Write recursive function `BinSrch` as a helper function in `SlstType.cpp`. Change the code of each member function, which requires a search, to use `BinSrch`. Test your class using the driver written for Exercise 6 in Lesson 13–3.

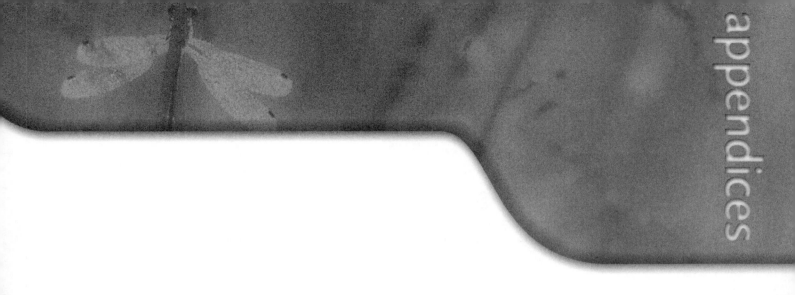

Appendix A

Java Reserved Words

The following identifiers are *reserved words*—identifiers with predefined meanings in the C++ language. The programmer cannot declare them for other uses in a C++ program.

and	double	not	this
and_eq	dynamic_cast	not_eq	throw
asm	else	operator	true
auto	enum	or	try
bitand	explicit	or_eq	typedef
bitor	export	private	typeid
bool	extern	protected	typename
break	false	public	union
case	float	register	unsigned
catch	for	reinterpret_cast	using
char	friend	return	virtual
class	goto	short	void
compl	if	signed	volatile
const	inline	sizeof	wchar_t
const_cast	int	static	while
continue	long	static_cast	xor
default	mutable	struct	xor_eq
delete	namespace	switch	
do	new	template	

Appendix B

Operator Precedence

The following is a list of the C++ operators, which are covered in the manual. Operators are binary unless marked unary.

Operators	Associativity
:: (scope resolution)	Left to right
() [] -> .	Left to right
++(postfix) --(postfix)	Right to left
! +(unary) –(unary) new delete (cast) sizeof *(unary) &(unary)	Right to left
->* .*	Left to right
* / %	Left to right
+ -	Left to right
<< >>	Left to right
< <= > >=	Left to right
== !=	Left to right
&	Left to right
^	Left to right
|	Left to right
&&	Left to right
||	Left to right

Appendix C

Description of Selected Operators

Type of Operator	Operator	Meaning
arithmetic	*	Unary plus
	-	Unary minus
	+	Addition
	-	Subtraction
	*	Multiplication
	/	Floating point operands: floating point result
		Integer operands: quotient
		Mixed operands: floating point result
	%	Modulus (remainder from integer division, operands must be integral)
	++	Increment by one; postfix form covered in text
	—	Decrement by one; postfix form covered in text
	`sizeof`	returns the size in bytes of its operand
assignment I/O	=	Assignment; evaluate expression on the right and store in variable named on the left
	<<	Insertion; insert the characters (if a string) or the value (if a variable or constant) in the output stream named on the left of the first insertion operator
	>>	Extraction; extract the value from the input stream named on the left of the first extraction operator and store in the place named on the right

relational	==	Equal to
	!=	Not equal to
	>	Greater than
	<	Less than
	>=	Greater than or equal to
	<=	Less than or equal to
logical	&&	AND is a binary Boolean operator. If both operands are true, the result is true. Otherwise, the result is false.
	||	OR is a binary Boolean operator. If at least one of the operands is true, the result is true. Otherwise, the result is false.
	!	NOT is a unary Boolean operator. NOT changes the value of its operand: if the operand is true, the result is false; if the operand is false, the result it true.
pointer related	*	(postfix on a type or prefix on a variable in a pointer variable declaration) Declare a variable that is a *pointer to* a place that can contain a variable of the type; must be dereferenced to access the place pointed to
	*	(prefix on a pointer variable in an expression) Dereferencing operator; accesses *place pointed to*
	&	(postfix on a type or prefix on a variable in a reference variable declaration) Declare a variable that is a *pointer to* a place that can contain a variable of the type; dereferenced automatically by the compiler
	&	(prefix on a variable) *Address of* a variable
	->	(infix between a pointer variable to `struct` or `class` and member name) Dereferences a pointer variable and accesses a member

	`new`	Returns the address of new space allocated for a dynamic variable of the type named on the right
	`delete`	Returns the space allocated for the dynamic variable on the right to the heap to be allocated again
selection	.	(infix: `struct` variable.member) Accesses the member field of the `struct` variable
	.	(infix: `class` variable.member) Accesses the member data or function of the `class` variable
	`[]`	(postfix: encloses an integral expression) Accesses a position within the array variable named on the left
scope resolution	`::`	(infix: `class` type`::`method) Associates a method with the `class` in which it is declared

Appendix D

C++ Library Routines and Constants

Header File `cctype`

isalnum(ch)	Returns true if **ch** is a letter or a digit; false otherwise.
isalpha(ch)	Returns true if **ch** is a letter; false otherwise.
iscntrl(ch)	Returns true if **ch** is a control character; false, otherwise.
isdigit(ch)	Returns true if **ch** is a digit; false otherwise.
isgraph(ch)	Returns true if **ch** is a nonblank printable character; false otherwise.
islower(ch)	Returns true if **ch** is lowercase; false otherwise.
isprint(ch)	Returns true if **ch** is a printable character; false otherwise.
ispunct(ch)	Returns true if **ch** is a nonblank printable character (i.e., not a letter or a digit); false otherwise.
isspace(ch)	Returns true if **ch** is a whitespace character; false otherwise.
isupper(ch)	Returns true if **ch** is an uppercase letter; false otherwise.
toupper(ch)	Returns **ch** in uppercase regardless of original case.
tolower(ch)	Returns **ch** in lowercase regardless of original case.

Header File `string`

str.c_str()	Converts string object **str** to a C string.
str.find(str2)	Searches **str** for **str2**. If found, returns the character position in **str** at which the match begins. If not found, returns **npos**, the largest value within the return value type of the function.
str.length()	Returns the number of characters in **str**.
str.size()	Returns the number of characters in **str**.
str.substr(pos, len)	Returns a substring of the object **str** beginning at the position **pos** and continuing until the substring is **len** characters or the end of **str** is reached. If the beginning position is outside the string, the program crashes.
getline(inData, str)	Reads and collects characters into **str** until a newline character is encountered. The newline character is read but not stored in **str**.

Header File `cstring`

cstrcat(s1, s2)	Returns the base address of **s1** with **s2** concatenated on the end.
cstrcmp(s1, s2)	Returns a negative integer if **s1** comes before **s2**; returns zero if **s1** is equal to **s2**; and returns a positive integer if **s2** comes before **s1**.
cstrcpy(s1, s2)	returns the base address of **s1** with **s2** copied in it.
cstrlen(s)	Returns the number of characters in **s**.

Header File `cstddef`

NULL	The system-dependent null pointer constant (usually 0).

Header File `cfloat`

FLT_DIG	Approximate number of significant digits in a **float** value on your machine.
FLT_MAX	Maximum positive **float** value on your machine.
FLT_MIN	Minimum positive **float** value on your machine.
DBL_DIG	Approximate number of significant digits in a **double** value on your machine.
DBL_MAX	Maximum positive **double** value on your machine.
DBL_MIN	Minimum positive **double** value on your machine.
LDBL_DIG	Approximate number of significant digits in a **long double** value on your machine.
LDBL_MAX	Maximum positive **long double** value on your machine.
LDBL_MIN	Minimum positive **long double** value on your machine.

Header File `climits`

CHAR_BITS	Number of bits in a byte on your machine.
CHAR_MAX	Maximum **char** value on your machine.
CHAR_MIN	Minimum **char** value on your machine.
SHRT_MAX	Maximum **short** value on your machine.
SHRT_MIN	Minimum **short** value on your machine.
INT_MAX	Maximum **int** value on your machine.
INT_MIN	Minimum **int** value on your machine.
LONG_MAX	Maximum **long** value on your machine.
LONG_MIN	Minimum **long** value on your machine.
UCHAR_MAX	Maximum **unsigned char** value on your machine.
USHRT_MAX	Maximum **unsigned short** value on your machine.
UINT_MAX	Maximum **unsigned int** value on your machine.
ULONG_MAX	Maximum **unsigned long** value on your machine.

Appendix E

The Character Sets

The following charts show the ordering of characters in two widely used character sets: ASCII (American Standard Code for Information Interchange) and EBCDIC (Extended Binary Coded Decimal Interchange Code). The internal representation for each character is shown in decimal. For example, the letter *A* is represented internally as the integer 65 in ASCII and as 193 in EBCDIC. The space (blank) character is denoted by a "□".

Left Digit(s) \ Right Digit	0	1	2	3	4	5	6	7	8	9
					ASCII					
0	NUL	SOH	STX	ETX	EOT	ENQ	ACK	BEL	BS	HT
1	LF	VT	FF	CR	SO	SI	DLE	DC1	DC2	DC3
2	DC4	NAK	SYN	ETB	CAN	EM	SUB	ESC	FS	GS
3	RS	US	□	!	"	#	$	%	&	'
4	(	)	*	+	,	-	.	/	0	1
5	2	3	4	5	6	7	8	9	:	;
6	<	=	>	?	@	A	B	C	D	E
7	F	G	H	I	J	K	L	M	N	O
8	P	Q	R	S	T	U	V	W	X	Y
9	Z	[	\	]	^	_	`	a	b	c
10	d	e	f	g	h	i	j	k	l	m
11	n	o	p	q	r	s	t	u	v	w
12	x	y	z	{	|	}	~	DEL		

Codes 00–31 and 127 are the following nonprintable control characters:

NUL	Null character	VT	Vertical tab	SYN	Synchronous idle
SOH	Start of header	FF	Form feed	ETB	End of transmitted block
STX	Start of text	CR	Carriage return	CAN	Cancel
ETX	End of text	SO	Shift out	EM	End of medium
EOT	End of transmission	SI	Shift in	SUB	Substitute
ENQ	Enquiry	DLE	Data link escape	ESC	Escape
ACK	Acknowledge	DC1	Device control one	FS	File separator
BEL	Bell character (beep)	DC2	Device control two	GS	Group separator
BS	Back space	DC3	Device control three	RS	Record separator
HT	Horizontal tab	DC4	Device control four	US	Unit separator
LF	Line feed	NAK	Negative acknowledge	DEL	Delete

Left Digit(s) \ Right Digit	EBCDIC									
	0	1	2	3	4	5	6	7	8	9
6					_					
7					¢	.	<	(	+	|
8	&									
9	!	$	*	)	;	_	–	/		
10							^	,	%	_
11	>	?								
12		_	:	#	@	'	=	"		a
13	b	c	d	e	f	g	h	i		
14						j	k	l	m	n
15	o	p	q	r						
16		~	s	t	u	v	w	x	y	z
17								\	{	}
18	[	]								
19				A	B	C	D	E	F	G
20	H	I								J
21	K	L	M	N	O	P	Q	R		
22							S	T	U	V
23	W	X	Y	Z						
24	0	1	2	3	4	5	6	7	8	9

Nonprintable control characters—codes 00–63, 250–255, and those for which empty spaces appear in the chart—are not shown.

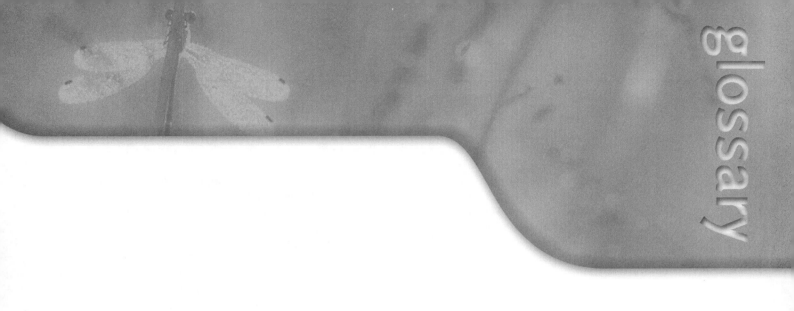

abstract data type a class of data objects with a defined set of properties and a set of operations that process the data objects while maintaining the properties

abstract step an algorithmic step for which some implementation details remain unspecified

abstraction a model of a complex system that includes only the details essential to the perspective of the viewer of the system; the separation of the logical properties of data or actions from their implementation details

abstraction (in OOD) the essential characteristics of an object from the viewpoint of the user

actual parameter a variable, constant, or expression listed in the call to a function or procedure

aggregate operation an operation on a data structure as a whole, as opposed to an operation on an individual component of the data structure

algorithm a logical sequence of discrete steps that describes a complete solution to a given problem computable in a finite amount of time; a step-by-step procedure for solving a problem in a finite amount of time; a verbal or written description of a logical sequence of actions

ALU see *arithmetic/logic unit*

anonymous type a user-defined type that does not have an identifier (a name) associated with it

arithmetic/logic unit (ALU) the component of the central processing unit that performs arithmetic and logical operations

array data type a collection of components, all of the same type, ordered on N dimensions ($N >= 1$); each component is accessed by N indices, each of which represents the component's position within that dimension

assembler a program that translates an assembly language program into machine code

assembly language a low-level programming language in which a mnemonic represents each of the machine language instructions for a particular computer

assertion A logical proposition that is either true or false

assignment expression a C++ expression with a value and the side effect of storing the expression value into a memory location

assignment statement a statement that stores the value of an expression into a variable

atomic data type a data type that allows only a single value to be associated with an identifier of that type

automatic variable a variable for which memory is allocated and deallocated when control enters and exits the block in which it is declared

auxiliary storage device a device that stores data in encoded form outside the computer's memory

base case the case for which the solution can be stated nonrecursively

base class the class being inherited from

big-O notation a notation that expresses computing time (complexity) as the term in a function that increases most rapidly relative to the size of a problem

binary expressed in terms of combinations of the numbers 1 and 0 only

binary search a search algorithm for sorted lists that involves dividing the list in half and determining, by value comparison, whether the item would be in the upper or lower half; the process is performed repeatedly until either the item is found or it is determined that the item is not on the list

bit short for binary digit; a single 1 or 0

block in C++, a group of zero or more statements enclosed in braces

body the statement(s) to be repeated within the loop; the executable statement(s) within a function

Boolean a data type consisting of only two values: true and false

Boolean expression an assertion that is evaluated as either true or false, the only values of the Boolean data type

Boolean operators operators applied to values of the type Boolean; in C++ these are the special symbols &&, ||, and !

booting the system the process of starting up a computer by loading the operating system into its main memory

branch a code segment that is not always executed; for example, a Switch statement has as many branches as there are case labels

branching control structure see *selection control structure*

byte eight bits

call the point at which the computer begins following the instructions in a subprogram is referred to as the subprogram call

cancellation error a form of representational error that occurs when numbers of widely differing magnitudes are added or subtracted

central processing unit (CPU) the part of the computer that executes the instructions (program) stored in memory; consists of the arithmetic/logic unit and the control unit

char data type whose values consist of one alphanumeric character (letter, digit, or special symbol)

character set a standard set of alphanumeric characters with a given collating sequence and binary representation

class an unstructured type that encapsulates a fixed number of data components with the functions that manipulate them; the predefined operations on an instance of a class are whole assignment and component access

class constructor a special member function of a class that is implicitly invoked when a class object is defined

class destructor a special member function of a class that is implicitly invoked when a class object goes out of scope

class member a component of a class; class members may be either data or functions

class object (class instance) a variable of a class type

client software that declares and manipulates objects (instances) of a particular class

code walk-through a verification process for a program in which each statement is examined to check that it faithfully implements the corresponding algorithmic step, and that the preconditions and postconditions of each module are preserved

coding translating an algorithm into a programming language; the process of assigning bit patterns to pieces of information

collating sequence the ordering of the elements of a set or series, such as the characters (values) in a character set

compiler a program that translates a high-level language (such as C++, Pascal, or FORTRAN) into machine code

compiler listing a copy of a program into which have been inserted messages from the compiler (indicating errors in the program that prevent its translation into machine language if appropriate)

complexity a measure of the effort expended by the computer in performing a computation, relative to the size of the computation

composite type a data type that allows a collection of values to be associated with an object of that type

composition (containment) a mechanism by which an internal data member of one class is defined to be an object of another class type

computer a programmable device that can store, retrieve, and process data

computer program a list of instructions to be performed by a computer

computer programming the process of planning a sequence of steps for a computer to follow

concrete step a step for which the implementation details are fully specified

conditional test the point at which the Boolean expression is evaluated and the decision is made to either begin a new iteration or skip to the first statement following the loop

constant an item in a program whose value is fixed at compile time and cannot be changed during execution

constant time an algorithm whose Big-O work expression is a constant

control abstraction the separation of the logical properties of a control structure from its implementation

control structure a statement used to alter the normally sequential flow of control

control unit the component of the central processing unit that controls the action of other components so that instructions (the program) are executed in sequence

conversion function a function that converts a value of one type to another type so that it can be assigned to a variable of the second type; also called transfer function or type cast

copy-constructor a special member function of a class that is implicitly invoked when passing parameters by value, initializing a variable in a declaration, and returning an object as the value of a function

count-controlled loop a loop that executes a predetermined number of times

counter a variable whose value is incremented to keep track of the number of times a process or event occurs

CPU see *central processing unit*

crash the cessation of a computer's operations as a result of the failure of one of its components; cessation of program execution to an error due to an error

cursor control keys a special set of keys on a computer keyboard that allow the user to move the cursor up, down, right, and left to any point on the screen

data information that has been put into a form a computer can use

data abstraction the separation of a data type's logical properties from its implementation

data encapsulation the separation of the representation of data from the applications that use the data at a logical level; a programming language feature that enforces information hiding

data flow the flow of information from the calling code to a function and from the function back to the calling code

data representation the concrete form of data used to represent the abstract values of an abstract data type

data structure a collection of data elements whose organization is characterized by accessing operations that are used to store and retrieve the individual data elements; the implementation of the composite data members in an abstract data type

data type the general form of a class of data items; a formal description of the set of values (called the domain) and the basic set of operations that can be applied to it

data validation a test added to a program or a function that checks for errors in the data

debugging the process by which errors are removed from a program so that it does exactly what it is supposed to do

decision see *selection control structure*

declaration a statement that associates an identifier with a process or object so that the user can refer to that process or object by name

deep copy an operation that not only copies one class object to another but also makes copies of any pointed-to data

delete a C++ operator that returns the space allocated for a dynamic variable back to the heap to be used again

demotion (narrowing) the conversion of a value from a "higher" type to a "lower" type according to a programming language's precedence of data types. Demotion may cause loss of information

dereference operator an operator that when applied to a pointer variable denotes the variable to which the pointer points

derived class the class that inherits

deskchecking tracing an execution of a design or program on paper

development environment a single package containing all of the software required for developing a program

documentation the written text and comments that make a program easier for others to understand, use, and modify

down a descriptive term applied to a computer when it is not in a usable condition

driver a simple dummy main program that is used to call a function being tested; a main function in an object-oriented program

dynamic allocation allocation of memory space for a variable at run time (as opposed to static allocation at compile time)

dynamic binding the run-time determination of which implementation of an operation is appropriate

dynamic data structure a data structure that can expand and contract during program execution

dynamic variable a variable created during execution of a program by the new operator

echo printing printing the data values input to a program to verify that they are correct

editor an interactive program used to create and modify source programs or data

encapsulation (in OOD) the bundling of data and actions in such a way that the logical properties of the data and actions are separated from the implementation details; the practice of hiding a module implementation in a separate block with a formally specified interface

enumeration data type a data type in which the formal description of the set of values is an ordered list of literal values

enumerator one of the values in the domain of an enumeration type

event counter a variable that is incremented each time a particular event occurs

event-controlled loop a loop that terminates when something happens inside the loop body to signal that the loop should be exited

executing the action of a computer performing as instructed by a given program

execution trace a testing procedure that involves simulating by hand the computer executing a program

expression an arrangement of identifiers, literals, and operators that can be evaluated to compute a value of a given type

expression statement a statement formed by appending a semicolon to an expression

external file a file that is used to communicate with people or programs and is stored externally to the program

external pointer a named pointer variable that references the first node in a linked list

external representation the printable (character) form of a data value

fetch-execute cycle the sequence of steps performed by the central processing unit for each machine language instruction

field a group of character positions in a line of output

field identifier (member identifier in C++) the name of a component in a record (struct)

field of a record a component of a record data type

field member selector the expression used to access components of a record variable; formed by using the record variable name and the field identifier, separated by a period

file a named area in secondary storage that is used to hold a collection of data; the collection of data itself

finite state machine an idealized model of a simple computer consisting of a set of states, the rules that specify when states are changed, and a set of actions that are performed when changing states

flag a Boolean variable that is set in one part of the program and tested in another to control the logical flow of a program

flat implementation the hierarchical structure of a solution written as one long sequence of steps; also called inline implementation

floating point number the value stored in a type **float** variable, so called because part of the memory location holds the exponent and the balance of the location the mantissa, with the decimal point floating as necessary among the significant digits

flow of control the order of execution of the statements in a program

formal parameter a variable declared in a function heading

formal parameter declaration the code that associates a formal parameter identifier with a data type and a passing mechanism

formatting the planned positioning of statements or declarations and blanks on a line of a program; the arranging of program output so that it is neatly spaced and aligned

free store (heap) A pool of memory locations reserved for dynamic allocation of data

function a subprogram in C++

function call an expression or statement in the main program requiring the computer to execute a function subprogram

function definition ta function declaration that includes the body of the function

function prototype a function declaration without the body of the function

function result   the value computed by the function and then returned to the main program; often just called the result

function result type   the data type of the result value returned by a function; often referred to simply as function type

function type   see *function result type*

functional cohesion   a property of a module in which all concrete steps are directed toward solving just one problem, and any significant subproblems are written as abstract steps

functional equivalence   a property of a module that performs exactly the same operation as the abstract step it defines, or when one module performs exactly the same operation as another module

functional modules   in top-down design, the structured tasks and subtasks that are solved individually to create an effective program

functional problem description   a description that clearly states what a program is to do

general (recursive) case   the case for which the solution is expressed in terms of a smaller version of itself

global   a descriptive term applied to an identifier declared outside any function, so-called because it is accessible to everything that follows it

hardware   the physical components of a computer

heuristics   assorted problem-solving strategies

hierarchical implementation   a process in which a modular solution is implemented by subprograms that duplicate the hierarchical structure of the solution

hierarchical records   records in which at least one of the fields is itself a record

hierarchy (in OOD)   structuring of abstractions in which a descendant object inherits the characteristics of its ancestors

high-level programming language   any programming language in which a single statement translates into one or more machine language instructions

homogeneous   a descriptive term applied to structures in which all components are of the same data type (such as an array)

identifier   a name associated with a process or object and used to refer to that process or object

implementation phase   the second set of steps in programming a computer: translating (coding) the algorithm into a programming language; testing the resulting program by running it on a computer, checking for accuracy, and making any necessary corrections; using the program

implementing   coding and testing an algorithm

implementing a test plan   running the program with the test cases listed in the test plan

implicit matching   see *positional matching*

in place   describes a kind of sorting algorithm in which the components in an array are sorted without the use of a second array

index   a value that selects a component of an array

infinite loop   a loop whose termination condition is never reached and which therefore is never exited without intervention from outside of the program

infinite recursion   the situation in which a subprogram calls itself over and over continuously

information   any knowledge that can be communicated

information hiding   The practice of hiding the details of a function or data structure with the goal of controlling access to the details of a module or structure; the programming technique of hiding the details of data or actions from other parts of the program

inheritance A design technique used with a hierarchy of classes by which each descendant class inherits the properties (data and operations) of its ancestor class; the language mechanism by which one class acquires the properties—data and operations—of another class; a mechanism for automatically sharing data and methods among members of a class and its subclasses

inline implementation see *flat implementation*

input the process of placing values from an outside data set into variables in a program; the data may come from either an input device (keyboard) or an auxiliary storage device (disk or tape)

input prompts messages printed by an interactive program, explaining what data is to be entered

input transformation an operation that takes input values and converts them to the abstract data type representation

input/output (I/O) devices the parts of a computer that accept data to be processed (input) and present the results of that processing (output)

integer number a positive or negative whole number made up of a sign and digits (when the sign is omitted, a positive sign is assumed)

interactive system a system that allows direct communication between the user and the computer

interface a connecting link (such as a computer terminal) at a shared boundary that allows independent systems (such as the user and the computer) to meet and act on or communicate with each other; the formal definition of the behavior of a subprogram and the mechanism for communicating with it

internal file a file that is created but not save; also called a scratch file

interpreter a program that inputs a program in a high-level language and directs the computer to perform the actions specified in each statement; unlike a compiler, and interpreter does not produce a machine language version of the entire program

invoke to call on a subprogram, causing the subprogram to execute before control is returned to the statement following the call

iteration an individual pass through, or repetition of, the body of a loop

iteration counter a counter variable that is incremented with each iteration of a loop

iterator an operation that allows us to process all the components in an abstract data type sequentially

length the actual number of values stored in a list or string

lifetime the period of time during program execution when an identifier has memory allocated to it

linear time for an algorithm, when the Big-O work expression can be expressed in terms of a constant times N, where N is the number of values in a data set

linked list a list in which the order of the components is determined by an explicit link field in each node, rather than by the sequential order of the components in memory

listing a copy of a source program, output by a compiler, containing messages to the programmer

literal value any constant value written in a program

local variable a variable declared within a block; it is not accessible outside of that block

logarithmic order for an algorithm, when the Big-O work expression can be expressed in terms of the logarithm of N, where N is the number of values in a data set

logging off informing a computer—usually through a simple command—that no further commands follow

logging on   taking the preliminary steps necessary to identify yourself to a computer so that it accept your commands

logical order   the order in which the programmer wants the statements in the program to be executed, which may differ from the physical order in which they appear

loop   a method of structuring statements so that they are repeated while certain conditions are met

loop control variable (LCV)   a variable whose value is used to determine whether the loop executes another iteration or exits

loop entry   the point at which the flow of control first passes to a statement inside a loop

loop exit   that point when the repetition of the loop body ends and control passes to the first statement following the loop

loop invariant   assertions about the characteristics of a loop that must always be true for a loop to execute properly; the assertions are true on loop entry, at the start of each loop iteration, and on exit from the loop, but are not necessarily true at each point in the body of the loop

loop test   the point at which the loop expression is evaluated and the decision is made either to begin a new iteration or skip to the statement immediately following the loop

machine language   the language, made up of binary-coded instructions, that is used directly by the computer

mainframe   a large computing system designed for high-volume processing or for use by many people at once

maintenance   the modification of a program, after it has been completed, in order to meet changing requirements or to take care of any errors that show up

maintenance phase   period during which maintenance occurs

mantissa   with respect to floating point representation of real numbers, the digits representing a number itself and not its exponent

member selector   the expression used to access components of a **struct** or **class** variable. It is formed by using the variable name and the member name, separated by a dot (period)

memory leak   the loss of available memory space that occurs when memory are allocated dynamically but never deallocated

memory unit   internal data storage in a computer

metalanguage   a language that is used to write the syntax rules for another language

method   a function declared as a member of a class object

microcomputer   see *personal computer*

minicomputer   a computer system larger than a personal computer but smaller than a mainframe; sometimes called an entry-level mainframe

mixed mode expression   an expression that contains operands of different data types

modular programming   see *top-down design*

modularity (in OOD)   meaningful packaging of objects

module   a self-contained collection of steps that solves a problem or subproblem; can contain both concrete and abstract steps

module nesting chart   a chart that depicts the nesting structure of modules and shows calls among them

name precedence   the priority treatment accorded a local identifier in a block over a global identifier with the same spelling in any references that the block makes to that identifier

named constant   a location in memory, referenced by an identifier, where a data value that cannot be changed is stored

named type a type that has an identifier (a name) associated with it

nested control structure a program structure consisting of one control statement (selection, iteration, or subprogram) embedded within another control statement

nested If an If statement that is nested within another If statement

nested loop a loop that is within another loop

new a C++ operator that returns the address of new space allocated for a dynamic variable

nodes the building blocks of dynamic structures, each made up of a component (the data) and a pointer (the link) to the next node

nonlocal a descriptive term applied to any identifier declared outside of a given block

nonlocal access access to any identifier declared outside of its own block

null statement an empty statement

nybble four bits; half of a byte

object class (class) the description of a group of objects with similar properties and behaviors; a pattern for creating individual objects

object program the machine-language version of a source program

object-based programming language a programming language that supports abstraction and encapsulation, but not inheritance

object-oriented design a building-block design technique that incorporates abstraction, encapsulation, modularity, and hierarchy

object-oriented programming a method of implementation in which programs are organized as cooperative collections of objects, each of which represents an instance of some class, and whose classes are all members of a hierarchy of classes united via inheritance relationships

observer an operation that allows us to observe the state of an instance of an abstract data type without changing it

one-dimensional array a structured collection of components of the same type given a single name; each component is accessed by an index that indicates its position within the collection

operating system a set of programs that manages all of the computer's resources

out-of-bounds array index an index value that, in C++, is either less than zero or greater than the array size minus one

output transformation an operation that takes an instance of an abstract data type and converts it to a representation that can be output

overflow the condition that arises when the value of a calculation is too large to be represented

overloading giving the same name to more than one function or using the same operator symbol for more than one operation; usually associated with static binding

overriding reimplementing a member function inherited from a parent class

parameter a literal, constant, variable, or expression used for communicating values to or from a subprogram

parameter list a mechanism by which functions communicate with each other

pass by address a parameter-passing mechanism in which the memory address of the actual parameter is passed to the formal parameter; also called pass by reference

pass by name a parameter-passing mechanism in which the actual parameter is passed to a function as a literal character string and interpreted by a thunk

pass by reference see *pass by address*

pass by value a parameter-passing mechanism in which a copy of an actual parameter's value is passed to the formal parameter

password a unique series of letters assigned to a user (and known only by that user) by which that user identifies himself or herself to a computer during the logging-on procedure; a password system protects information stored in a computer from being tampered with or destroyed

path a combination of branches that might be traversed when a program or function is executed

path testing a testing technique whereby the tester tries to execute all possible paths in a program or function

PC see *personal computer*

peripheral device an input, output, or auxiliary storage device attached to a computer

personal computer (PC) a small computer system (usually intended to fit on a desktop) that is designed to be used primarily by a single person

pointer a simple data type consisting of an unbounded set of values, each of which addresses or otherwise indicates the location of a variable of a given type; operations defined on pointer variables are assignment and test for equality

polymorphic operation an operation that has multiple meanings depending on the type of the object to which it is bound at run time

polymorphism The ability to determine which of several operations with the same name is appropriate; a combination of static and dynamic binding

positional matching a method of matching actual and formal parameters by their relative positions in the two parameter lists; also called *relative* or *implicit* matching

postconditions assertions that must be true after a module is executed

postfix operator an operator that follows its operand(s)

precision a maximum number of significant digits

preconditions assertions that must be true before a module begins execution

prefix operator an operator that precedes its operand(s)

priming read an initial reading of a set of data values before entry into an event-controlled loop in order to establish values for the variables

problem-solving phase the first set of steps in programming a computer: analyzing the problem; developing an algorithm; testing the algorithm for accuracy

procedural abstraction the separation of the logical properties of an action from its implementation

programming planning, scheduling, or performing a task or an event; see also *computer programming*

programming language a set of rules, symbols, and special words used to construct a program

pseudocode a mixture of English statements and C++-like control structures that can easily by translated into a programming language

range of values the interval within which values must fall, specified in terms of the largest and smallest allowable values

real number a number that has a whole and a fractional part and no imaginary part

record (struct) data type a composite data type with a fixed number of components called fields (members); the operations are whole record assignment and selection of individual fields by name

recursion the situation in which a subprogram calls itself

recursive call a subprogram call in which the subprogram being called is the same as the one making the call

recursive case see *general case*

recursive definition a definition in which something is defined in terms of a smaller version of itself

reference parameter   a formal parameter that receives the location (memory address) of the caller's actual parameter

reference type   a simple data type consisting of an unbounded set of values, each of which is the address of a variable of a given type.   The only operation defined on a reference variable is initialization, after which every appearance of the variable is implicitly dereferenced

refinement   in top-down design, the expansion of a module specification to form a new module that solves a major step in the computer solution of a problem

relational operators   operators that state that a relationship exists between two values; in C++, symbols that cause the computer to perform operations to verify whether or not the indicated relationship exists

representational error   arithmetic error caused when the precision of the true result of arithmetic operations is greater than the precision of the machine

reserved word   a word that has special meaning in a programming language; it cannot be used as an identifier

result   see *function result*

return   the point at which the computer comes back from executing a function

right-justified   placed as far to the right as possible within a fixed number of character positions

robust   a descriptive term for a program that can recover from erroneous inputs and keep running

run-time stack   a data structure that keeps track of activation records during the execution of a program

scope   the region of program code where it is legal to reference (use) an identifier

scope rules   the rules that determine where in a program a given identifier may be accessed, given the point at which the identifier is declared

scratch file   see *internal file*

secondary storage device   see *auxiliary storage device*

selection control structure   a form of program structure allowing the computer to select one among possible actions to perform based on given circumstances; also called a *branching control structure*

self   the instance object (class) used in the invocation of a method

self-documenting code   a program containing meaningful identifiers as well as judiciously used clarifying comments

semantics   the set of rules that gives the meaning of instruction written in a programming language

semihierarchical implementation   a modular solution implemented by   functions in a manner that preserves the hierarchical design, except that a function used by multiple modules is implemented once, outside of the hierarchy, and called in each place it is needed

sentinel   a special data value used in certain event-controlled loops as a signal that the loop should be exited

sequence   a structure in which statements are executed one after another

shallow copy   an operation that copies one class object to another without copying any pointed-to data

side effect   any effect of one function on another that is not part of the explicitly defined interface between them

significant digits   those digits from the first nonzero digit on the left to the last nonzero digit on the right (plus any zero digits that are exact)

simulation   a problem solution that has been arrived at through the application of an algorithm designed to model the behavior of physical systems, materials, or processes

size (of an array)   the physical space reserved for an array

software computer programs; the set of all programs available on a computer

software engineering the application of traditional engineering methodologies and techniques to the development of software

software life cycle the phases in the life of a large software project including requirements analysis, specification, design, implementation, testing, and maintenance

software piracy the unauthorized copying of software for either personal use or use by others

sorting arranging the components of a list in order (for instance, words in alphabetical order, numbers in ascending or descending order)

source program a program written in a high-level programming language

stable sort a sorting algorithm that preserves the order of duplicates

stack frame see *activation record*

standardized made uniform; most high-level languages are standardized, as official descriptions of them exist

static binding the compile-time determination of which function to call for a particular object

static variable a variable for which memory remains allocated throughout the execution of the entire program

stepwise design see *top-down design*

stepwise refinement see *top-down design*

string a collection of characters that is interpreted as a single data item; in C++, a null-terminated sequence of characters stored in a **char** array

stub a dummy function that assists in testing part of a program; it has the same function that would actually be called by the part of the program being tested, but is usually much simpler

style the individual manner in which computer programmers translate algorithms into a programming language

subprogram see *function*

supercomputer the most powerful class of computers

switch expression the expression in a Switch statement whose value determines which case label is selected. It cannot be a floating point expression

syntax the formal rules governing how valid instructions (constructs) are written in a programming language

system software a set of programs—including the compiler, the operating system, and the editor—that improves the efficiency and convenience of the computer's processing

tail recursion a recursive algorithm in which no statements are executed after the return from the recursive call

team programming the use of two or more programmers to design a program that would take one programmer too long to complete

temporary file a file that exists only during the execution of a program

termination condition the condition that causes a loop to be exited

test driver see *driver*

test plan a document that specifies how a program is to be tested

test plan implementation using the test cases specified in a test plan to verify that a program outputs the predicted results

testing checking a program's output by comparing it to hand-calculated results; running a program with data sets designed to discover any errors

text file a file in which each component is a character; each numeric digit is represented by its code in the collating sequence

top-down design a technique for developing a program in which the problem is divided into more easily handled subproblems, the solutions of which create a solution to the overall problem; also called stepwise refinement and modular programming

transfer function see *conversion function*

transformer an operation that builds a new value of an ADT, given one or more previous values of the type

traverse a list to access the components of a list one at a time from the beginning of the list to the end

two-dimensional array a collection of components, all of the same type, structured in two dimensions; each component is accessed by a pair of indices that represent the component's position within each dimension

type cast see *conversion function*

type coercion an automatic conversion of a value of one type to a value of another type

type definition the association of a type identifier with the definition of a new data type

unary operator an operator that has just one operand

underflow the condition that arises when the value of a calculation is too small to be represented

unstructured data type a collection consisting of components that are not organized with respect to one another

user name the name by which a computer recognizes the user, and which must be entered to log on to a machine

value parameter a formal parameter that receives a copy of the contents of the corresponding actual parameter

value-returning function a function that returns a single value to its caller and is invoked from within an expression

variable a location in memory, referenced by an identifier, in which a data value that can be changed is stored

virtual function a function in which each invocation cannot be matched with the proper code until run time

virus a computer program that replicates itself, often with the goal of spreading to other computers without authorization, possibly with the intent of doing harm

visible accessible; a term used in describing a scope of access

void function (procedure) a function that does not return a function value to its caller and is invoked as a separate statement

word a group of 16, 32, or 64 bits; a group of bits processed by the arithmetic-logic unit in a single instruction

work a measure of the effort expended by the computer in performing a computation

workstation a minicomputer or powerful microcomputer designed to be used primarily by one person at a time